Home Plann

Guide to Residential Design

Charles Talcott

Don Hepler

Paul Wallach

McGRAW-HILL BOOK COMPANY

New York St. Louis San Francisco Auckland
Bogotá Hamburg Johannesburg London
Madrid Mexico Montreal New Delhi
Panama Paris São Paulo Singapore
Sydney Tokyo Toronto

Library of Congress Cataloging in Publication Data

Talcott, Charles W.
    Home Planners' guide to residential design.

    Bibliography: p.
    Includes index.
    1. Architecture, Domestic—United States—Designs
and plans. I. Hepler, Donald E. II Wallach, Paul I.
III. Home Planners, inc. IV. Title. V. Title: Guide to
residential design.
NA7205.T35   1985   728.3'7'0222   85-185
ISBN 0-07-028306-0

1234567890   HAL/HAL   898765

ISBN 0-07-028306-0

*The editors for this book were Joan Zseleczky and Kate Scheinman,
the designer was Naomi Auerbach, and the production supervisor was
Sally L. Fliess. It was set in Melior by Black Dot.*

Printed and bound by Halliday Lithograph Corporation

Contents

Preface

The Home Planners' Guide to Residential Design is just what the title implies. It's a practical guide to designing a residence, or in working more creatively and effectively with an architect or designer. The book is based on the reality that few "do-it-yourself" home designers (and professionals) actually design custom-planned residences from scratch. Most draw, in varying degrees, upon existing plans, ideas, or experiences in formulating new designs. This guide provides the neophyte home planner with simplified logical and practical methods for progressing through the design sequences used by professional designers. However, many shortcuts and practical "dos and don'ts" help guide the planner smoothly through the design process with minimum use of technical jargon and complicated architectural design procedures.

The Home Planners' Guide to Residential Design is presented in two parts. Part I covers the basic principles of residential design upon which the remainder of the book is based. Part II deals with the sequences used in identifying needs and wants, choosing the best-fit plan, and designing alterations to ensure completion of a technically appropriate and aesthetically pleasing final plan.

The illustrative material for this book draws heavily upon the vast library of architectural work of Home Planners, Inc. Established in 1946, this firm has created and published over 2500 house designs and 140 home plan books. Blueprints available for each of these designs have been shipped to plan book readers throughout the world. Home Planners' designs have been a frequent feature in national shelter magazines. Should readers of this book wish to obtain additional information about any of the illustrated designs, or information about Home Planners' current home plan book titles and blueprints, inquiries should be sent to Home Planners, Inc., Dept. MH, 23761 Research Dr., Farmington Hills, Michigan 48024. For ease of reference note the Illustrated Designs Index on page vi.

Illustrated Designs Index

PART 1

Principles of Residential Design

CHAPTER 1

Introduction

Designing a residence is similar to designing any functional object or structure. The designer must carefully study the functions of the structure and develop the design through progressive, logical steps to achieve a functional and aesthetically pleasing plan. However, before the first step can be taken in residential design, the home planner will find it extremely helpful to be able to read and understand basic architectural drawings. Architectural drawings are divided into two basic types: pictorial drawings and multiview drawings.

Reading Architectural Drawings

Pictorial drawings Confucius said, "One picture is worth ten thousand words." But neither a picture, a drawing as shown in Fig. 1–1, or ten thousand words could adequately describe this building in sufficient detail for construction purposes. Although words and pictures are used extensively to communicate design ideas, neither is precise enough to be used exclusively in the design process. Exterior (Fig. 1–1) and interior (see Fig. 1–2) pictorial drawings show several sides of an object in one drawing, but the other sides are always hidden. Therefore the precise layout of the interior cannot be shown on this type of drawing. For these reasons pictorial drawings are good for general interpretation, but multiview drawings are needed for planning and construction.

Multiview drawings Multiview (several views) drawings are used in the design process because they represent the exact form and scaled size of each side of an object. Multiview drawings are sometimes called "orthographic drawings." To visualize and understand multiview drawings, imagine a structure surrounded by an imaginary transparent plane, as shown in Fig. 1–3. If you draw the outline of the structure as seen from the outside on the imaginary transparent planes you create the various orthographic views. The front view is shown on the front plane, the side view is shown on the side plane and the top view is shown on the top plane. When the planes of the top, bottom, and sides are hinged (swung out from the front plane as shown in Fig. 1–4), the six views of an object are shown exactly as they are positioned on an orthographic drawing. In Fig. 1–4 look at the position of each view as it relates to the front view. The right side is to the right of the front view, the left side is to the left of the front view, the top (roof) view is on the top, and the bottom view is on the bottom, but the rear view is to the left of the left side view.

Notice that the lengths of the front view, top (roof) view, and bottom view are exactly the same as the length of the rear view. Also notice that the heights and alignments of the front right side, left side, and rear are also the same. Keep in mind the position of these views and remember that the lengths of the front, bottom, and top views are always the same. Likewise the heights of the rear, left, front, and right sides are also always the same.

Fig. 1-1   One picture is worth ten thousand words. (Design 2356)

Fig. 1-2   Interior pictorial drawing.

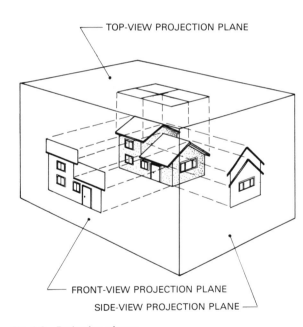

Fig. 1-3   Projection planes.

All six of these views are not used to depict architectural structures. Instead only four side elevation views are shown, and the top view is replaced with a section through the structure called a floor plan. A roof plan may also be developed from the top view, but the bottom view is never used in architectural work. There are therefore two basic types of orthographic drawings used for architectural design and construction purposes: elevation drawings and plan draw- ings. Elevation drawings are viewed from the side and plan views are viewed from the top.

Elevation drawings   Elevation drawings are the orthographic side views of an object as shown in Fig. 1–4. These are identified as the right side view, left side view, front view, and rear view. Figure 1–5 also shows the relationship of the projected elevation to the floor plan. Elevation drawings are similar to a picture of the front,

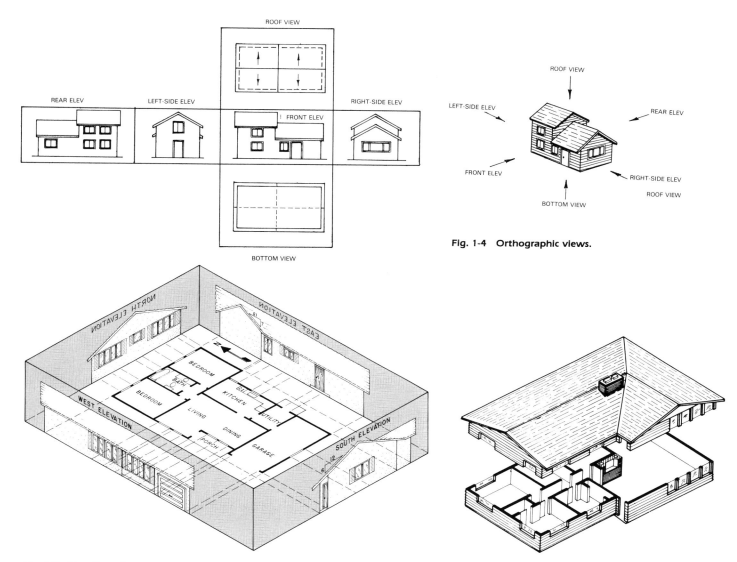

Fig. 1-4 Orthographic views.

Fig. 1-5 Elevation views.

Fig. 1-6 Floor Plan section.

sides, and rear of a building and are prepared to exact dimensions without pictorial receding angles as would be shown in a perspective drawing.

Floor plans A floor plan is a top orthographic view of a building as seen as if the building were cut through horizontally about 4 feet above the floor line as shown in Fig. 1–6. The floor plan is the basic plan used for designing the interior layout of a building. The floor plan is therefore the most significant of all architectural drawings since it contains more information pertaining to the design and construction of the structure than any other single drawing. Floor plans show the exact width and length of each room or subdivision of a structure. And for this reason floor plans are used as the basic design tool of the architect or designer. Floor plans which show width and length are developed first, and elevations which also show height are designed later to relate to the

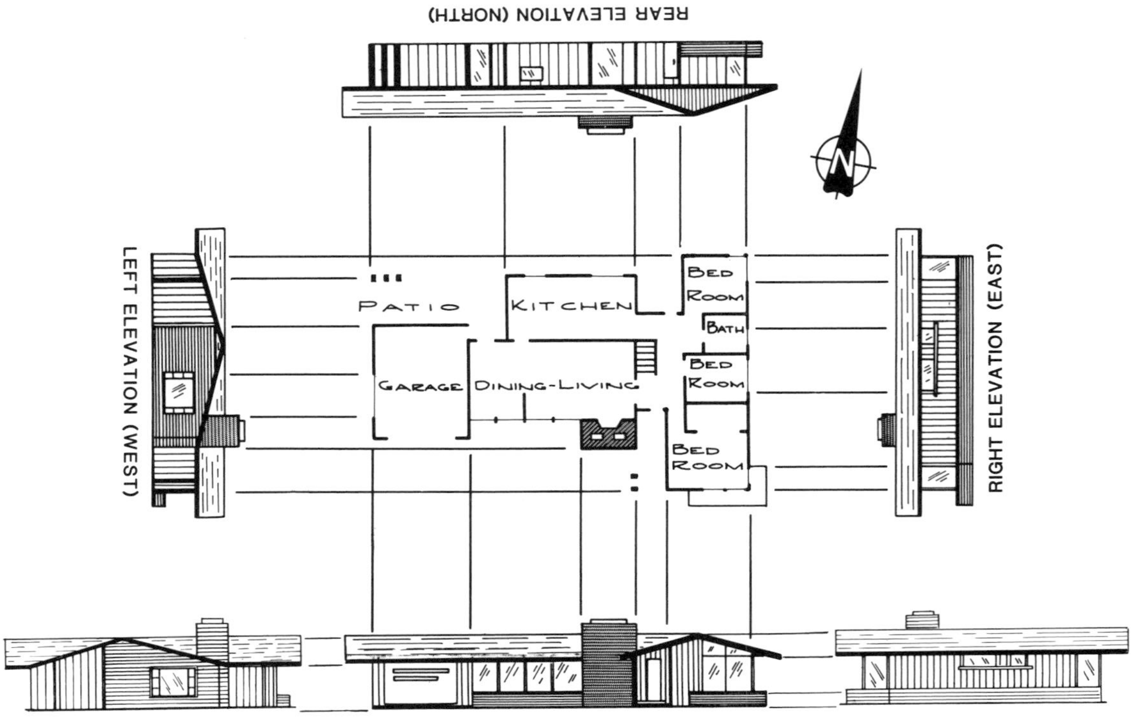

REAR ELEVATION (NORTH)

LEFT ELEVATION (WEST)

RIGHT ELEVATION (EAST)

PATIO

KITCHEN

BED ROOM

BATH

BED ROOM

GARAGE

DINING-LIVING

BED ROOM

N

LEFT ELEVATION (WEST)

FRONT ELEVATION (SOUTH)

RIGHT ELEVATION (EAST)

Fig. 1-7 Elevation projection.

floor plan. Figure 1–7 shows the relationship of the four basic elevation drawings to a floor plan. Note that the elevations are sometimes referred to by the compass direction—North, East, South, West—rather than left, right, front, and rear. In Fig. 1–7 the front elevation is the South elevation, therefore the rear elevation is the North elevation. Likewise, the left elevation is the West elevation and the right elevation is the East elevation.

There are several types of floor plans: floor plan sketches, general design floor plans, and working-drawing floor plans. Figure 1–8 is a floor plan sketch of the same plan shown in Figs. 1–9 and 1–10. Figure 1–9 is a general design floor plan and Fig. 1–10 is a working-drawing floor plan.

Floor plan sketches are used by the designer as a temporary design tool until the final plan layout is established. General design floor plans, also called "abbreviated plans," as shown in Fig. 1–9 are used only to show the basic layout of areas and design features. They do not include much detail nor are they fully dimensioned. They show only the approximate position of walls and partitions. They do not include sufficient information to be used for construction, but they are drawn to scale and do include approximate internal dimensions for each room and the total width and length dimensions for the structure. These plans are usually drawn at a reduced scale which is too small to include many construction details and symbols. These types of plans are prepared during early planning stages primarily for use in

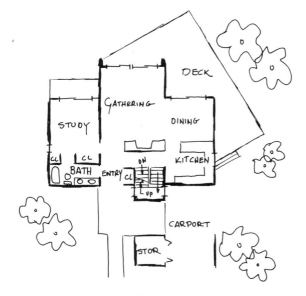

Fig. 1-8 Floor plan sketch.

development and consultation, and they can also be used as sales tools.

An accurate working-drawing floor plan, complete with detail dimensions and material symbols, is necessary for construction purposes. By using a plan of this type, a contractor can accurately interpret and implement the desires of the designer. The prime function of a working-drawing floor plan is to communicate specific

Fig 5-12m *continued.* (Design 2379)

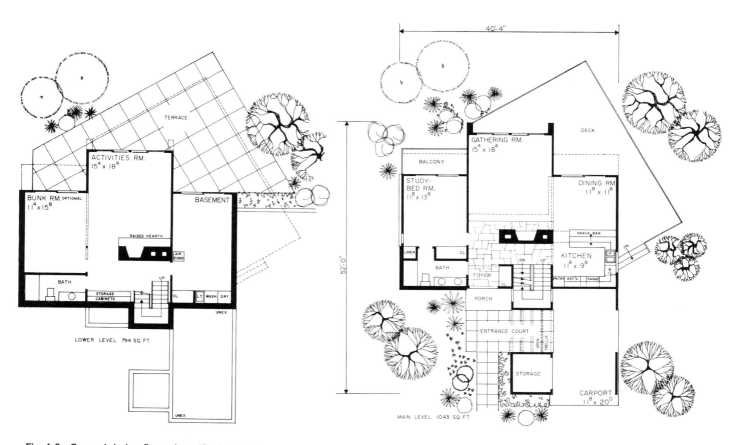

Fig. 1-9 General design floor plans. (Design 2511)

design and construction information to builders and various subcontractors. A complete floor plan eliminates misunderstandings between the designer and the builder, since the builder's judgment must be used to fill in omitted details if the floor plan is inaccurate, incomplete, or abbreviated. The floor plan shown in Fig. 1–10 is a complete working-drawing floor plan for construction purposes. In some cases electrical, air conditioning, and plumbing symbols are added to the working-drawing floor plan, eliminating the need for separate, specialized plans to describe these features.

Architectural symbols Architects substitute symbols for materials and fixtures just as stenographers substitute shorthand symbols for words or syllables. It is obviously more convenient and

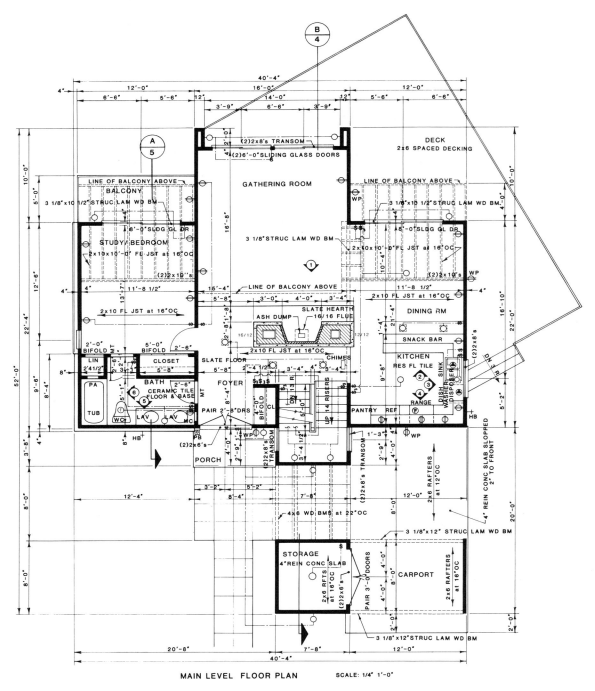

Fig. 1-10 Working drawing floor plan.

time saving to draw a symbol of a material than to repeat a description every time the material is used. It is also impractical to describe all construction materials or components shown on the floor plans—such as fixtures, doors, windows, stairs, and partitions—without the use of symbols and abbreviations. In addition to the symbols that represent materials and fixtures on floor plans and elevations, different types of lines are used as symbols. Heavier lines are used to show the outline of an object and thinner lines, or "dimen-

sion lines," are used with the building dimensions. Thin extension lines project out from the building and intersect dimension lines, showing the exact length of an area of a structure. Dotted lines are used to show areas that are not visible on the surface but which exist below the plane of projection. Dotted lines are also used on floor plans to show objects above the floor plan section line such as wall cabinets, arches, and beams. Center lines, a long dash, and a short dash are used to identify and locate the center of symmet-

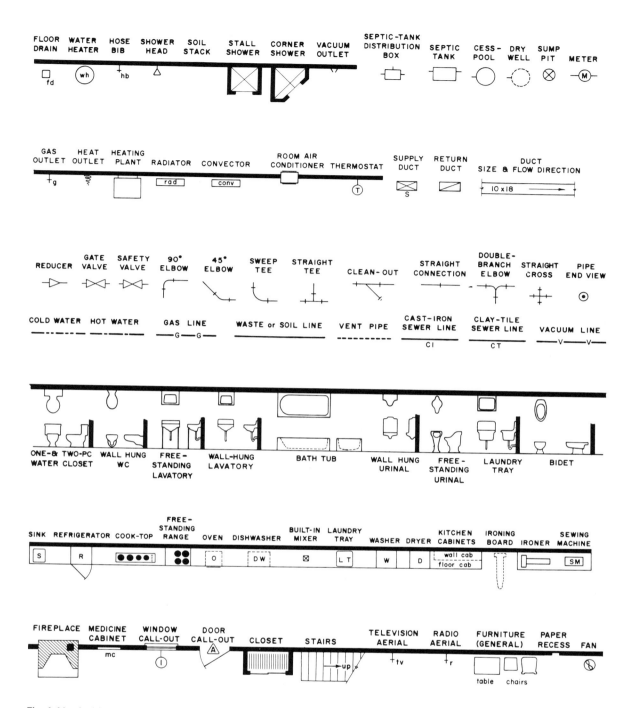

Fig. 1-11 Architectural symbols.

rical objects such as fixtures, doors, and windows. Center lines are also used for dimensioning purposes.

It is not necessary to develop total recall for each symbol, but it is important to recognize what material or component each symbol represents when you are reading architectural drawings. The symbols shown in Fig. 1–11 represent materials, equipment, or fixtures which appear in drawings viewed from the top (plan views) and as they appear from the side (elevation views).

Since plan views are sectional drawings, plan view symbols represent material in sectioned form. You'll notice that some floor plan symbols are designed to approximate the appearance of the material, fixture, or component represented. However, many elevation symbols very accurately represent the appearance of the material they depict. Other materials, usually because of size and space restrictions, are assigned a design symbol which must be remembered by rote if drawings are to be meaningful and consistently interpreted by each reader. Figure 1–12 shows the application of symbols to a typical floor plan. Figure 1–13 shows the application of symbols to a typical elevation drawing.

Design Factors

Factors affecting residential design are divided into two basic groups: floor plan design factors and elevation design factors. Floor plan design involves the most efficient and creative use of available space, while elevation design involves more use of the aesthetic aspects of design.

Principles of floor plan design Since the floor plan provides more specific information about the design of a building than any other drawing, it is the first plan developed by the designer. For a

Fig. 1-12 Floor plan symbols.

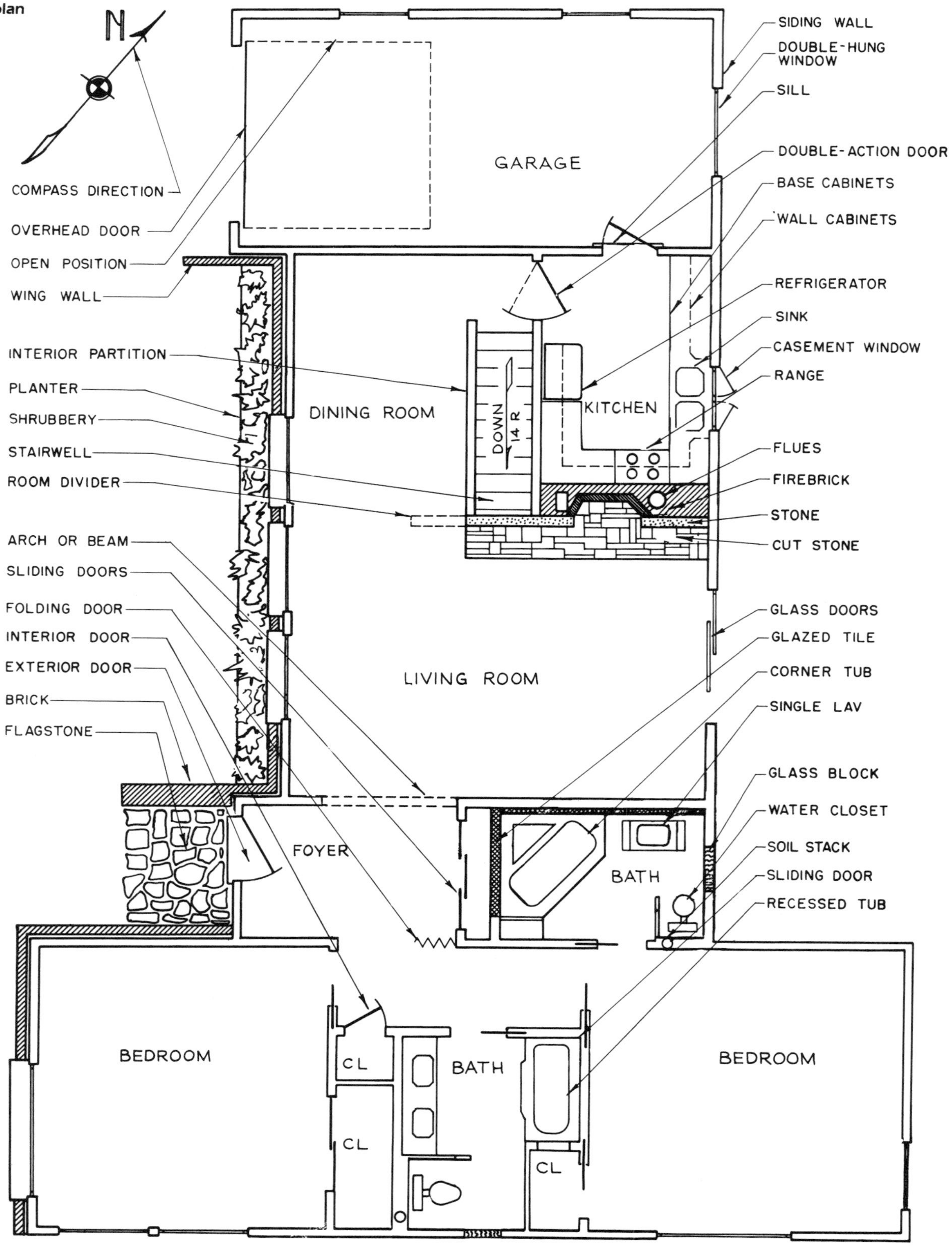

N

COMPASS DIRECTION
OVERHEAD DOOR
OPEN POSITION
WING WALL

INTERIOR PARTITION
PLANTER
SHRUBBERY
STAIRWELL
ROOM DIVIDER

ARCH OR BEAM
SLIDING DOORS
FOLDING DOOR
INTERIOR DOOR
EXTERIOR DOOR
BRICK
FLAGSTONE

GARAGE

DINING ROOM

DOWN 14 R

KITCHEN

LIVING ROOM

FOYER

BATH

BEDROOM

CL

CL

BATH

CL

BEDROOM

SIDING WALL
DOUBLE-HUNG WINDOW
SILL
DOUBLE-ACTION DOOR
BASE CABINETS
WALL CABINETS
REFRIGERATOR
SINK
CASEMENT WINDOW
RANGE
FLUES
FIREBRICK
STONE
CUT STONE
GLASS DOORS
GLAZED TILE
CORNER TUB
SINGLE LAV
GLASS BLOCK
WATER CLOSET
SOIL STACK
SLIDING DOOR
RECESSED TUB

Fig. 1-13 Elevation symbols.

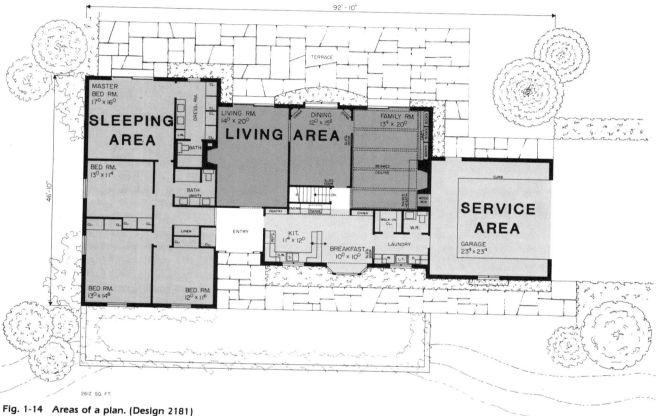

Fig. 1-14 Areas of a plan. (Design 2181)

floor plan to be accurate and functional, the designer must first determine what services or facilities should be included in the various areas of the building. These areas must then be combined into an integrated plan, with appropriately sized and proportioned rooms that are in the best locations and connected by the most efficient traffic patterns.

Area planning Figure 1–14 shows a very basic, well-designed floor plan. Note that in this floor plan rooms that function together are clustered together. For example, the living room, dining room, and family room are all adjacent to the entry. The kitchen is connected directly to both the dining room and the breakfast area.

The bedrooms and baths are all clustered in one

part of the plan, and the service facilities, laundry, and garage, are located at the opposite end. All of these areas are connected effectively by an entry hall which joins the sleeping area, living area, and the kitchen portion of the service area. Thus, each residence can be divided into three basic areas: the sleeping area, the living area, and the service area. The unusual plan shown in Fig. 1–15 illustrates a most distinct separation of this plan—the study provides a transition from the living area to the sleeping area, while the dining room, which is part of the living area, is directly adjacent to the kitchen portion of the service area.

Traffic patterns The major traffic areas of a residence include halls, entrance foyers, stairs, lanais, and areas of rooms through which people pass

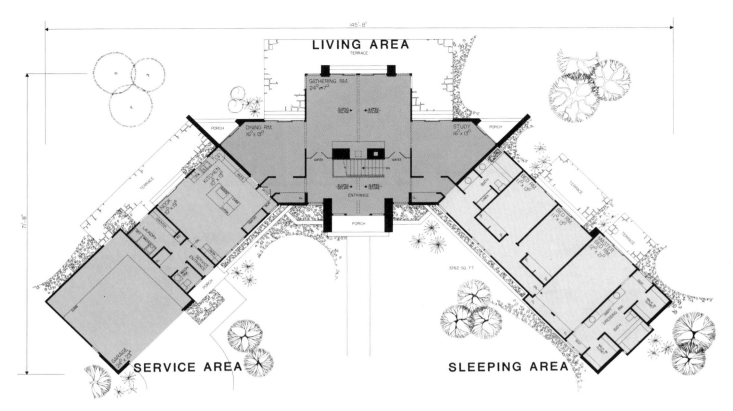

Fig. 1-15 Separation of areas. (Design 2534)

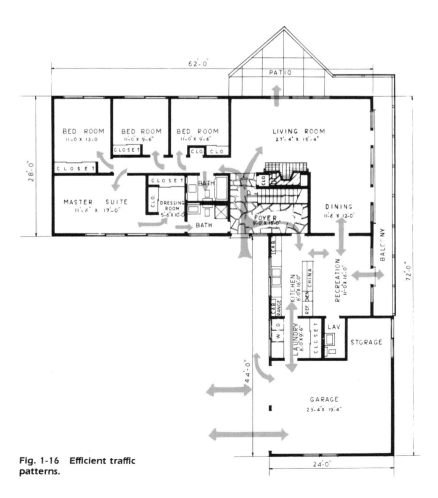

Fig. 1-16 Efficient traffic patterns.

to gain access to other areas. Traffic areas must be designed for each room that provide passage from one area to another or from one room to another, using the least amount of space. Always remember that space used for halls, foyers, and stairs leaves less space for living, sleeping, and service area functions. Therefore, extremely long halls or corridors should be avoided, not only because they provide no living space but also because they are difficult to light, heat, and cool. Traffic patterns that require passage through one room to reach another room should be generally avoided in the living area and absolutely avoided in the sleeping area.

The traffic pattern shown in Fig. 1–16 is both efficient and functional. It contains a minimum amount of wasted hall space without creating a boxed-in appearance. It also provides access to each of the areas without passing through the other areas. The arrows clearly show that the sleeping, living, and service areas are all accessible from the entrance. In this plan, the service entrance provides access to the kitchen from the carport and other parts of the service area, thus providing an effective channel for traffic. However, sometimes the use of an extremely open living area helps to facilitate traffic circulation as shown in Fig. 1–17.

One method of determining the effectiveness of traffic circulation in a house is to trace daily routine patterns through the house with a pencil on the floor plan. If you trace through a whole day's activities, you will see graphically where

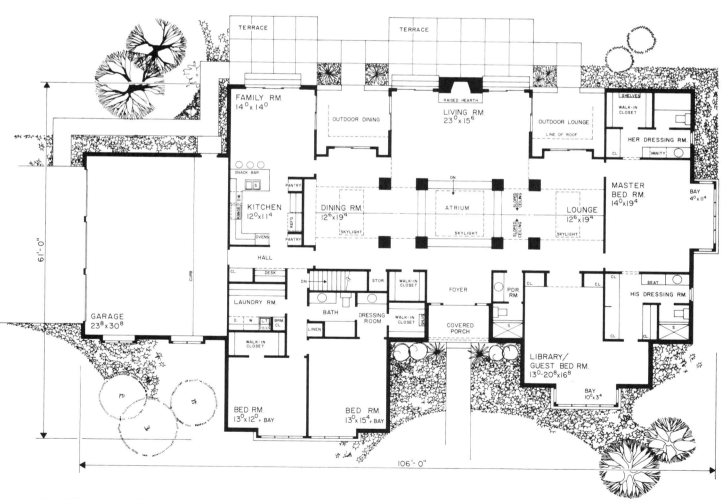

Fig. 1-17 Open traffic circulation. (Design 2791)

3809 SQ FT

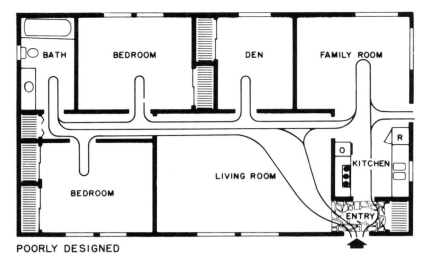

POORLY DESIGNED

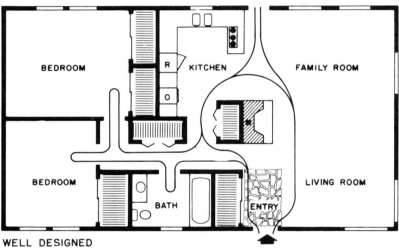

WELL DESIGNED

Fig. 1-18 Traffic circulation.

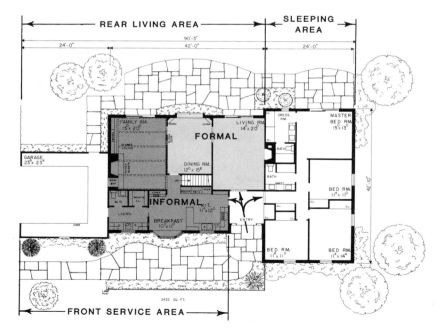

Fig. 1-19 Living area zones. (Design 2144)

the heaviest traffic occurs and whether the traffic areas have been planned effectively. Figure 1–18 shows the difference between poorly designed traffic patterns and well-designed traffic patterns through use of these traced routes.

Room locations   The location of each room in the correct position and relationship with other rooms is the key to designing a well-functioning plan.

Living room   The living room should be centrally located. It should be near the major outside entrance, but the entrance should not lead directly into the living room. In smaller residences the entrance may need to open into the living room, but this should be avoided wherever possible. If it is necessary, the entry should not be located in the center of the living room. It should be on the side close to the sleeping and service areas. The living room should not provide a traffic access to the sleeping and service areas of the house. Since the living room and dining room often function together, the living room should be directly adjacent to the dining room. Notice how this is achieved in Fig. 1–19. Notice also how the areas are divided into formal and informal zones.

Dining room   Dining facilities may be located in many different areas, depending on the capacity needed and the type of plan. However, the major dining facility should generally be located directly adjacent to the living room with direct access to the kitchen, as shown in Fig. 1–17. The ideal dining location is one that requires few steps from the kitchen to the dining table. However, the view of the preparation of food and other kitchen activities should be baffled (screened) from the dining room. Figure 1–20 illustrates another effective dining room-kitchen relationship, but without the living and dining rooms being adjacent.

The necessity of having the dining room near to both the kitchen and the living room requires that it normally be placed either between the kitchen and the living room or in a corner between the two, thus forming a triangle as shown in Figs. 1–19 and 1–21.

Family room   The family room should be located in an area accessible, but not visible, from the living area. Because of the normal accumulation of hobby materials and clutter, it is quite common to locate the family room adjacent to the kitchen, as shown in Fig. 1–21. This revives the concept of the old country kitchen in which many family activities were centered. It creates a distinct informal living area in the rear and a more private formal living room in the front. All this is possible because of the isolation of the sleeping area on the second floor.

When the family room is located adjacent to the living room or dining room, it becomes an extension of these rooms for social purposes. In this location the family room is often separated from

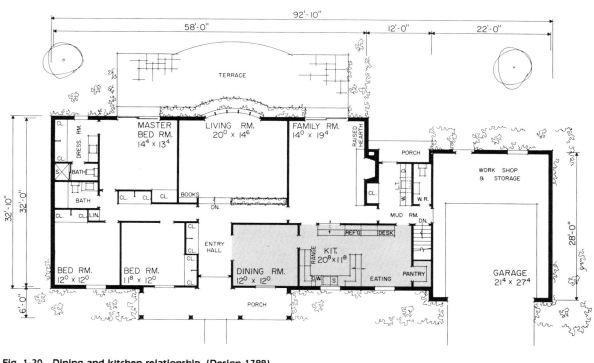

Fig. 1-20 Dining and kitchen relationship. (Design 1788)

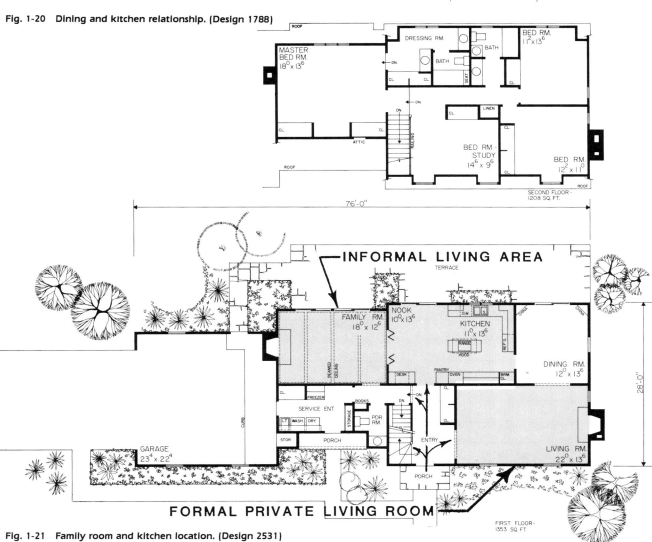

Fig. 1-21 Family room and kitchen location. (Design 2531)

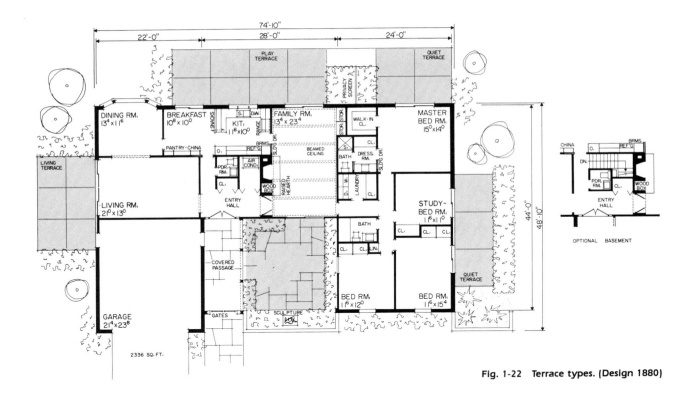

the other rooms by folding doors, screens, or sliding doors. Another popular location for the family room is between the service area and the living area, since the family room at one time or another may function as part of either area.

Recreation rooms Although family rooms may serve a dual function as family room and recreation room, recreation rooms are normally those rooms which are devoted to physical activities, such as table tennis, billiards, shuffleboard, dancing, exercise, and so forth. For this reason recreation rooms are frequently located in a basement in order to utilize space that would otherwise be wasted. However, when the recreation room is located on the ground level its function can often be expanded to a patio or terrace. Regardless of the level, the recreation room should be located away from the quiet areas of the home. If a recreation room cannot actually be separated from the main part of the house, it can often be included as part of the garage or carport design.

Porch The function of the porch must, of course, be considered before any location can be established. If the porch is to function simply as an extension of a living area then it should be located close to and accessible from the living room. If dining facilities are to be included on the porch then access must be available from the dining room or kitchen. In either case the porch should be located to provide maximum flexibility in functioning as an outdoor living area.

The primary functions of the porch should be considered when orienting the porch with the sun. If daytime use is anticipated and direct sunlight is desirable, a southern exposure should be planned. If little sun is wanted during the day, a northern exposure is preferable. If morning sun is desirable, an eastern exposure would be best, and for the afternoon sun, a western exposure is recommended.

Patios and terraces These two terms are currently being used interchangeably. Traditionally, a patio was an outdoor, covered surface adjacent to or directly accessible from the house. A terrace was generally thought to be an outdoor raised area with or without plantings. These days terraces and patios can be regarded as outdoor living areas with a variety of surfaces which function conveniently with indoor living areas. They may be covered or uncovered.

Patios ideally should be located adjacent to the area of the home to which they relate. They should also be somewhat secluded from the street or from the adjoining residences. There are three basic types of patios: living area patios, play area patios, and quiet patios.

Living area patios should be located close to the living room or the dining room. Play area patios should be located near to the service area and if possible be accessible from the family room or recreation room. Quiet patios can be planned as an extension of the bedroom area. These patios can be used for relaxation or for sleeping, and should be secluded from the normal traffic of the home.

Patios can be placed conveniently at the end of a building, between the corners of a building, wrapped around the sides of the house, or placed in the center of a U-shaped house or courtyard. In addition, a patio can be located completely apart from the house when a wooded area, a particular view, or a feature of the terrain is of interest. However, when patios are placed in this manner, accessibility from the house must be considered.

When the patio is placed on the north side of the house, the house itself is used to shade the patio. If sunlight is desired, the patio should be located on the south side of the house. The planner should take full advantage of the most pleasing view and should restrict the view of undesirable sights from the patio. Terraces (or patios), as shown in Fig. 1–22, can serve and function with different areas and zones of the house.

Lanais Lanais (covered exterior passageways) can be located to connect areas of a home on the exterior of a building. In some regions, lanais are known as "breezeways." Lanais commonly link either the garage and the kitchen, the patio and the kitchen or living area, or the living area and the service area. When lanais are carefully located, they can function as sheltered access from inside areas to outside facilities, such as patios, pools, or outdoor cooking areas. The use of lanais, especially in warm climates, can often eliminate the need for more expensive internal space such as indoor halls, as shown in Fig. 1–23. Notice how this lanai (loggia) is connected to an inside, windowed passageway (gallery) to also provide traffic lanes on the inside without sacrificing light.

Fig. 1-23 Courtyard lanais. (Design 2294)

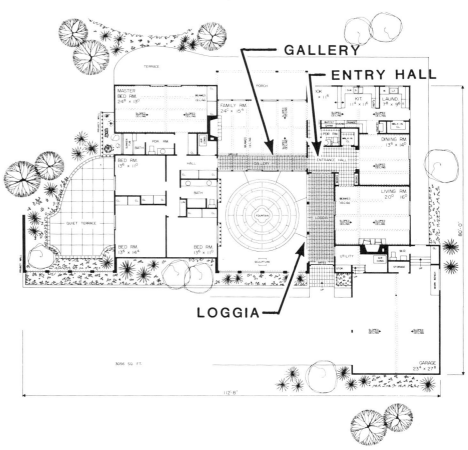

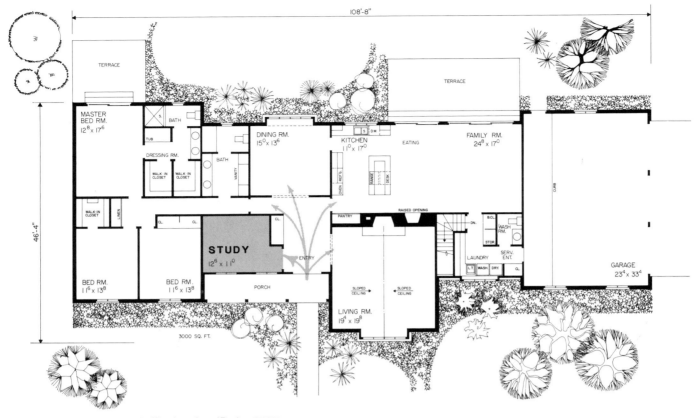

Fig. 1-24 Effective study and office location. (Design 2767)

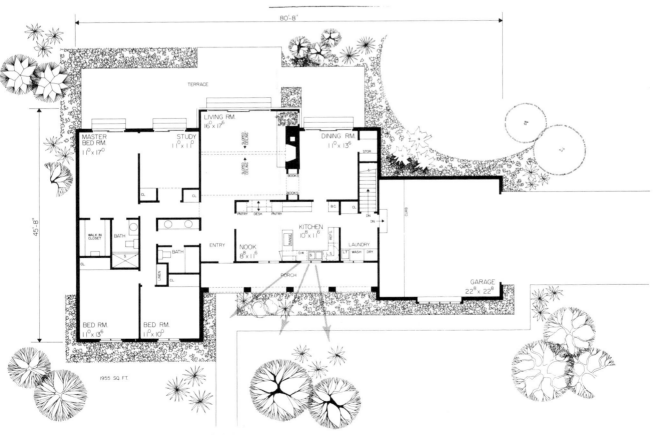

Fig. 1-25 Kitchen with front views. (Design 2557)

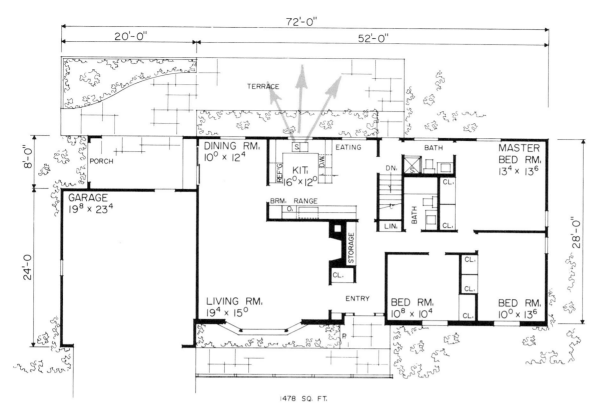

Fig. 1-26 Kitchen with rear views. (Design 1322)

Entrances There are three types of entrances: main access entrances, service entrances, and special-purpose entrances. The main entrance should be located centrally to provide easy access to each area and should be conveniently accessible from driveways, sidewalks, or the street. The service entrance should be located close to the driveway or garage and should be placed near the kitchen or laundry unit if possible. Special-purpose entrances are located adjacent to specific areas, such as between patios and living areas, dining areas, sleeping areas, and so forth. These are generally not accessible to the public, but are entered only from the nonpublic part of the property. For instance, a cellar-basement frequently has a direct access to the rear or side.

Dens or studies Dens or studies should be located in a private area of the residence. They can be incorporated as part of the sleeping area or located in a basement or attic away from the mainstream or functioning of the residence. However, if the study doubles as an office used by the public, then it must be located in an area accessible to the front entrance, as shown in Fig. 1–24.

Kitchen The kitchen is the core of the service area and should be located near the service entrance and the outdoor service area. The children's play area should also be visible from the kitchen. However, the main criterion for locating the kitchen must be the proximity to the dining area and outdoor eating areas. A basic planning decision should involve locating the kitchen (and often its adjacent breakfast nook) to the front or to the rear of the plan. Solar orientation preferences, enjoyment of surrounding landscape, desire to view front yard activities versus overseeing rear yard events are among the points to consider when weighing the choice of kitchen locations. Notice how the kitchen in Fig. 1–25 provides occupants with a view of approaching callers. On the other hand, Fig. 1–26 shows a kitchen with a full view of the rear yard.

Laundry The location of the laundry is often a matter of personal preference. In many cases it can be a matter of economics. In a house with a basement, if space permits, its location on the first floor is most convenient. Plumbing economy can be realized when the laundry equipment is situated near kitchen and/or bath facilities. In a non-basement home, its location in the utility room adjacent to the hot water heater and heating and cooling equipment is a wise choice. When space is extremely restricted, the laundry unit can be located in the kitchen or in a closet. In warmer climates the service porch, garage, or carport are acceptable locations. Personal preference may

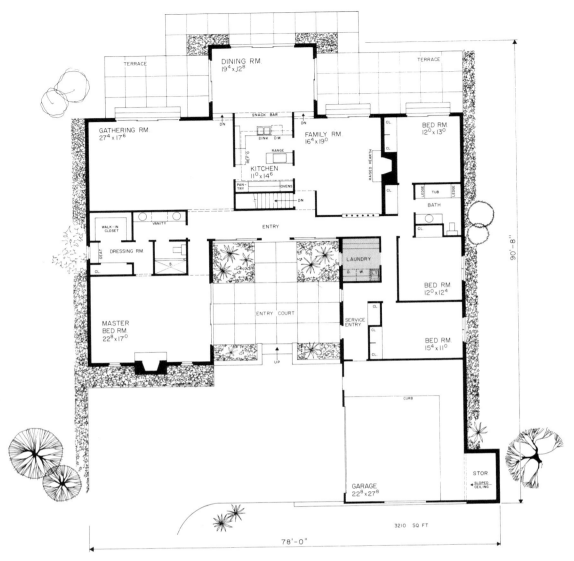

Fig. 1-27 Laundry location. (Design 2783)

lead you to locate the laundry in the sleeping area, from which so much soiled linen and clothing emanate (see Fig. 1–27).

Garages Garages may be attached to the house or located elsewhere on the site. But regardless of the location, the garage greatly affects the traffic pattern of the entire plan.

Attached garages can make a contribution to energy efficiency. If you are in an area where strong northwest winds are a problem in winter, the garage can serve as a buffer. On the other hand, locating the garage away from the path of the sun allows an additional measure of sunlight to reach the interior of the plan. In southern regions you may wish to use the garage, or carport, to protect against the hot summer sun.

Storage areas Areas should be provided for general storage, and for specific storage within each room. Areas that would otherwise be consid-ered wasted space should be used as general storage areas. Parts of the basement, attic, or garage fall into this category. Effective storage planning is necessary to provide storage facilities within each room that will create the least amount of inconvenience in securing stored arti-cles. Wardrobe closets, walk-in closets, wall clos-ets, and furniture such as chests and dressers can be used effectively for local storage.

Bedrooms Bedrooms and the entire sleeping area should be located away from the major activities of the home and from street noises. If possible, the master bedroom should be isolated from other bedrooms by halls, closets, or bath space. It can even be completely isolated from other bedrooms, as shown in Fig. 1–28.

Baths One full bath should be located within or adjacent to the master bedroom, and at least one other bath should be accessible from the

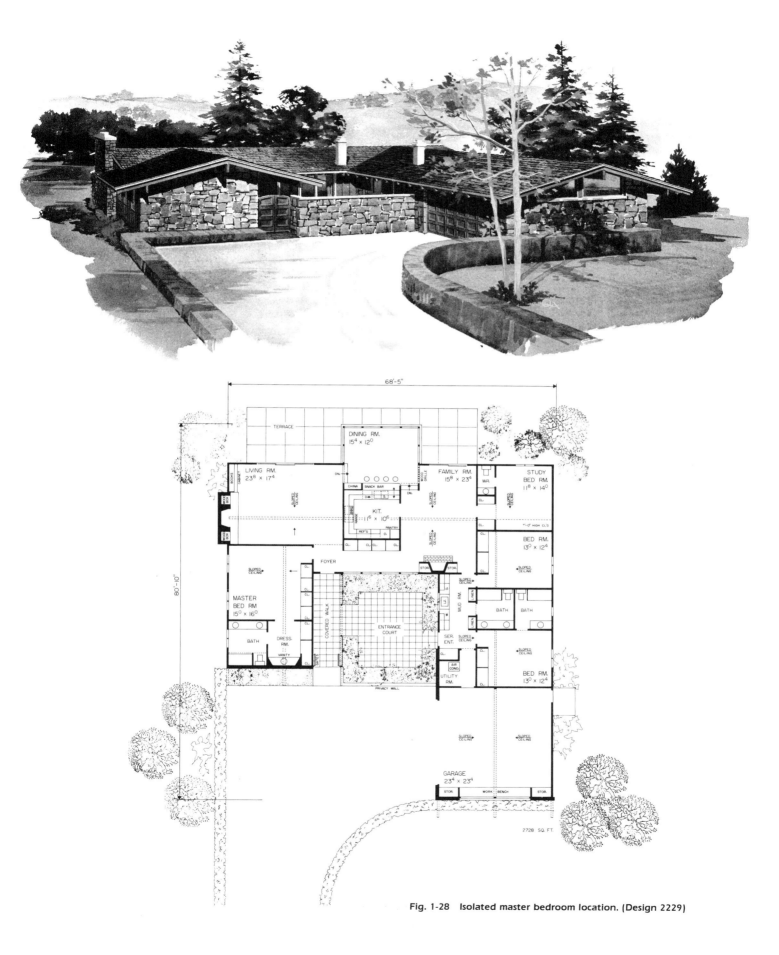

Fig. 1-28 Isolated master bedroom location. (Design 2229)

remainder of the bedrooms in the sleeping area. One of these baths should be accessible to guests, or a separate half bath should be provided adjacent to the living area. A bath can be located to effectively serve two distinct areas of the house, as in Fig. 1–29. By locating it near the center of the plan and providing double access a bath's utility is greatly enhanced, as shown in Fig. 1–30. A single bath may serve two bedrooms exclusively, as depicted in Fig. 1–31. Then, too, everybody can have their own bath, if space is provided, as illustrated by Fig. 1–32.

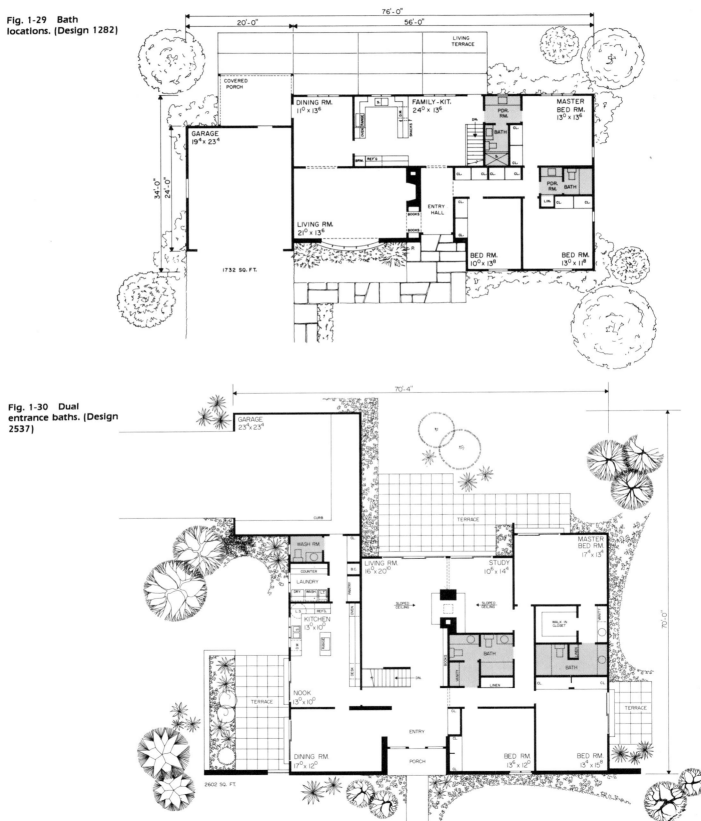

Fig. 1-29 Bath locations. (Design 1282)

Fig. 1-30 Dual entrance baths. (Design 2537)

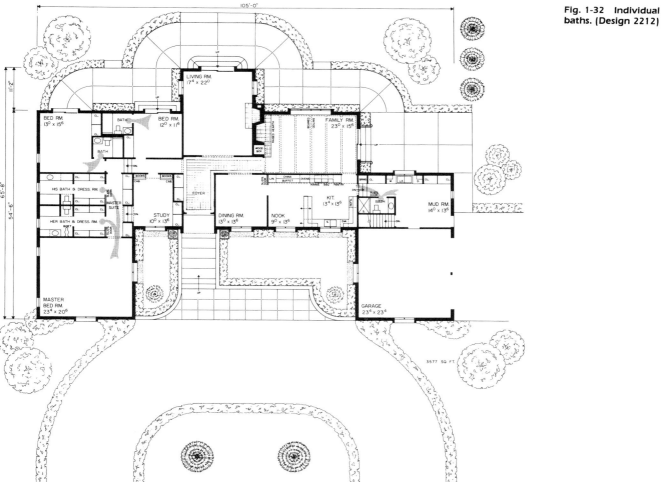

Fig. 1-31 Effective bath accesses. (Design 2613)

TERRACE

TERRACE

PORCH

NOOK
10' x 9'

FAMILY RM.
12⁸ x 18⁴

DINING RM.
11⁰ x 11⁰

LIVING RM.
18⁰ x 13⁰

MASTER
BED RM.
13⁰ x 14⁰

KITCHEN
10⁴ x 10⁰

BEAMED
CEILING

ENTRANCE

PORCH

BED RM.
12⁸ x 11⁰

BATH

BED RM.
10⁸ x 10⁸

BATH

BED RM.
10⁸ x 10⁸

BATH

STORAGE

STORAGE

2132 SQ. FT.

CURB

GARAGE
23⁴ x 23⁸

70'-8"

64'-8"

FAMILY RM.

PANTRY

BATH

BED RM.
12⁸ x 11⁴

GARAGE

STORAGE

CURB

OPTIONAL NON-BASEMENT

Fig. 1-32 Individual baths. (Design 2212)

105'-0"

LIVING RM.
17⁴ x 22⁰

BED RM.
13⁰ x 15⁶

BATH

BED RM.
12⁰ x 11⁶

FAMILY RM.
23⁰ x 15⁶

BEAMED CEILING

RAISED HEARTH

WOOD
BOX

BOOKS

BOOKS
CAB

CHINA
BUFFET

OVENS

RANGE

HIS BATH & DRESS. RM.

MASTER
SUITE

FOYER

KIT.
13⁴ x 13⁶

MUD RM.
14⁰ x 13⁶

BATH

HER BATH & DRESS. RM.

STUDY
10⁰ x 13⁶

DINING RM.
13⁰ x 13⁶

NOOK
9⁰ x 13⁶

MASTER
BED RM.
23⁴ x 20⁶

GARAGE
23⁴ x 23⁴

3577 SQ. FT.

11'-2"

65'-8"

54'-6"

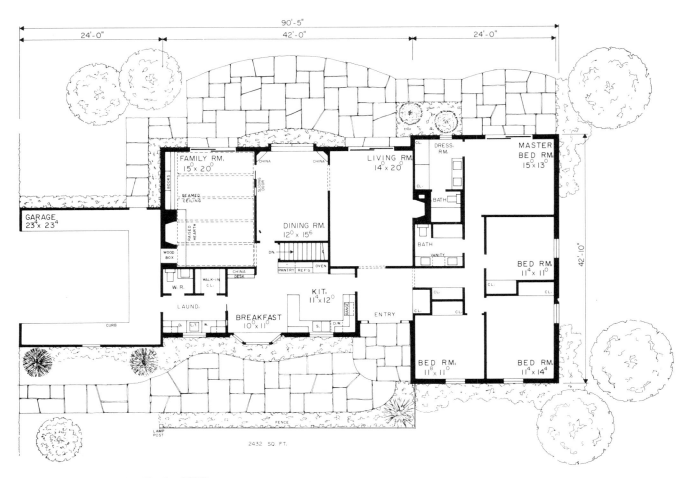

Fig. 1-33 One-level plan. (Design 2675)

Effect of levels on room locations Different living requirements may affect the location of rooms in one-story residences compared to two-story homes. Figure 1–33 shows a one-story plan with rooms located effectively. Notice the distinct separation of the sleeping area, and the relationship between the living, dining, and breakfast-kitchen areas. Notice also the formal zones and the informal zones, which include part of the service area, kitchen, breakfast room, laundry, and garage. In this plan the laundry room is strategically placed to function as a mud room. The outdoor living area functions with both the family room and living room, and the front outdoor zone functions as an access from the garage to the main service area without going through each. Also, the central entrance is a very short distance from the entrance to the sleeping, living, and service areas.

In the two-story plan shown in Fig. 1–34, all the bedrooms are placed on the second level, with the master bedroom isolated by an adjacent dressing room and bath and another bath serving the other three bedrooms. On the first level the service and living areas are well separated but equally accessible from the main entrance. The living room can be extremely private with no unnecessary traffic, but the adjacent dining room has access to the rear terrace as do the family room and breakfast areas. Here again, the informal living area is adjacent to the service area. Also, the powder room is close to the living area for guest use. However, the most unique feature of this plan is the dual entrance to the service area from the second front porch or from the garage.

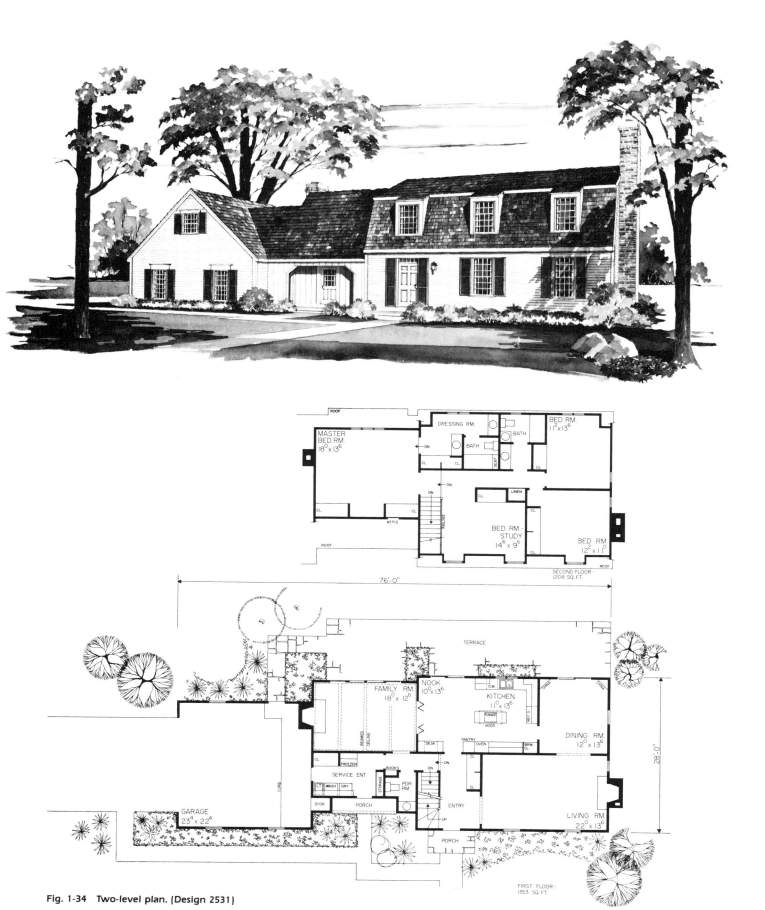

Fig. 1-34   Two-level plan. (Design 2531)

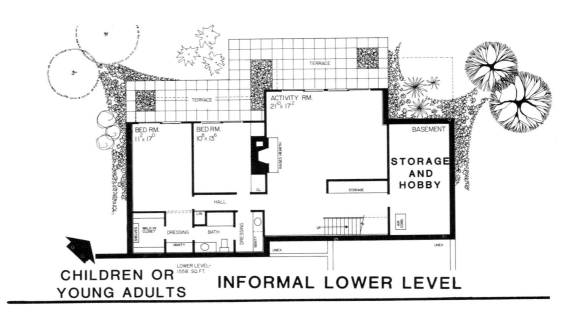

CHILDREN OR YOUNG ADULTS   INFORMAL LOWER LEVEL

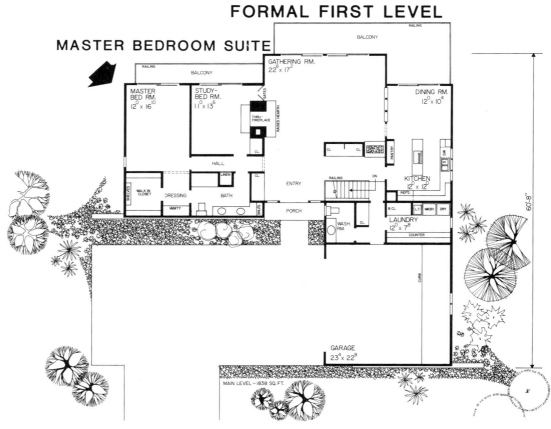

FORMAL FIRST LEVEL

MASTER BEDROOM SUITE

Fig. 1-35   Hillside two-level plan. (Design 2583)

Another variation of a two-story plan is shown in Fig. 1–35. In this plan, designed for a hillside lot, the back of the house is exposed at the top level. The functions can be divided between levels; for example, a master bedroom suite and study area are located on the top level with the formal living room and dining room, while the other bedrooms are located on the lower level with the activities room, which is more informal and is more likely to be used by children or young adults.

Room sizes The size of each room in a residence is greatly influenced by budget considerations and determined by the functions of that room and the amount and size of furniture necessary to serve those functions. The need for a grand piano in a living room could easily double the planned size of the room. Likewise, a bedroom planned for a king-size bed will necessarily need to be much larger than a room designed for a single bed. Therefore, the furniture requirements of each room must be considered seriously before room sizes are determined. Figure 1–36 gives general guidelines for room size design. However, since the cost of a home is largely determined by the size and number of rooms, room sizes should be adjusted to conform to the acceptable price range for each residence.

In addition to establishing appropriate room sizes, *room proportions* also play an important role in creating an effective floor plan design.

Typical Room Sizes (Feet)			
Basic Rooms	Small	Average	Large
1. Living room	12 × 18	16 × 20	22 × 28
2. Dining room	10 × 12	12 × 15	15 × 18
3. Kitchen	5 × 10	10 × 16	12 × 20
4. Utility room	6 × 7	6 × 10	8 × 12
5. Bedroom	10 × 10	12 × 12	14 × 16
6. Bathroom	5 × 7	7 × 9	9 × 12
Additional Rooms/ Areas			
7. Halls	3′ wide	3′–6″ wide	3′–9″ wide
8. Area	10 × 20	20 × 20	22 × 25
9. Storage wall	6″ deep	12″ deep	18″ deep
10. Den	8 × 10	10 × 12	12 × 16
11. Family room	12 × 15	15 × 18	15 × 22
12. Wardrobe closet	2 × 4	2 × 8	2 × 15
13. One-rod walk-in closet	4 × 3	4 × 6	4 × 8
14. Two-rod walk-in closet	6 × 4	6 × 6	6 × 8
15. Porch	6 × 8	8 × 12	12 × 20
16. Entry	6 × 6	8 × 10	8 × 15
17. One-car garage	11 × 19	13 × 25	16 × 25
18. Two-car garage	20 × 20	22 × 22	25 × 25

Fig. 1-36 Typical room sizes.

Fig. 1-37 A 1500-square-foot plan. (Design 2106)

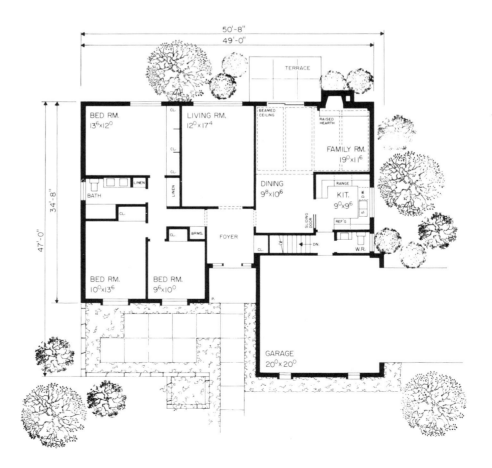

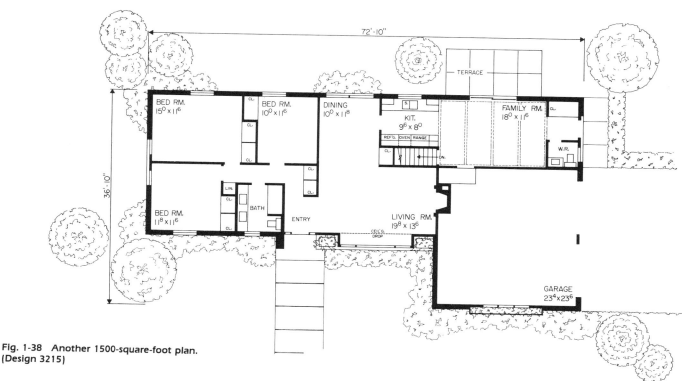

Fig. 1-38 Another 1500-square-foot plan. (Design 3215)

Rectangular rooms, for example, are easier to furnish than perfectly square rooms or rooms with angular walls. Rooms with offsets or blind corners should be avoided.

Floor plan sizes The total size of the overall plan is dependent on the number and size of each room, but it also depends heavily on the arrangement of rooms and features. Different floor plans of the same size which include identical features

can be arranged quite differently. For example, Figs. 1–37 and 1–38 are approximately the same size, 1500 square feet, and contain the identical features: three bedrooms, one sleeping-area bath, one living-service area half-bath, formal living and dining area adjacent to a kitchen and a family room. And yet the layout of each plan is very different.

Conversely, a plan with identical features and numbers of rooms can vary in size depending on

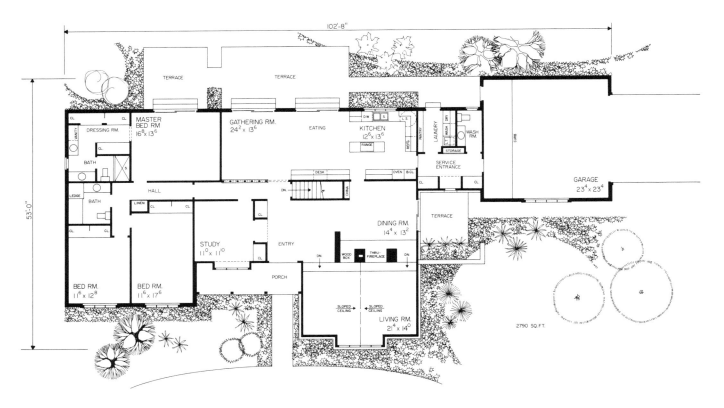

Fig. 1-39 A 2700-square-foot plan. (Design 2746)

the size and arrangement of those rooms. For example, Figs. 1–39 and 1–40 vary greatly in size, and the plans differ in layout. The first is 2700 square feet and the latter is 3200 square feet, but each contains the identical number of rooms: four bedrooms, including a master bedroom, dressing room, and bath; living room; dining room; gathering room; kitchen with an eating area; laundry-

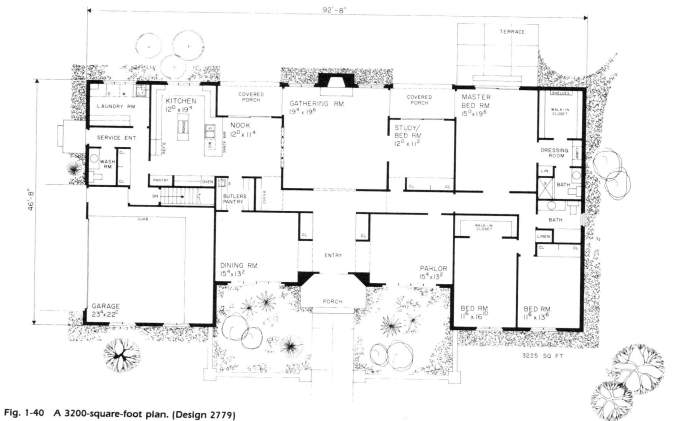

Fig. 1-40   A 3200-square-foot plan. (Design 2779)

Fig. 1-41 Similar plan to Fig. 1-42 except size. (Design 1917)

wash room; and garage.

Plans (Figs. 1–41 and 1–42) can vary greatly in size without significantly changing the basic arrangements of rooms. Notice these two plans are similar, but not identical in size. The first is 1700 square feet and the latter 2400 square feet. Thus even a smaller plan can be changed significantly in size and arrangement. In changing the size, the integrity of the original plan is maintained, yet Fig. 1–42 includes an additional study and dressing room.

Fundamentals of elevation design The aesthetic design of the interior is not as related to the basic floor plan layout as it is to the treatment of surfaces, walls, floors, ceilings, and the furnishing of the interior. Thus, the interior can be "decorated" after the plan is complete, but the exterior must be designed from the start by using the basic elements and principles of design. The designing of the exterior elevation of a residence is both a functional and an aesthetic activity. The functional part involves the correct placement of windows

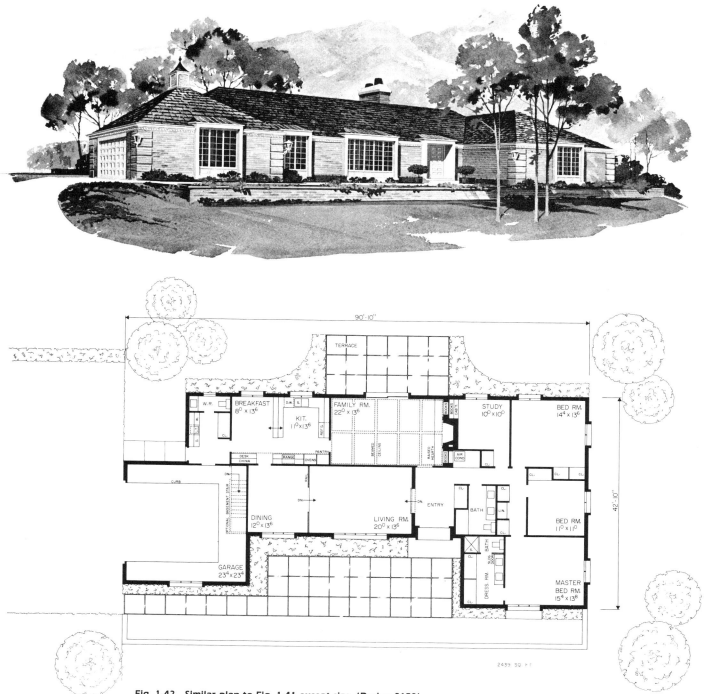

Fig. 1-42 Similar plan to Fig. 1-41 except size. (Design 2179)

and doors, balconies, roof overhangs, and siding, but much of this also involves aesthetic design since many styles and configurations of doors, windows, roofs, sidings, and chimneys are possible for the same floor plan. The aesthetic part involves the manipulation of material and space according to the principles and elements of design.

Elements of design The elements of design are the tools of the designer and the ingredients of every successful design. These elements are line, form (space and shape), color (light and shadow), and texture (materials).

The element of line is used to produce a sense of movement. Lines are either curved or straight. Curved lines have an infinite number of directional variables. Curved lines indicate soft, graceful, and flowing movements. Figure 1–43a shows the use of curved lines in an elevation design. Straight lines are either vertical, horizontal, or diagonal. A vertical line creates the illusion of an

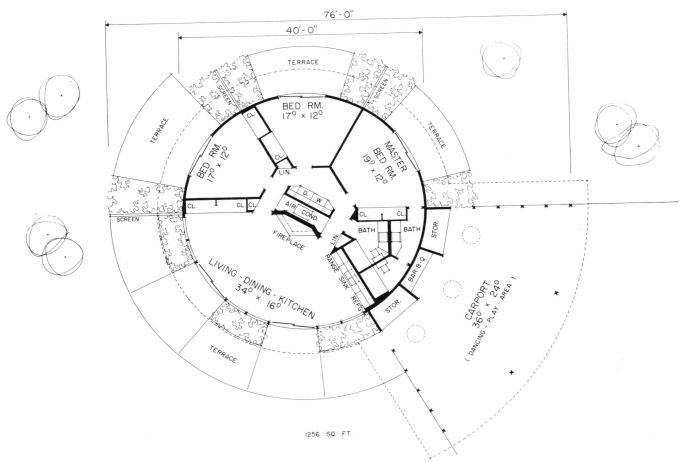

76'-0"

40'-0"

TERRACE

TERRACE

BED RM.
17⁰ x 12⁰

MASTER
BED RM.
19⁰ x 12⁰

BED RM.
17⁰ x 12⁰

SCREEN

SCREEN

TERRACE

CL.

CL.

LIN.

SCREEN

CL.

CL. CL.

D. W.

AIR COND.

CL.

CL.

BATH

BATH

STOR.

FIREPLACE

LIVING - DINING - KITCHEN
34⁰ x 16⁰

LIN.

RANGE

SINK

BAR-B-Q.

STOR.

REFG.

STOR.

CARPORT
36⁰ x 24⁰
(DANCING - PLAY AREA)

TERRACE

1256 SQ. FT.

Fig. 1-43a Curved line design. (Design 1428)

Street View

Garden View

Fig. 1-43b Vertical line emphasis. (Design 2123)

increase of height, as the eye is led upward to follow the line. In Fig. 1–43b vertical line emphasis is created through the use of the vertically oriented front window walls. In Fig. 1–44 horizontal line emphasis is achieved by the long eave line emphasis. Straight vertical lines create a feeling of strength, simplicity, and alertness. Hor-

izontal lines, however, suggest relaxation and repose. Diagonal lines create a feeling of restlessness or transition.

Materials are the raw substances with which designers create. Materials possess their own color, form, and degree of harshness and texture. Surfaces of rough, dull texture such as concrete, stone, and brick suggest strength and informality. Figure 1–45 shows the effective use of natural materials.

Lines join together to produce forms and shapes. The form of an object may be closed and solid, closed and volume-containing, or open as implied in Fig. 1–46. But regardless, the form of any structure must always be determined by its function. Space surrounds form and may be contained within it. A design can create the feeling of space, as shown in Fig. 1–46, by extending the form in many different directions. Thus, much architectural design work is the art of defining form and space relationships in a manner that allows all the elements of design to function effectively in the most aesthetic manner.

Fig. 1-44 Horizontal line emphasis. (Design 1959)

Fig. 1-45 Use of natural materials. (Design 2782)

Color is either an integral part of an architectural material or must be added to create the desired effect. Color in architecture serves to distinguish items, strengthen interest, and reduce eye fatigue. Color combinations are therefore varied depending on the purpose to be served. Colors must be used in harmonies that create the most pleasing visual effect. Red is associated with warmth; yellow is related to cheer and exuberance; orange is associated with light and heat; violet, the color of shadows, creates a feeling of mystery; green depicts coolness and restraint; blue is associated with coolness, repose, and formality.

The natural color or appearance of a surface can be changed by the light reflected by forms and shadows which appear in areas that light cannot reach. Light and shadow both give a sense of depth to any structure. Notice how the light and shadow in Fig. 1–47 help define and strengthen the features of the design.

Principles of design The principles of design are the guidelines for using the elements of design to create aesthetically functional buildings. The basic principles of design are balance, variety, emphasis, unity, opposition, proportion, rhythm, subordination, transition, and repetition.

Balance is the achievement of equilibrium in design. Buildings are either formally balanced if they are symmetrical, or informally balanced if there is a variety and yet a harmonious relationship in the distribution of space, form, light,

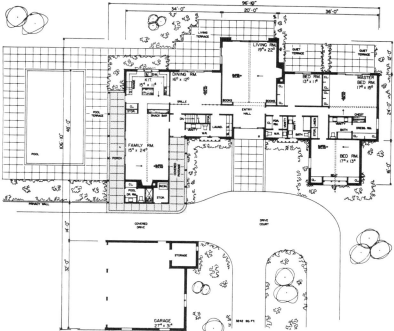

Fig. 1-46 Open form design. (Design 1725)

Fig. 1-47 Light and shadow defuse shapes. (Design 2357)

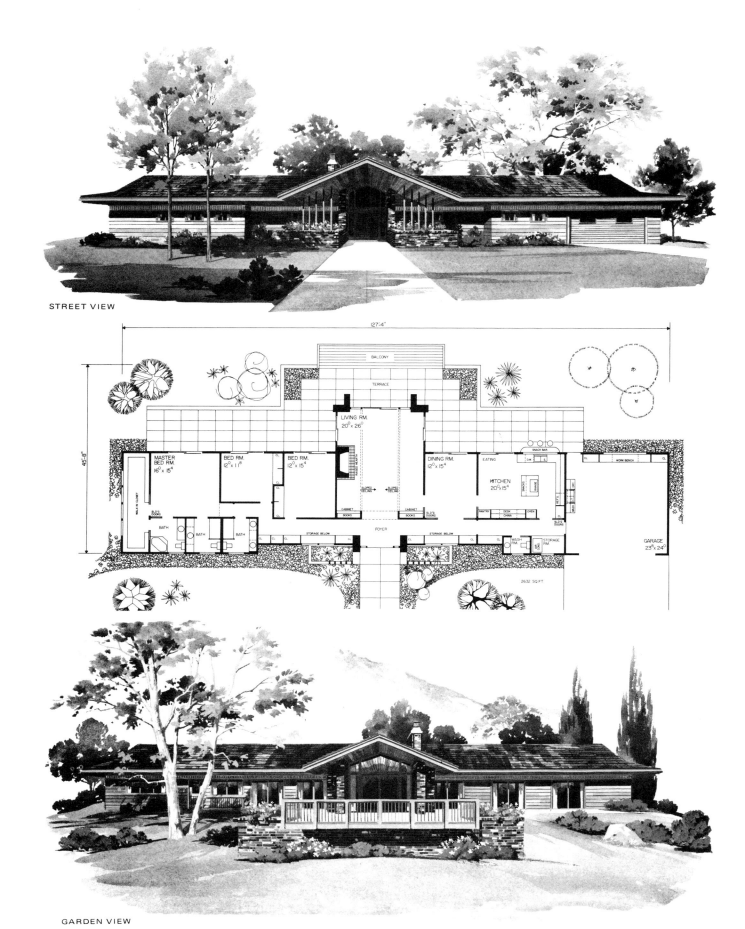

STREET VIEW

GARDEN VIEW

Fig. 1-48 Symmetrically balanced design. (Design 2256)

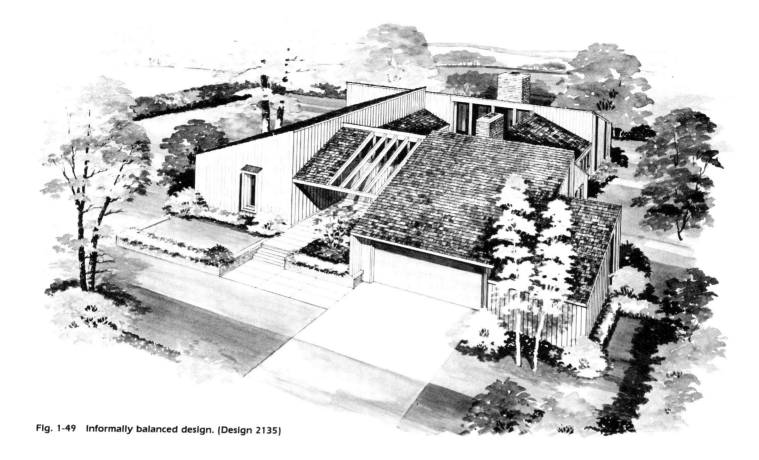

Fig. 1-49 Informally balanced design. (Design 2135)

color, and shade. The residence shown in Fig. 1–48 is formally balanced because of the symmetrical relationship of the sleeping area wing and the service area wing to the front entrance. The residence shown in Fig. 1–49 is informally balanced owing to the varying roof slopes which give an unsymmetrical balance around the entrance area.

The principle of emphasis (or domination) is used by designers to draw attention to an area or subject. Emphasis is achieved through the use of color, form, texture, or line. The contrasting shade and line of the entrance shown in Fig. 1–50 provides the emphasis on the entrance to this residence. Some key feature should dominate every elevation design. For this reason too many different building materials or too much mixing of different colors, textures, or lines should be avoided.

When lines, planes, and surface treatments are repeated in a regular sequence a sense of rhythm is achieved. Rhythm is used in design to create motion and carry the viewer's eye to various parts of the space. See Fig. 1-51.

The proportional dimensions (scale of a building) are important. Large components in small areas should be avoided; likewise small components in large areas should not be used.

Unity is the expression of wholeness in design. Every structure should appear complete. No part should appear as an appendage or afterthought.

Variety in design is needed to keep any structure from becoming dull and tiresome to the eye. Too much rhythm, too much repetition, too much unity, and so forth can ruin the sense of variety or contrast.

Unity is often achieved through *repetition*. Vertical lines, space, and textures are often repeated throughout the design to tie the structure together aesthetically.

Opposition in design adds interest. Opposition involves creating elements such as short and long, thick and thin, straight and curved, black and white, and so forth. Opposite forms, colors, and lines in a design, when used effectively with other principles of design, achieves balance, emphasis, and variety.

When emphasis is achieved through some design feature, other features naturally become subordinate. Thus *subordination* of a feature is the opposite of emphasis. There cannot be any emphasis on a feature without the subordination of other features and vice versa.

A change from one color to another or from a curved to a straight line, if done while maintaining the unity of design, is known as transition. The designer's task in achieving transition in all aspects of design contributes to the harmony of the different elements of design without sacrificing unity.

Architectural design involves not only how a

Fig. 1-50   Entrance emphasis. (Design 2599)

structure appears but also how it functions. However, functional success alone does not guarantee that a design is aesthetically pleasing. The task of the designer is to combine functional efficiency and aesthetics into a unified design. But remember: *form follows function* and no design should exist in isolation but must be always related to the situations that influence it. Thus, the creation of a successful design involves manipulating the entire environment.

Fig. 1-51   Rhythm gained through repetition of vertical window lines. (Design 2178)

CHAPTER 2

Defining Personal Requirements

Before beginning to design, redesign, or alter any residential plan, the personal requirements of the occupants must be clearly defined and agreed to by all involved. This requires the designer to assess lifestyles, determine wants and needs, and consider the financial status of the occupants.

Assessing Lifestyles

Lifestyles, living habits, and needs vary greatly throughout the population, from person to person, from family to family, and even from individual to individual within a family. There are basic, minimal facilities which must be included in each residence—a living area, bath, bedroom, cooking and dining facilities. Once these are included the features required to satisfy the wide range and variety of living habits are extremely diverse. Since a wide range of furniture, equipment, and/or separate rooms are needed to satisfy different requirements the designer must first consider and identify the specific living habits that relate these requirements to the architectural plan. In addition, the designer must consider the personal tastes and financial restrictions of the potential home buyer. Figure 2–1 shows graphically the development of an architectural plan, beginning with the identification of living habits, tastes, needs, and style through the finalizing of a floor plan.

Determining Needs and Wants

To develop an effective residential plan the designer must first clearly define the *needs* and *wants* of the occupants. In designing, altering, or redesigning your own residence you must probe your *real* needs even more carefully to overcome the tendency to feel you need what everyone else needs or wants. You must not believe that every want is a need.

Needs in architectural terms means absolute—a must. A need is something the occupant cannot or will not do without under any circumstances. But needs are not universal. A territorial sales representative may need a home office, a business executive may want a home office, and a bus driver may have no need or want for a home office. Likewise, a large family may need four bedrooms, while a slightly smaller family may want or prefer four bedrooms but only absolutely need three bedrooms. One person's needs may therefore be another person's wants.

Determining the difference between individual needs and wants is a matter of defining basic requirements versus identifying desirable or preferable features. Simply stated, an architectural need is a feature you will not live without. A want, on the other hand, is a preferred feature which can, though reluctantly, be omitted if space, circumstances, or budget restrictions demand.

For these reasons it is extremely important to define and differentiate between needs and wants before beginning to design, alter, or redesign a residence. Only then can the features of a residence be designed in the proper perspective and with meaningful priorities.

Figure 2–2 shows a list of needs and wants of a typical prospective home builder. Wants should

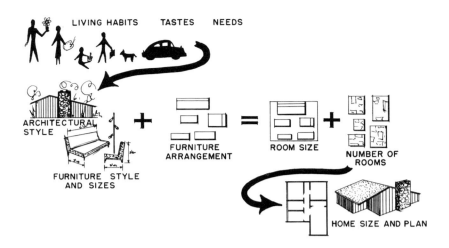

Fig. 2-1 Architectural plan development.

LIVING HABITS   TASTES   NEEDS

ARCHITECTURAL STYLE

FURNITURE STYLE AND SIZES

FURNITURE ARRANGEMENT

ROOM SIZE

NUMBER OF ROOMS

HOME SIZE AND PLAN

Fig. 2-2   Typical residential needs and wants.

Needs (absolute)	Wants (if possible)
1. Contemporary exterior with large front entrance	11. Fireplace
2. Spacious foyer	12. Quiet terrace off master bedroom
3. Large living room with large glass area and view	13. Powder room in living area
4. Large study	14. Study to double as fourth/guest bedroom
5. *a.* Large master bedroom with dressing room and bath	15. Living area walk-in closet
5. *b.* Two additional bedrooms	16. Basement
6. Living and dining patio	17. One level
7. Formal separate dining with access to terrace	18. Sauna
8. Large breakfast area	19. Rec room for ping pong and billiards
9. Separate laundry room	20. Tennis court
10. Three car garage	21. Bath for each bedroom

be ranked in order of importance so that if there are any trade-offs, that is, if there is not enough space or budget available for all items, there will be a clear understanding of which items can be deleted from the design. Since needs are all absolutely necessary, ranking is not required. So prioritize "wants" and list "needs."

Figure 2–3 shows a residence designed to match the needs and most of the wants outlined in Fig. 2–2. The needs are numbered in Fig. 2–3. How many of the wants can you identify in Fig. 2–3? As required, all needs have been met (items 1–10). In addition, the first seven wants were also incorporated into the plan (items 11–17). Only the last four wants were not included. However, by including a basement the sauna and rec room can be added at a later time.

Figure 2–4 shows a list of needs and wants for a

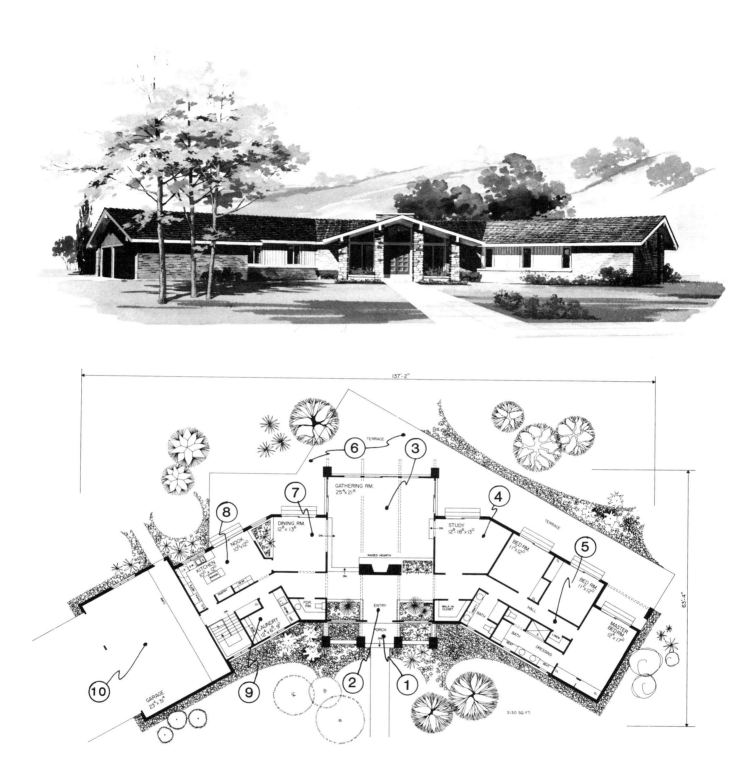

Fig. 2-3 Plan matching Fig. 2-2 needs and wants. (Design 2720)

smaller residence. Figure 2–5 shows how these needs and wants were incorporated into an actual residential plan. In this case, all the needs were met as required, and also the first three wants were included in the design—the fireplace, the study, and the two-level design.

Figure 2–6 shows a list of needs and wants for a vacation home, and Fig. 2–7 shows how these needs and wants were accomplished in the development of the design. All the needs plus the first four wants were accomplished, although the powder room for guests doubles as a lavatory for the first bedroom. A comparison of Fig. 2–7 with Figs.

2–3 and 2–5 shows the wide variety of needs, depending on the anticipated living habits and requirements of the occupants. This comparison clearly shows the need to carefully define individual needs in order to ensure the development of a plan which fulfills these needs.

Designers who create architectural plans for the general public without reference to specific individual needs must speculate on the needs and wants of most as related to space and budget restrictions. For this reason prospective home builders should carefully assess their wants and needs and diligently study existing plans to effect

Fig. 2-4 Needs and wants for a smaller residence.

Needs	Wants
1. Kitchen with breakfast area	9. Fireplace
2. Full bath	10. Study
3. Master bedroom bath	11. Entry area
4. Half bath main level	12. Family room
5. 3 bedrooms	13. Fourth bedroom
6. Living area with adjacent dining room	14. Two car garage
7. One car garage	15. Hot tub
8. Two story house	16. Pool

Fig. 2-6 Vacation home needs and wants.

Needs	Wants
1. Master bedroom with bath	9. Quiet terrace
2. Second bedroom	10. Cathedral ceilings
3. 2nd bath	11. Raised hearth for fireplace
4. Open living room area	12. Large glass area on both sides of living room
5. Kitchen with dining bar	13. Attached garage
6. Outdoor living areas	14. Master bedroom dressing room
7. Fireplace	15. Third bedroom
8. Boat landing	16. Utility room
	17. Hot tub

Fig. 2-5 Plan matching Fig. 2-4 needs and wants. (Design 1723)

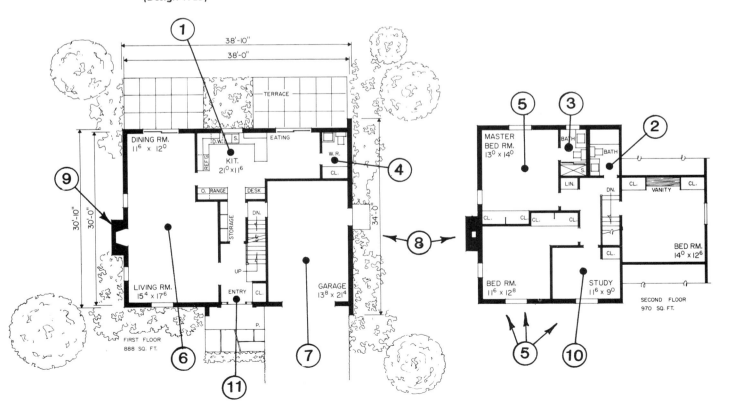

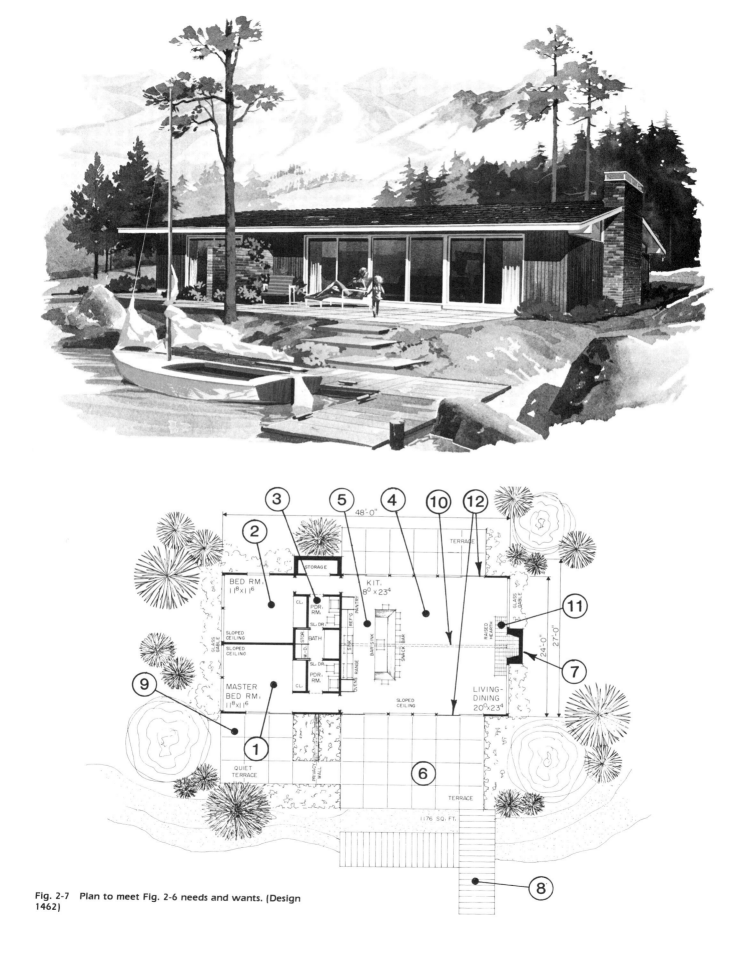

Fig. 2-7   Plan to meet Fig. 2-6 needs and wants. (Design 1462)

the best match-up between the features of the plan and the requirements of the prospective occupant.

Compromise is a term which must be recognized and understood in the process of planning a home. Compromise will play an important part in arriving at a final list of needs and wants. Even in cases where budgeting considerations are not a factor, compromise is often necessary if a family is to reach agreement on the features each member would like to incorporate in a new home. Everyone's preferences for living patterns, room arrangements, exterior styling, and use of materials are not identical. There must be a mutual respect for the exercise of give and take among the members of the family, since all the wants and needs of each individual cannot be fully satisfied. There must be practical limitations; therefore, a spirit of compromise must exist.

General Financial Considerations

Although the size of a residence has the greatest effect on the cost, the type, and the location of the site, building materials and labor costs also have a great effect on the total cost of the house.

Principal Items	Percentage of total cost
Excavation and site improvements	4.45%
Foundations	7.28
Structural frame	9.52
Cement finish	5.44
Exterior masonry	6.58
Interior partitions	4.89
Carpentry and millwork	4.84
Sash and glazing	4.77
Roofing	2.47
Insulation	2.28
Waterproofing and dampproofing	0.12
Metal lath, furring, and plastering	3.56
Hollow metal work	1.14
Miscellaneous iron and ornamental metal	1.90
Tile, terrazzo, and marble	1.50
Floor covering	1.04
Painting	1.71
Finish hardware	1.55
Acoustical ceiling	3.60
Plumbing	7.43
Heating, ventilating, and air conditioning	14.99
Electrical work and light fixtures	8.94
TOTAL	100%

Fig. 2-8 Building materials as percentage of total cost. (Engineering News Record).

Site The location of the site is extremely important. An identical house built on an identically sized lot can vary many thousands of dollars in cost, depending on whether it is located in a city, in a suburb, or in the country. Site costs also vary greatly from one part of the country or region to another. In addition to the initial cost of the lot, the expense of altering or building on the site must also be considered in estimating the cost of the residence. A building can be erected at less cost on a flat lot with no trees than on a hillside lot that is heavily wooded. Excavating large boulders or filling unwanted depressions can also add considerably to the cost of the site preparation.

Building materials Approximately 40 percent of the cost of an average house in this country is spent on building materials (see Fig. 2-8). However, the cost of construction materials also varies greatly from one part of the country to another, depending on whether materials are native to the region or must be imported. For example, redwood is relatively inexpensive in California but very expensive on the East Coast. Probably the greatest variable affecting the cost of building materials is the use of standard sizes of components versus the custom construction of components. For example, if kitchen cabinets are built on the site, the cost could easily be double the price of preconstructed factory units. Also, designing the residence in modular units will enable the builder to use standard size framing materials with a minimum of waste. So there is a direct relationship between the amount of on-site construction and the cost of construction. Also, specifying unique or exotic materials, such as rare stone or paneling, may not be worth the additional cost, depending on the budget restrictions of the builder. Regional climate conditions may also have a serious effect on the cost of building. For example, in moderate climates many costs can be eliminated by excluding large heating equipment, frost-deep foundation storm doors, double or triple glazing, and by reducing the amount of insulation a little.

Specifications Specifications for building a house can be divided into two groups. The first group may be referred to as "construction specifications." These involve the various materials and methods of installation which will ensure a well-built house in conformance with local building codes and restrictions. Included in this group are the numerous phases of construction, from excavating to painting. Basic decisions relating to construction specifications are generally left to the architect and builder because of their technical nature. Prior to signing any contract, an owner should review these specifications with the architect or builder.

A second group of specifications are often referred to as "individual specifications." These involve the selection of materials, fixtures, and equipment which are subject to the personal preference of the owner. They can have a big influence on the final contract price of a house. In a custom-designed house, it is the owner who has the right to decide upon such items as the type of brick or other exterior surfaces, color and quality of bathroom facilities, price range of lighting fixtures, floor and wall surface treatment, the type of heating and cooking equipment, and the type and extent of insulation. The choices an owner makes are influenced by likes and dislikes, plus the size of the building budget.

Labor costs Labor costs also vary greatly from one part of the country to another and from urban to rural areas. Normally, labor costs are lower in rural areas. However, the amount of customized construction affects the labor cost of a building most dramatically. Not only does customizing take additional time, but it requires the services of more highly paid technicians. The labor cost factor can be reduced to whatever extent the owner may wish and is capable of becoming involved in some phase of the construction process. Labor costs can also be significantly reduced through the extensive use of prefabricated components.

Estimating costs There are two basic methods of determining the cost of a house. One is by adding the total cost of all materials to the hourly outlay for labor, multiplied by the anticipated number of hours it will take to build the home. The cost of the lot, the landscaping, and various architects' fees must also be added to this figure. This process requires careful computation and experience in estimating construction costs.

Two quicker and easier methods for estimating the cost of a house are the "square foot method" and the "cubic foot method." These methods are not as accurate as itemizing; however, they do provide a quick and rough estimate for speculative and budgetary purposes.

The square foot method of estimating housing costs simply involves multiplying the number of square feet on the floor plan by a fixed dollar rate per square foot. This construction cost per foot varies from time to time and from region to region. Figure 2–9 shows various square foot rates for different floor levels, which is more accurate than using a 1 square foot rate for all levels.

The cubic foot method of estimating compensates for these levels by providing a 1 cubic foot fixed dollar rate figure which is multiplied by the total cubage of the house. The total cubage (volume) is arrived at by multiplying the square footage of the floor area by the height of the building. A 10 percent factor may be applied for houses with steeply pitched roofs.

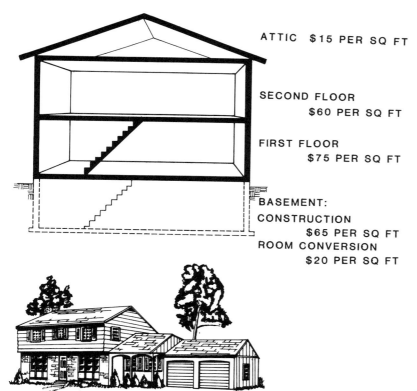

ATTIC $15 PER SQ FT

SECOND FLOOR
$60 PER SQ FT

FIRST FLOOR
$75 PER SQ FT

BASEMENT:
CONSTRUCTION
$65 PER SQ FT
ROOM CONVERSION
$20 PER SQ FT

Fig. 2-9 Typical square foot rates.

Mortgage planning Once the total cost of the house is determined, including the cost of the lot, the monthly payments needed to purchase and maintain the residence can be computed. Since most personal budgets are established on a monthly basis, the monthly payments are often more significant than the total cost of the home. Monthly payments are divided into four categories: principal, interest, taxes, and insurance. Monthly payments of the principal will depend on the amount of the down payment, the interest rate on the balance due, and the number of years needed to repay. The prevailing interest rate must then be added to this principal, in addition to the monthly taxes and insurance costs. Variable costs, such as utilities, furnishings, and landscaping, must also be added to the fixed costs to arrive at the monthly estimate.

More detailed information on mortgages is found in Chapter 12. However, as a rule of thumb, the monthly payments for principal, interest, tax, insurance (PITI) should not exceed one-quarter to one-third of the net monthly income. An individual family's standard of living and lifestyle will help determine what is an acceptable proportion of income to be used for housing.

Expandable plans If the cost of the home selected or designed is too expensive for the prospective home owner, several options are available. First, the entire structure can be scaled down in size by selectively reducing the size of minimally used rooms or areas. Second, some expensive wants that were available on the first design can be eliminated, but none of the needs. Third, an expandable plan can be considered which will satisfy the needs for years to come but expand, in stages, into a more spacious home as the budget permits and/or as the family grows. Figure 2–10 shows how a plan begins with a basic unit, consisting of living room, kitchen, dining

Fig. 2-10 Two-stage expansion plan. (Design 1425)

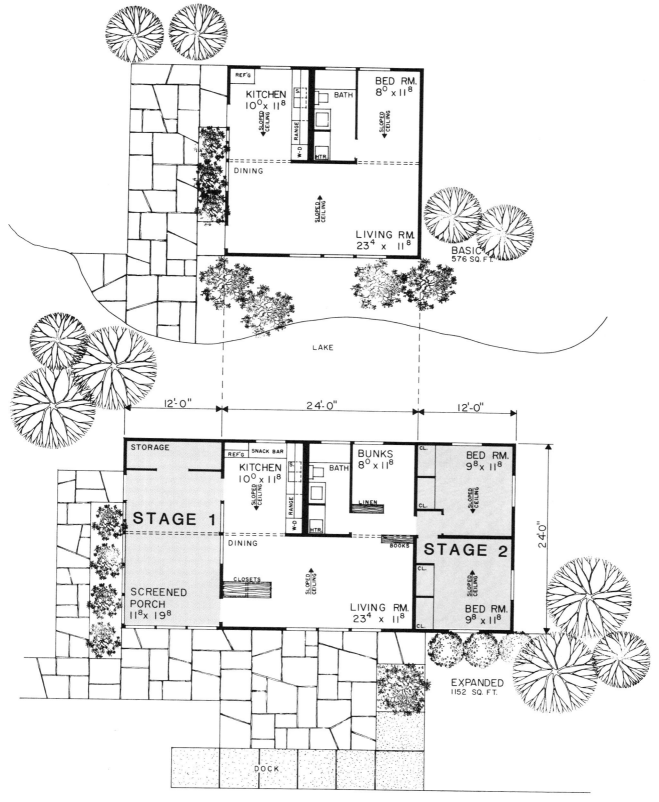

REF'G

KITCHEN
10⁰ x 11⁸

SLOPED CEILING

RANGE

S

W-D

HTR

BATH

BED RM.
8⁰ x 11⁸

SLOPED CEILING

DINING

SLOPED CEILING

LIVING RM.
23⁴ x 11⁸

BASIC
576 SQ. FT.

LAKE

12'-0"   24'-0"   12'-0"

STORAGE

REF'G   SNACK BAR

KITCHEN
10⁰ x 11⁸

SLOPED CEILING

RANGE

S

W-D

HTR

BATH

BUNKS
8⁰ x 11⁸

LINEN

CL.

CL.

BED RM.
9⁸ x 11⁸

SLOPED CEILING

STAGE 1

DINING

CLOSETS

SLOPED CEILING

BOOKS

STAGE 2

CL.

CL.

SLOPED CEILING

24'-0"

SCREENED
PORCH
11⁸ x 19⁸

LIVING RM.
23⁴ x 11⁸

BED RM.
9⁸ x 11⁸

EXPANDED
1152 SQ. FT.

DOCK

LAKE

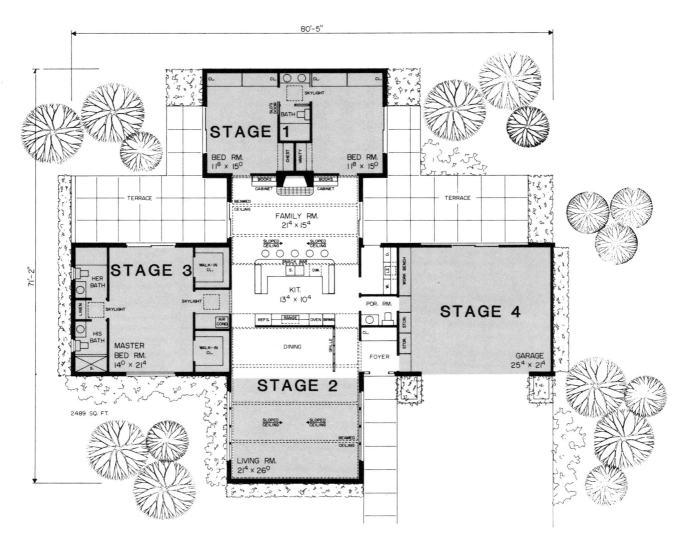

Fig. 2-11 Four-stage expansion plan. (Design 2244)

alcove, bath, and bedroom, and can expand in two stages to include two additional bedrooms and/or a porch or family room. In the expandable plan shown in Fig. 2–11, the family room functions as the bedroom and the powder room and utility room function as the family bathroom by adding a temporary bathtub or shower. The first stage is the addition of two bedrooms and a bathroom. The second stage occurs when the family needs require two additional bedrooms. Stage three in this plan involves the addition of the master bedroom suite. Stage four involves the addition of a garage. These stages, of course, can

be interchanged, depending on the specific developing needs of the home owner.

Perhaps the easiest way to cut costs and still allow for expansion involves the construction of a story-and-a-half residence, as shown in Fig. 2–12. As with any expandable plan, the residence should be planned with the final design completed, then only the construction is completed in phases, not the basic design. In this case, either stage 1, 2, or 3 could be completed at any time, depending on the needs or financial position of the owner. A reverse of this method of expansion is shown in Fig. 2–13, which simply involves the

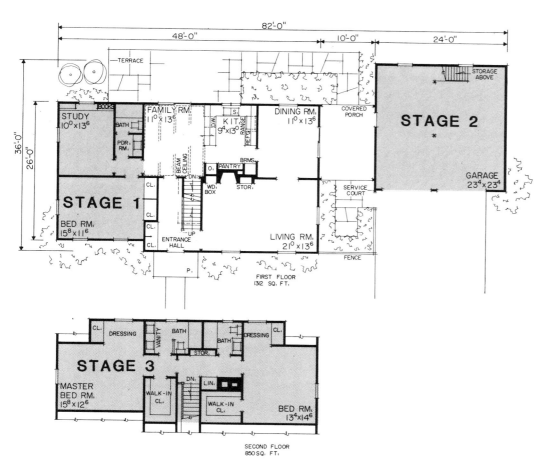

Fig. 2-12 One and one-half story expansion. (Design 1902)

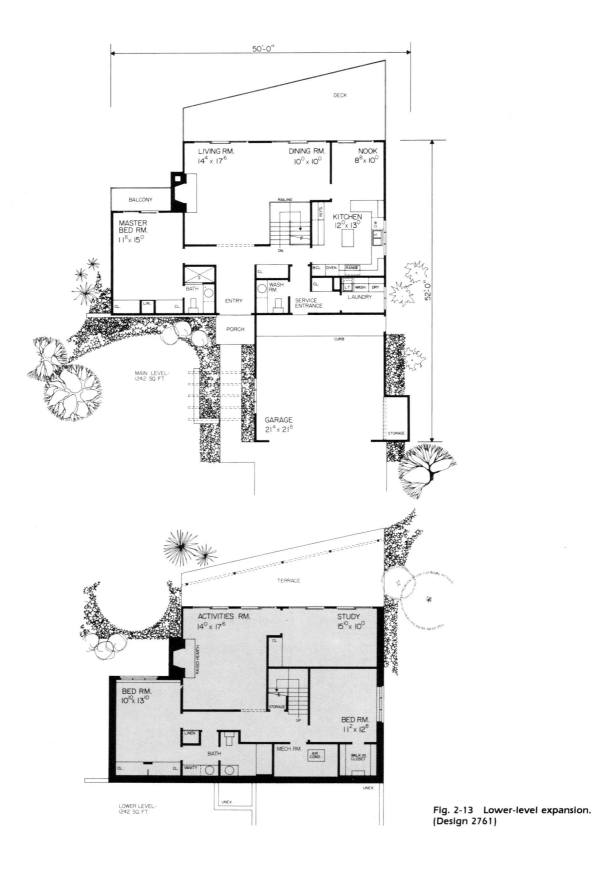

Fig. 2-13 Lower-level expansion. (Design 2761)

construction of a two-level residence without finishing the lower level initially. In this case the plan must be developed to provide all necessary services on the top level. In this plan a minimum master bedroom is included on the top level, then additional bedrooms, activity rooms, and study are added when the lower level is ready to be completed.

CHAPTER 3

Site Considerations

Every house should be designed as an integral part of the site, regardless of the shape of the terrain. It should not appear as an appendage to the land but as a functional part of the site. For the indoor and outdoor living areas to effectively *function* as part of the same plan, the house and the lot must be *designed* as part of the same plan. A particular plan may be compatible with one lot and site and yet appear totally out of place in another location. Sloping sites offer a variety of conditions. Bilevel and trilevel houses are well adapted to an almost endless combination of site contours. A careful selection of house type, when coordinated with effective grading, can result in a successful integration of house and site.

Orientation

In order to achieve the maximum compatibility of the house with the lot, the house must be oriented effectively to its environment. In order to do this the conditions of the building site must be studied for climatic factors, such as air temperature, type and amount of precipitation, humidity, wind speed and wind direction, and available sunlight. The position of the sun must also be considered.

In addition to climatic factors, the designer must also consider the specific physical characteristics of the site, such as hills, valleys, fences, other buildings, and trees. Physical obstructions such as these may effect wind patterns and the amount and direction of available sunlight in different seasons. Large bodies of water may also affect air temperature and air movements, and

surrounding pavement areas and buildings can raise or lower temperatures because concrete and asphalt collect and store the sun's heat. When the characteristics of a site are known, the designer can then begin orienting and designing a structure to utilize the site's benefits and minimize its disadvantages. A well-oriented structure is designed to take full advantage of the environmental factors shown in Fig. 3–1. The sun's heat and light, existing vegetation, desirable and undesirable views, objectionable noise, velocity and direction of the prevailing winds or breezes, land form and shapes, and relation of the site to the neighborhood must all be considered in orienting a house.

To take full advantage of the sun, rooms and outdoor living areas requiring sun in the morning should be located on the east side of the floor plan. Those requiring the sun in the evening should be placed on the west side. Remember that the midday sun in the western hemisphere shines from the south, which means that the north side of the building receives no direct sunlight. Consequently, the north may be the appropriate side for placing the sleeping area since it provides the greatest darkness in the morning and evening and is also the coolest side. Many designers prefer to place living areas on the south or west side because they receive the late-day rays of the sun, but it basically depends on your lifestyle and in what rooms you want the sun at various parts of the day.

Don't forget to consider the view options in orienting the house. Orientation toward the best

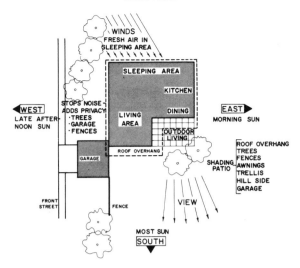

NORTH
COOLEST AREA

WINDS
FRESH AIR IN
SLEEPING AREA

SLEEPING AREA

KITCHEN

STOPS NOISE
ADDS PRIVACY
·TREES
·GARAGE
·FENCES

WEST
LATE AFTER-
NOON SUN

LIVING
AREA

DINING

EAST
MORNING SUN

OUTDOOR
LIVING

ROOF OVERHANG

GARAGE

ROOF OVERHANG
TREES
FENCES
AWNINGS
TRELLIS
HILL SIDE
GARAGE

SHADING
PATIO

FRONT
STREET

FENCE

VIEW

MOST SUN
SOUTH

Fig. 3-1   Factors affecting orientation.

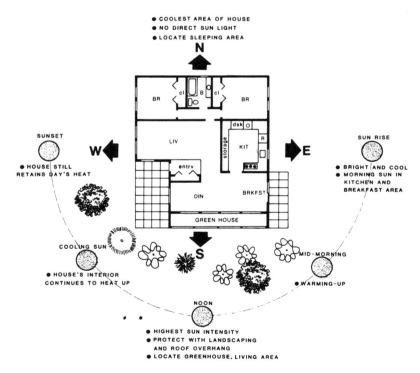

● COOLEST AREA OF HOUSE
● NO DIRECT SUN LIGHT
● LOCATE SLEEPING AREA

N

BR   cl B cl   BR

SUNSET

● HOUSE STILL
RETAINS DAY'S HEAT

W

LIV

dsk
storage
KIT
R

E

SUN RISE

● BRIGHT AND COOL
● MORNING SUN IN
KITCHEN AND
BREAKFAST AREA

entry

DIN

BRKFST

GREEN HOUSE

COOLING SUN

● HOUSE'S INTERIOR
CONTINUES TO HEAT UP

S

MID-MORNING

● WARMING-UP

NOON

● HIGHEST SUN INTENSITY
● PROTECT WITH LANDSCAPING
AND ROOF OVERHANG
● LOCATE GREENHOUSE, LIVING AREA

Fig. 3-2a   Passive solar
consideration.

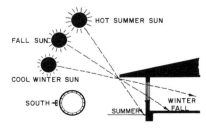

HOT SUMMER SUN

FALL SUN

COOL WINTER SUN

SOUTH

SUMMER

WINTER
FALL

Fig. 3-2b   Seasonal sun angles.

view, or away from an objectionable view, usually means careful planning of the position of the living area.

Soft, gentle breezes are often desirable, especially in warm weather, but harsh prevailing winds are usually objectionable. Once the wind patterns are known for the site, the house should be located to take full advantage of the cooling effect of prevailing winds without subjecting outdoor living areas to harsh prevailing winds. Also determine the source, if any, of noise pollution and baffle it or orient the house to reduce the noise level as much as possible.

When orientation cannot solve all problems, effective landscaping can be used to enhance views, baffle noise and wind, and provide privacy. But landscaping should not be used as a substitute for site-house orientation.

Solar Planning

Professional designers and builders are rediscovering the natural cooling, heating, and lighting potential offered in different climates. This awareness can be combined with technology to bring about effective alternative directions in design and in construction. We no longer need to sacrifice quality or comfort in order to design houses that place less demand on energy sources. Natural systems can be used to regulate heating and cooling, often as effectively as artificially controlled environments. But certain design principles must be adhered to in order to achieve maximum natural energy efficiency.

Passive solar planning. Passive solar planning of residences makes use of natural environmental elements without the technical assistance of devices such as solar panels or heat pumps. Briefly stated, passive solar planning involves taking the fullest advantage of the sun to provide heat when and where it is needed and to block the heat of the

sun where and when it is *not* wanted. The first and most important factor in solar planning is the correct orientation of the house to the sun. In a solar-efficient home, the use of the sun's heat must be maximized in the winter and minimized in the summer. A large southern exposure and south-facing windows collect the largest amount of heat from sunlight (see Fig. 3–2a).

A car parked in direct sunlight with the windows closed illustrates a basic principle used in passive solar planning. The interior of the car becomes heated because sunlight enters through the windows. The heat is absorbed by the interior surfaces of the car and trapped inside the car as stored heat. This is known as the "greenhouse effect." In a similar manner, heat from the winter sun enters the house through the windows. It can then be stored in a thermal mass so that the heat can be used later when the sun's heat is not available. Thermal mass is any material that will absorb heat from the sun and later radiate the heat back into the air. The seats in the car act as a thermal mass. Walls, floors, and fireplaces can all work in this manner in a building designed for maximum solar effectiveness.

In the summer it is unnecessary to collect the sun's heat; rather, protection against the sun's heat may be needed. Fortunately, the sun's angle changes conveniently from summer to winter. Thus it is possible to design buildings that bar the summer sun's heat and collect the winter sun's heat, as shown in Fig. 3–2b. To aid in this process, vents and windows should be located to provide optimal natural air convection and circulation. Using heavy brick or concrete construction will delay entry of daytime heat into the house. Since hot air rises, the use of ceiling fans to flush out hot air will also keep the house cooler during the summer months. Figure 3–3 shows the use of a passive solar system for cooling and heating. This system uses water tanks to store heat. A similar

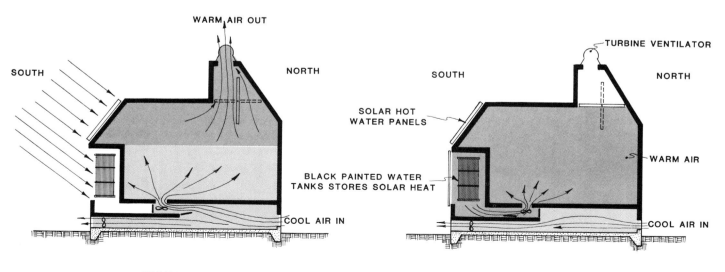

WARM DAYS   COOL NIGHTS

Fig. 3-3 Passive solar system.

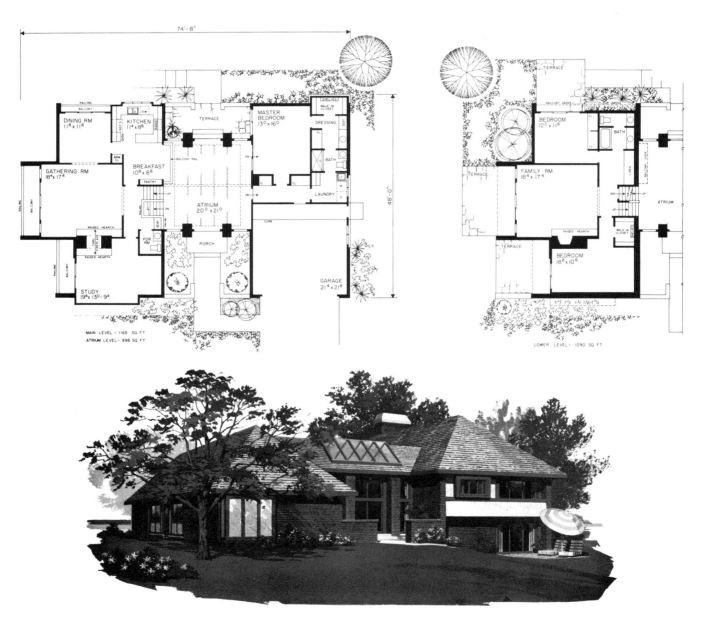

DINING RM
11⁸ x 11⁸

KITCHEN
11⁴ x 8⁶

GATHERING RM
18⁴ x 17⁴

BREAKFAST
10⁸ x 8⁶

TERRACE

MASTER BEDROOM
13⁰ x 16⁰

DRESSING

WALK-IN CLOSET

BATH

ATRIUM
20⁰ x 21⁰

LAUNDRY

STUDY
19⁴ x 13⁰ - 9⁴

PDR RM

RAISED HEARTH

PORCH

GARAGE
21⁴ x 21⁸

74' - 8"

48' - 0"

MAIN LEVEL - 1165 SQ FT
ATRIUM LEVEL - 998 SQ FT

TERRACE

BEDROOM
12⁰ x 11⁸

BATH

BALCONY ABOVE

TERRACE

FAMILY RM
18⁴ x 17⁴

ATRIUM

RAISED HEARTH

WALK-IN CLOSET

BEDROOM
18⁸ x 10⁸

TERRACE

LOWER LEVEL - 1090 SQ FT

Fig. 3-4a Residence with passive solar features. (Design 2837)

effect can be achieved by placing windows on the south side, which is almost constantly exposed to the sun. Note how the hot air is trapped on warm days and released on cool nights through the use of the ventilators. All of this is based on the very basic principle of the natural rise of warm air. Thus, anything that can be done to accelerate the rise of warm air when the warm air is not wanted, or trap the hot air when desired, is in effect trapped-air solar planning (see Fig. 3–3).

Figure 3–4a shows a passive solar–designed residence using an atrium skylight to admit the sun's heat when required and block the sun's heat when undesirable. Since the solarium shown in Fig. 3–4b can be opened or closed from either the foyer, master bedroom, breakfast room, or terrace, opening or closing any or all of the solarium doors or windows can adjust the amount of heat admitted from the solarium. Therefore, the occupant has control not only of the heat gain from the solarium through use of the skylight panels, but also of the dissipation of solarium heat into other parts of the house. Figure 3–4b also shows how a studio can be added to this plan above the foyer if extra living space is needed.

Other construction devices and features that contribute to better energy efficiency include the effective use of roof overhangs; vegetation; insulation materials that collect heat; insulation of walls, floors, and ceilings; exhaust fans and vents; pipe and duct insulation; thermopane windows; sun control shades for windows; weatherstripping and caulking; flue heating recovery devices,

energy saving thermostats; and fuel-saving devices.

Active solar systems. Active solar systems are mechanical devices used for solar heat collection, storage, distribution, and control. Active solar systems use south-facing solar collectors set at an angle perpendicular to the sun. However, these collectors should have full access to the sun from at least 10 a.m. until 2 p.m., since most solar heat is emitted during these middle hours of the day. Each solar collector panel acts as a small greenhouse. Sunlight enters through the glass and warms water or air circulating in the pipes. The heat is trapped and pumped into storage areas. Even on a cold day with bright or filtered sunlight, these panels can be heated to over 200°F. Then, either hot air can be blown or hot water piped from the storage tanks to other parts of the house as heat is needed. In active solar systems some thermostatic control is required to automate the distribution of heat to the various rooms as required. Figure 3–5a shows a residence designed for active solar heat utilization. Remember, a house designed for an active solar system must be oriented so that the solar panels face south and the roof angle is perpendicular to the sun's rays at midday. This perpendicular angle can vary somewhat in either direction without a significant loss of energy. However, for maximum efficiency the sun's southern rays should strike the solar panels as perpendicularly as possible, as shown in Fig. 3–5b. In this plan the solar equipment area houses the storage tanks for the hot water created in the

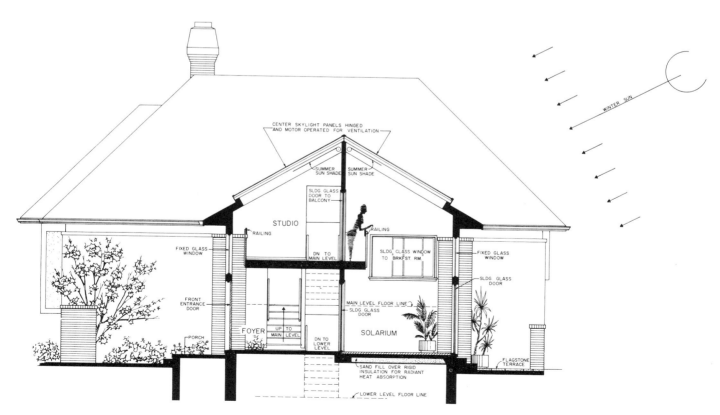

Fig. 3-4b Solarium. (Design 2836)

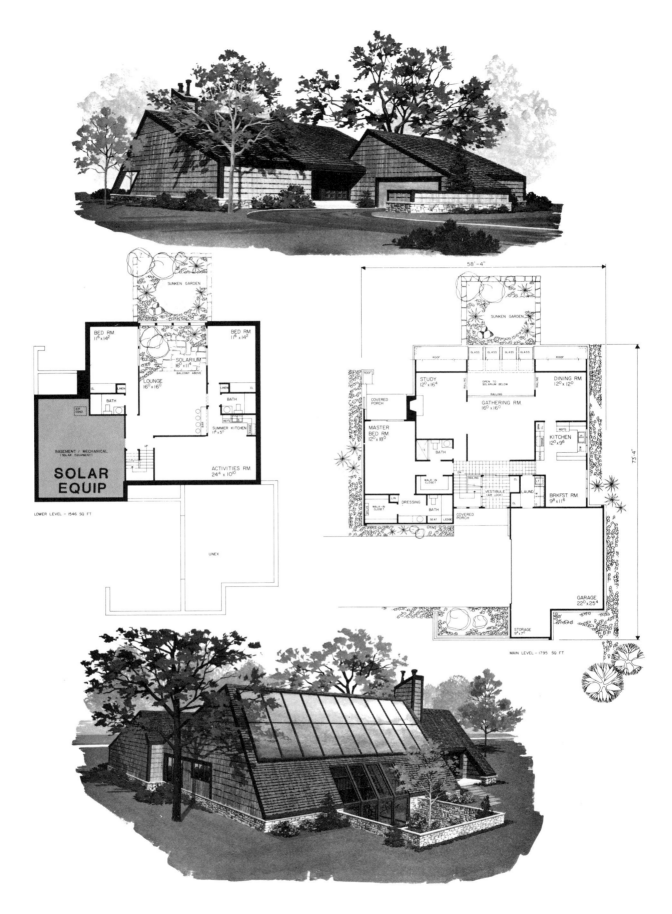

Fig. 3-5a Residence with active solar system. (Design 2830)

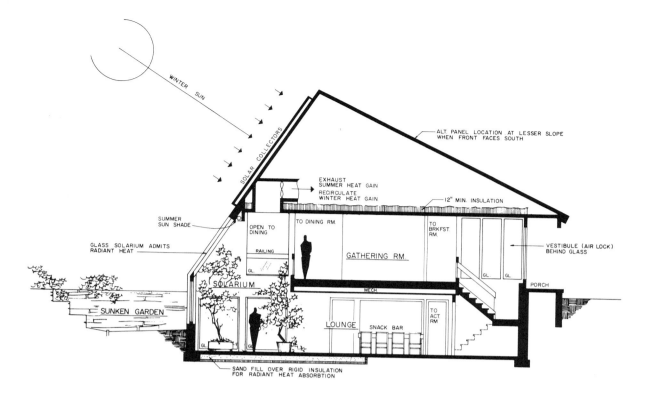

WINTER SUN

SOLAR COLLECTORS

ALT PANEL LOCATION AT LESSER SLOPE WHEN FRONT FACES SOUTH

EXHAUST
SUMMER HEAT GAIN
RECIRCULATE
WINTER HEAT GAIN

12" MIN. INSULATION

SUMMER SUN SHADE

GLASS SOLARIUM ADMITS RADIANT HEAT

OPEN TO DINING

TO DINING RM.

TO BRKFST. RM.

VESTIBULE (AIR LOCK) BEHIND GLASS

RAILING

GATHERING RM.

GL.

GL.

GL.

SOLARIUM

PORCH

SUNKEN GARDEN

MECH.

LOUNGE

TO ACT. RM.

SNACK BAR

GL.

GL.

SAND FILL OVER RIGID INSULATION FOR RADIANT HEAT ABSORBTION

SECTION

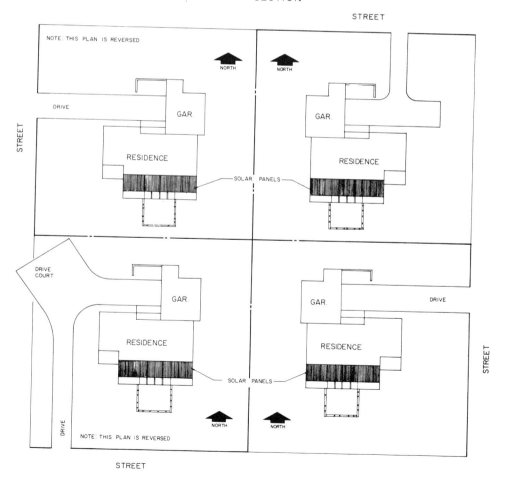

STREET

NOTE: THIS PLAN IS REVERSED

NORTH

NORTH

DRIVE

GAR.

GAR.

STREET

RESIDENCE

RESIDENCE

SOLAR PANELS

SOLAR PANELS

DRIVE COURT

GAR.

GAR.

DRIVE

RESIDENCE

RESIDENCE

STREET

SOLAR PANELS

SOLAR PANELS

DRIVE

NOTE: THIS PLAN IS REVERSED

NORTH

NORTH

STREET

SITE ORIENTATION

Fig. 3-5b Section and site orientation for Fig. 3-5a. (Design 2830)

solar panels. A residence designed to utilize active solar devices should also incorporate as many *passive* solar features as possible to increase the efficiency of the active devices. In this plan the solarium creates a greenhouse effect which produces heat that can be circulated out or recirculated back into the house as the needs change.

Earth Sheltered Housing

Sloping sites lend themselves to houses that make

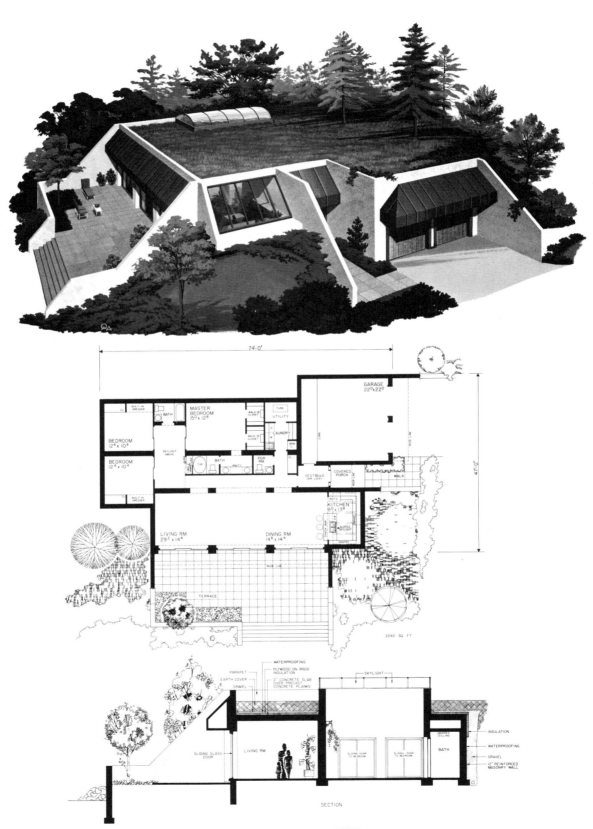

Fig. 3-6 Earth-sheltered home with earth roof covering. (Design 2860)

use of the earth for sheltering. Figure 3–6 shows a house with the earth covering the roof area. This is commonly referred to as an underground house. Although such houses gain significant insulation qualities, their construction specifica-tions are highly specialized. Construction should proceed only after consultation with experts and with great caution. Figure 3–7 illustrates a berm house showing the sidewalls covered with earth. Here, again, significant energy-efficient qualities

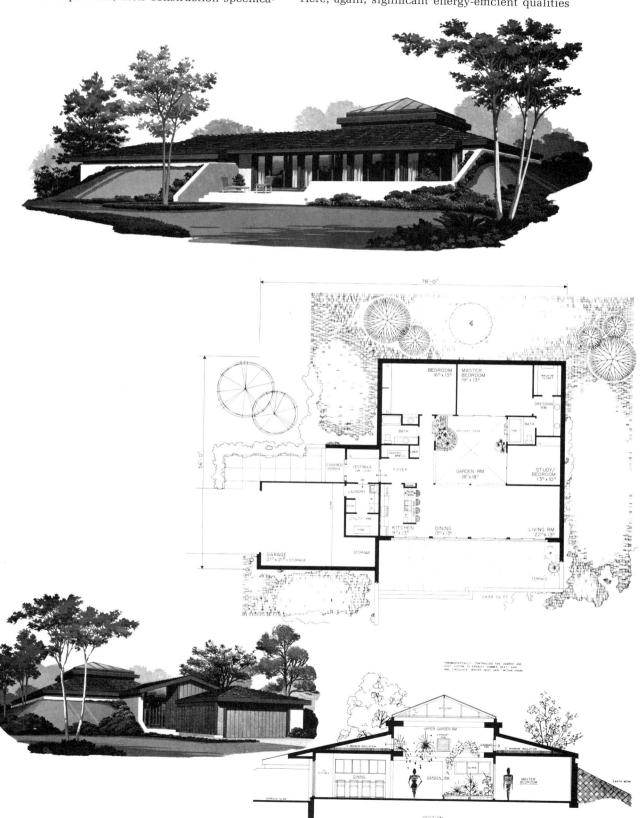

Fig. 3-7 Earth-sheltered home with earth-covered walls. (Design 2861)

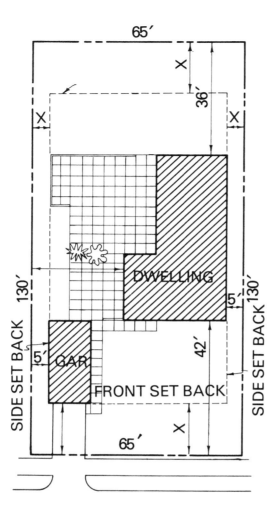

Fig. 3-8 Setback lines.

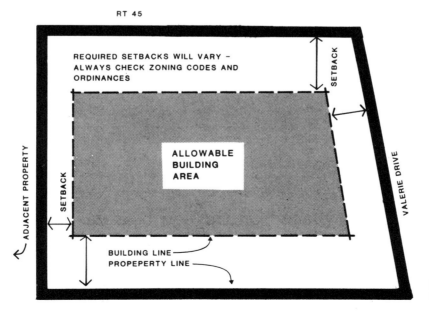

Fig. 3-9 Allowable building areas.

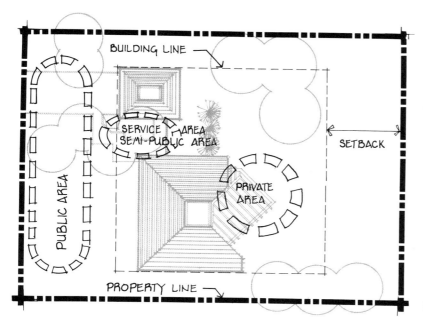

Fig. 3-10 Areas of a lot.

are realized, but not before specialized construction procedures have been followed by experts in the field. For maximum energy efficiency, both underground and berm houses should have their living areas facing south.

Building Code Considerations

A house plan should not be selected or designed until a building site is identified by size, slope, solar orientation, and access area. All of these factors affect the flexibility of choice in selecting, designing, and locating a house on a site. For example, some building codes require that a house be placed no closer than 10 feet from the property line, others require a distance of 50 feet or more. A line drawn within and parallel to the property line on all sides represents the building line. The area contained within the building lines is the area in which buildings can be located, as shown in Fig. 3–8. Building codes also restrict the distance from the house to the street. These

distances are known as "setbacks," as shown in Fig. 3–9. On small lots there is often little flexibility in orienting the home. Larger lots offer the greatest opportunity to use a variety of positions for house orientation.

Lots may be divided into three areas, according to function: the private area, the public area, and the service area. These three areas are shown in Fig. 3–10. The private area includes the outdoor living space. In temperate climates a southern exposure is usually desirable for the outdoor living area. In warmer climates outdoor living may be more comfortable on the north side. The public area is the area of the lot that can be viewed by the public. This area is usually located at the front of the house and should provide off-street access to the main entrance and parking space. The service area, or children's play area, of the lot should be located adjacent to the service area of the house. The placement of the house on the lot determines the relative size, shape, and relationship of these areas, as shown in Fig. 3-11.

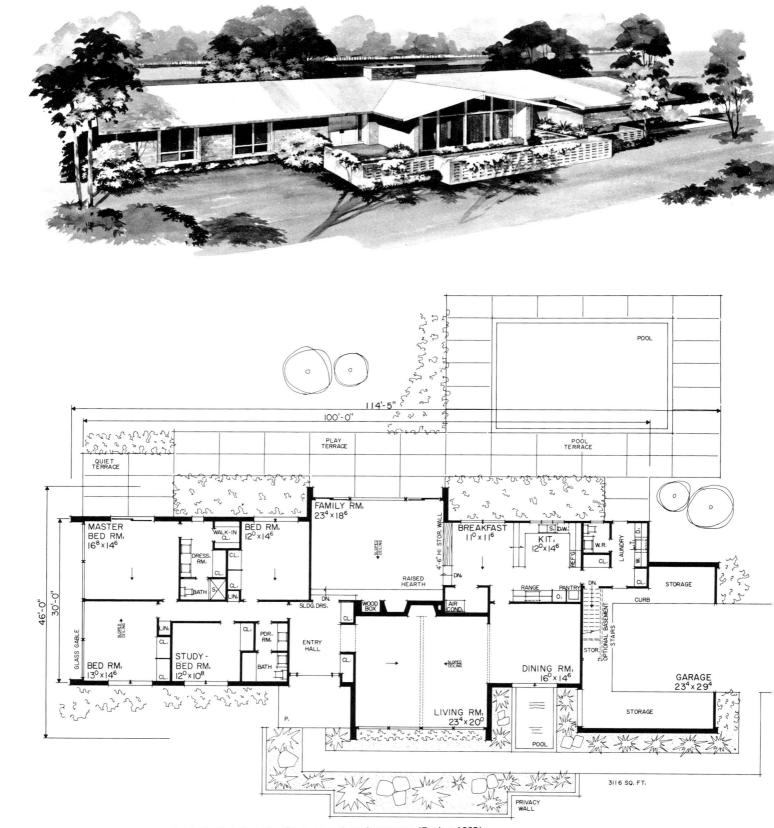

Fig. 3-11   Relationship of indoor and outdoor areas. (Design 1883)

Area Planning

In creating any architectural design, the designer should progress logically step by step through the design process. The first step in this process is to divide the functions of building into specific areas. For example, a school would be divided into such areas as administration, classroom, service, physical activity, and so forth. A hospital would likewise be divided into such areas as reception, emergency services, food service, maintenance, patient rooms, laboratory functions, and so forth. In the same manner a house can be divided into three major functional areas for planning purposes: the living area, the service area, and the sleeping area. Areas are subdivided into rooms so that all the rooms in an area will relate to its basic function. Figure 4–1 shows a floor plan divided into the three basic areas. In this plan the living area is centered and the bedroom area is clustered on the right, with the service area clustered on the left. Figure 4–2 shows various possible relationships between the living, service, and sleeping areas.

Living Area

The living area is exactly what the name describes —the area where most of the living occurs. Here the occupants entertain, relax, dine, listen to music, watch television, enjoy hobbies, and participate in other recreational activities. Subdivisions of most living areas include the living room, dining room, recreation or game room, family room, patio entrance, foyer, den or study, and guest lavatories. Other specialized rooms, such as the library and music or sewing room, are often included as part of the living area in larger homes that have space to devote to such specialized functions. In smaller homes many of the specialized room functions are combined into one room. For example, the living room and the dining room are often combined. In extremely small homes the living room may constitute the entire living area and provide all the facilities normally assigned to other rooms in the living area. Living area facilities may be provided for formal or informal pursuits, depending on lifestyle needs. In recent years, because of ever-increasing construction costs, the gathering room has become popular. This single room serves as a replacement for the living and family rooms. Its function is to satisfy both the formal and informal living pursuits of the family.

Service Area

The service area includes the kitchen, laundry, garage, workshops, storage centers, and utility rooms. Since a great number of different activities take place in the service areas, it should be designed for the greatest efficiency. The service area includes facilities for the maintenance and servicing of other areas of the home. The functioning of the living and sleeping areas is greatly dependent on the efficiency of the service area.

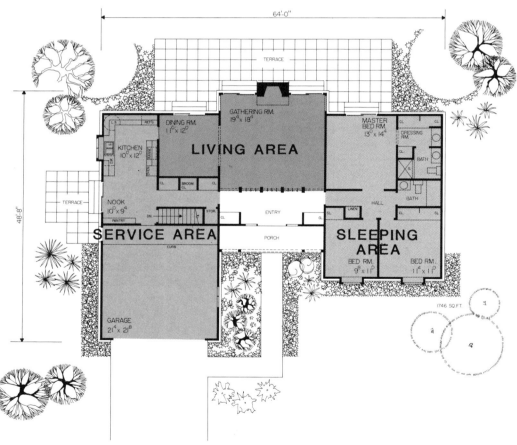

Fig. 4-1   Three basic areas. (Design 2706)

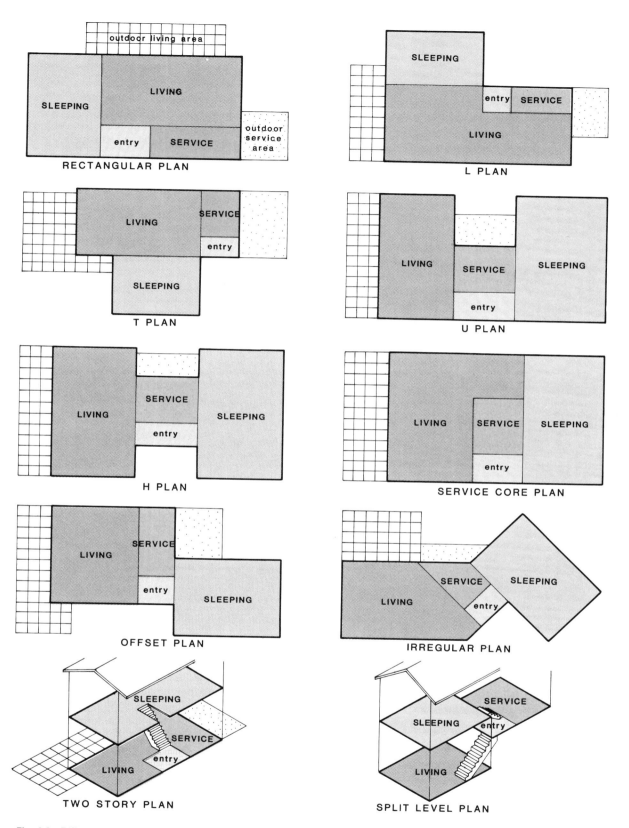

Fig. 4-2 Different area relationships.

Sleeping Area

One-third of our time is spent sleeping. Because of its importance, the sleeping area should be planned to provide facilities for maximum comfort and relaxation. Sleeping areas are usually located in a quiet part of the house and contain bedrooms, baths, dressing rooms, and nurseries. Houses are usually classified by size according to the number of bedrooms. For example, a three bedroom home, a four bedroom home, etc. The sleeping area must also provide adequate facilities for both bath and bedroom linen storage. Also, planning for sufficient wardrobe storage must not be overlooked. Although most of our waking time is spent in the living and service areas, a large block of time is spent in the sleeping area and it should be planned accordingly.

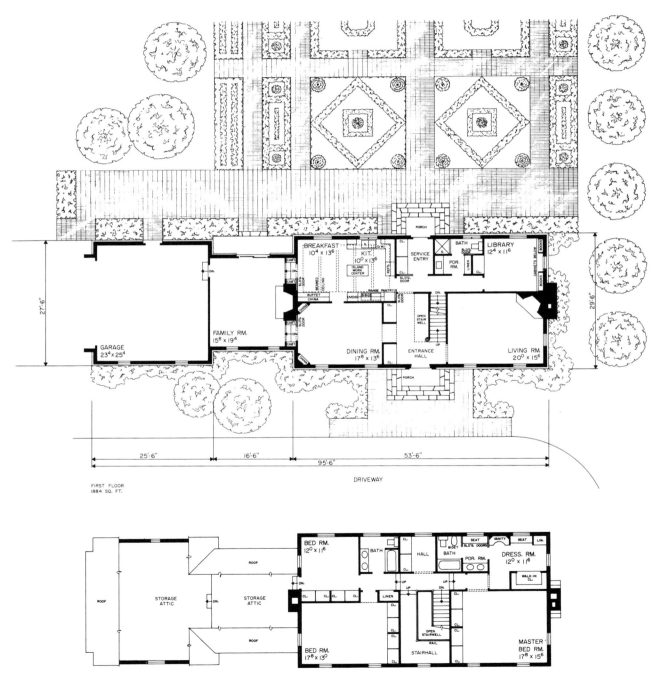

Fig. 4-3 Closed type plan. (Design 2192)

Types of Plans

When the rooms of a plan are divided by solid partitions, doors, or arches, the plan is known as a "closed plan." Most traditional plans are of the closed type, such as the one shown in Fig. 4–3. Closed plans like this one are more formal because they isolate specific functions. For example, the living room is totally separated from the formal dining room and even from the entrance hall. A closed plan offers the greatest amount of privacy. For this reason home buyers and designers who prefer closed plans often also prefer traditional (formal) style architecture.

If partitions between the rooms of an area are eliminated or kept to a minimum, as shown in Fig. 4–4, the plan is known as an informal plan, or "open plan." The open plan is used mostly and to best advantage in the living area. Here the walls that separate the entrance foyer, living room, dining room, activities room, and sometimes recreation room can be removed or partially eliminated. Hence living patterns tend to be more informal. These open areas are created to provide a sense of spaciousness, to add lighting efficiency, and to increase the circulation of air throughout the area. Obviously, not all areas of a residence lend themselves well to open planning. For example, an open plan is almost never used in the sleeping or service areas. In the open plan shown in Fig. 4–4, the area between the family room, dining room, living room, and atrium are partially

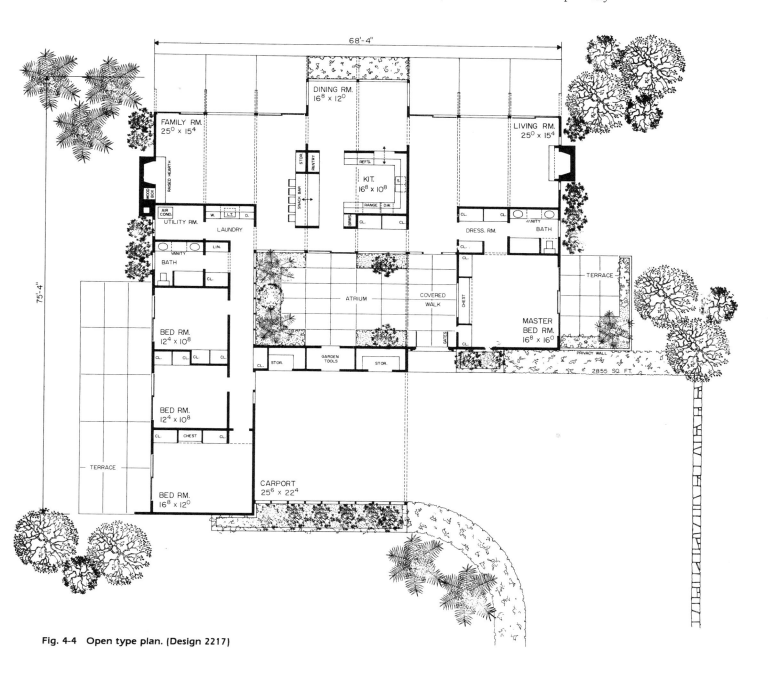

Fig. 4-4 Open type plan. (Design 2217)

open, which maximizes light and air circulation. But the location of the kitchen does break the sight level from one room to another.

Levels

Effective area planning is most difficult on small, single-level residences, such as the one shown in Fig. 4–5. The difficulty arises from not being able to spread the plan either horizontally as in large ranch style homes, or vertically as in split-level or two-story homes. Even though the residence shown in Fig. 4–6 is located on one level, there is sufficient space to separate the sleeping area al-

most totally from the living and service area through the use of a center courtyard and gallery. However, the plan shown in Fig. 4–5 covers only 1200 square feet, while the plan shown in Fig. 4–6 is over 3000 square feet.

Separation of the three areas of a residence by level is preferred by many designers because of the natural separation it provides between the sleeping area and other areas without using additional surface area of the lot. In designing second-floor plans, tracing paper is placed directly over the first-floor plan to ensure alignment of walls and varying partitions. Once the major outline has been traced, the first-floor plan is removed. Figure

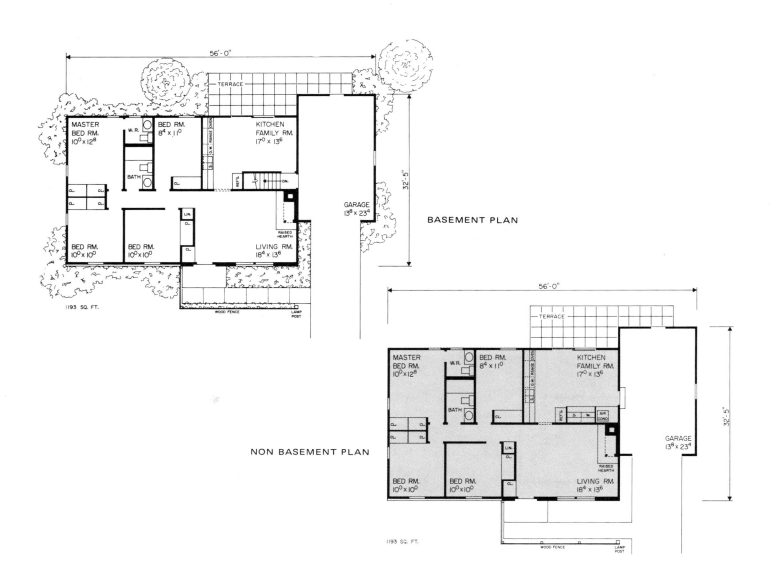

Fig. 4-5 Small single-level plan. (Design 2198)

STREET VIEW

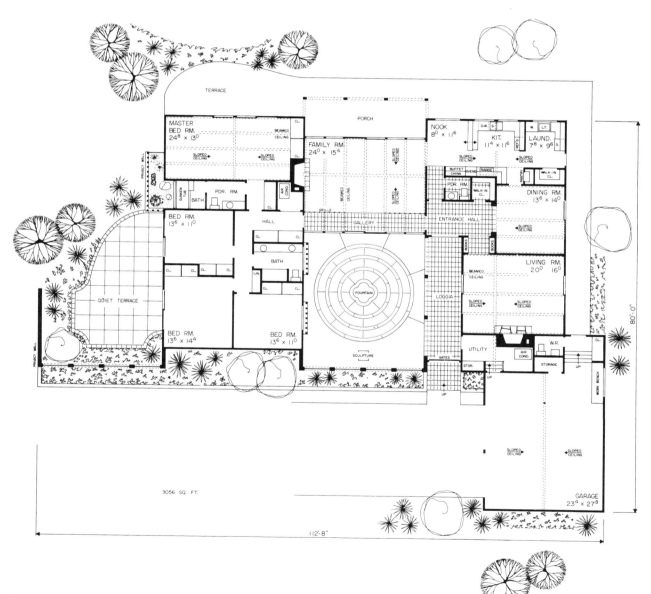

Fig. 4-6 Large single-level plan. (Design 2294)

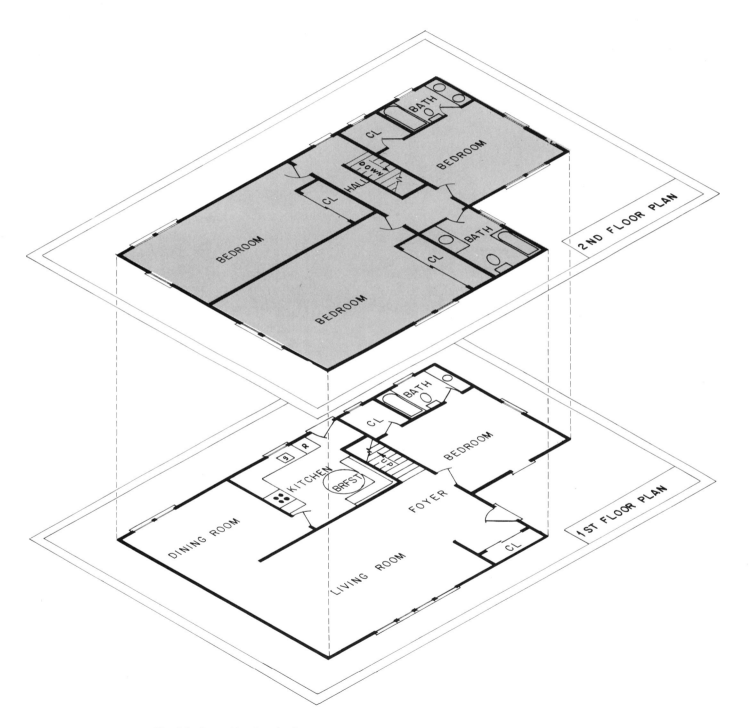

Fig. 4-7 Second-level projection.

4–7 shows a second-floor plan projected from a first-floor plan. Alignment of features such as stair openings (see Fig. 4–8), outside walls, plumbing walls, and chimneys is critical in preparing the second-floor plan. Keep in mind that wherever there is a chimney or stairwell on the first floor it must pass through the second floor in a straight vertical line. Likewise if plumbing is needed on the second floor it must pass from the first floor through a partition. For this reason second-floor plans are always designed on tracing paper laid over a first-floor plan so that the designer can see the position of these first-floor features (see Fig. 4–8).

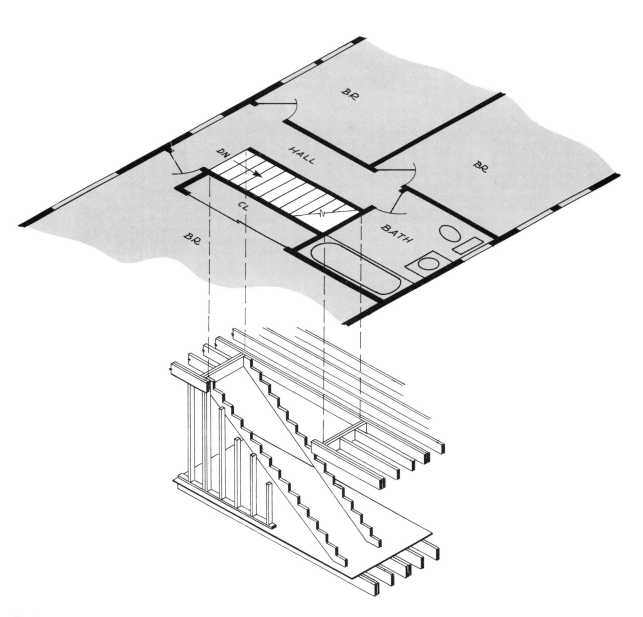

Fig. 4-8 Alignment of features.

Bi-level When residences are planned with two full levels, as shown in Fig. 4–9, the entire sleeping area (or zone) can be conveniently placed on the second level. It is then much easier to separate the service and living functions on the first floor. Figure 4–9 is a very common closed plan of this type, with the dining room, kitchen, and living room forming a circle, and the garage and family room extended at the opposite end and buffered by the breakfast nook. This is the plan, with its variations, that is most commonly used in traditional homes.

Perhaps one of the most popular bilevel designs is the two-level plan with a split foyer, as shown in Fig. 4–10. In this plan the sleeping area is separated to the right while the living and service areas are located on two levels at the left and on the first level. This type of plan is extremely

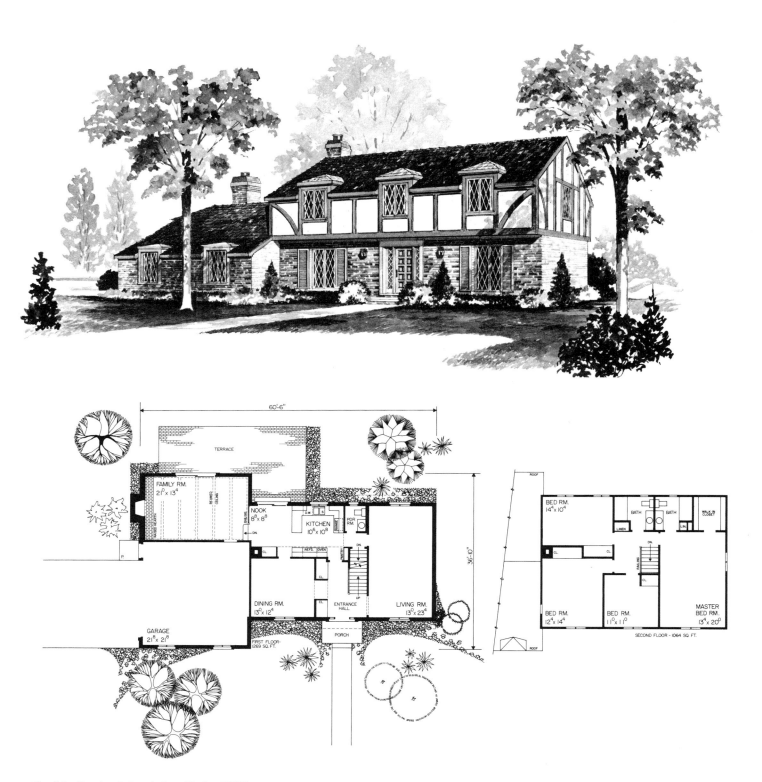

Fig. 4-9   Two-level closed plan. (Design 2618)

Fig. 4-10 Bi-level split foyer plan. (Design 1850)

popular because of the immediate access to the family room, living area, and sleeping area with a minimum of hall space. Consequently, this plan maximizes the amount of actual living space in a relatively small area.

Another variation of the two-story plan is the alignment of two levels on one end and only one level on the other. This type of plan maximizes the features of a hillside lot, because the lower end of the slope can expose two levels and the upper end can provide access to the top level. This is especially advantageous for lots below street level. For example, the first floor of the house shown at the top of Fig. 4–11 is at street level. But because of the slope of the lot, the rear of the house is exposed at both levels. In designing this type of two-level plan, remember that the bottom level inside wall and side walls are underground and have no windows. Consequently, additional light must be provided from the opposite wall. For this reason the hobby-laundry area, or other specialized or occasionally used rooms such as shops, exercise rooms, and so forth, can be located conveniently in this area. When a one–two split (one level at front and two at the rear) is designed, balconies are often used to provide outdoor area extensions to the top level. Notice how this is accomplished in the residence shown in Fig. 4–11. Balconies are provided for the master bedroom, study, living room, and dining room. Ground-level terraces are then added below the balconies to provide additional outdoor living space for the lower bedrooms and family room.

Another variation on the concept of multilevel

Fig. 4-11a   Bi-level designs back to front. (Design 2504)

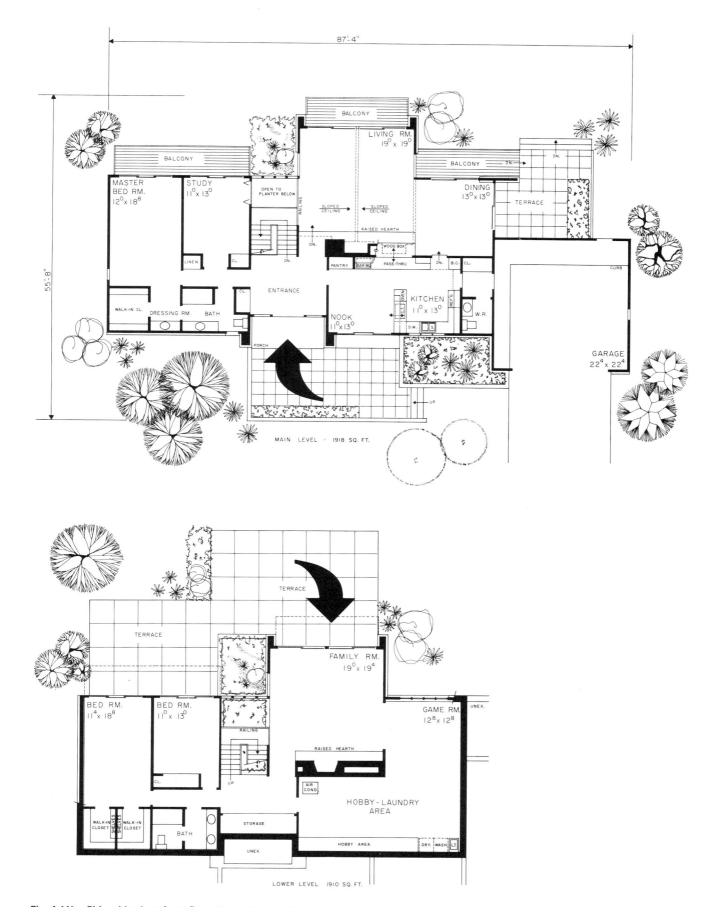

Fig. 4-11b *Bi-level back to front floor plans. (Design 2504)*

residence planning is the two–three front-to-back split, in which two levels are exposed on the front or top of a sloping lot and three levels are exposed at the back or bottom. An example of this type of design is shown in Fig. 4–12a and b. In this case the center (main) level is the street level. This level and the level above are exposed on all sides, but the lower level, as in the one–two split, is exposed only in the back. In this plan the occasionally used rooms—laundry, storage, and guest

Fig. 4-12a   Tri-level back to front. (Design 2716)

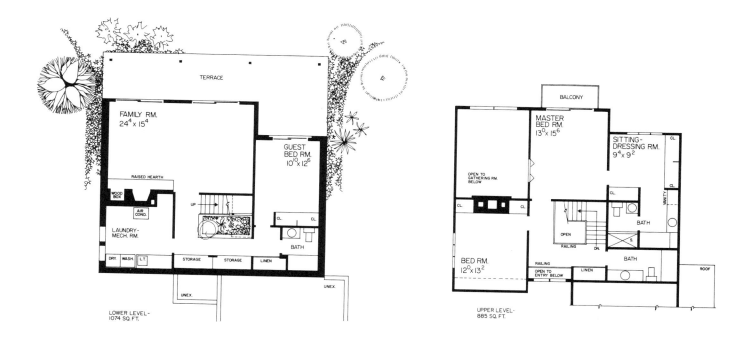

LOWER LEVEL-
1074 SQ. FT.

UPPER LEVEL-
885 SQ. FT.

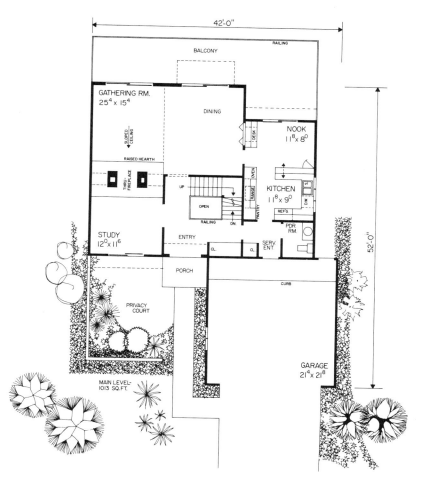

MAIN LEVEL-
1013 SQ. FT.

Fig. 4-12b Tri-level floor plans.

bath—are conveniently placed in the dead-end area, since they are less affected by lack of sunlight.

Split-level Not all multilevel residences need include full levels of living space. When the slope of the lot is excessive and limits the construction of full levels, construction of a partial level can result in a split-level house. There are two basic types of split-level homes, the side-by-side split as shown in Fig. 4–13, and the front-to-back split as shown in Fig. 4–14.

In the side-by-side split, the lot may vary in grade level parallel to the front of the house or street. To compensate for the slope of the lot, the

Fig. 4-13 Side-by-side split level. (Design 2254)

front entrance is placed at street level and one area, usually the living zone (see Fig. 4–13), is placed at this level. The other levels are split, one level above the other. In Fig. 4–13 the sleeping level is located on the upper of these two levels, and the garage, laundry, and family room on the lower level. While this type of split level lends itself to a side sloping site, it can be effectively adapted to a flat site.

The front-to-rear type of split level residence is exemplified by the plan shown in Fig. 4–14. In this plan the entire front area is parallel to the street and is consistently level with the front of the lot. But the rear of the lot slopes downward

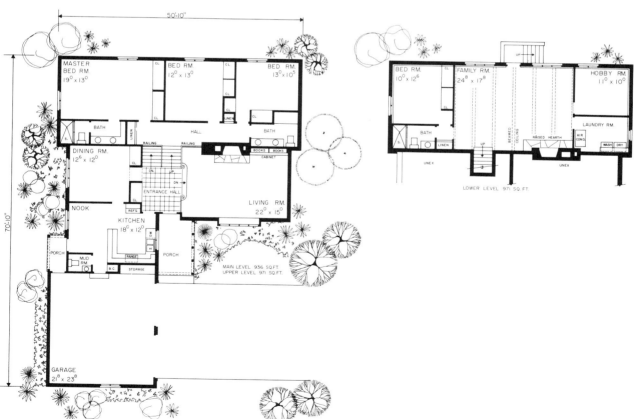

Fig. 4-14 Front-to-back split. (Design 2354)

from this level. In Fig. 4–14 the front entrance is located on the upper level with the living area and the sleeping area. The family room, hobby room, and guest bedroom (all occasionally used rooms) are located on the partial lower level. This type of plan also lends itself to phased building,

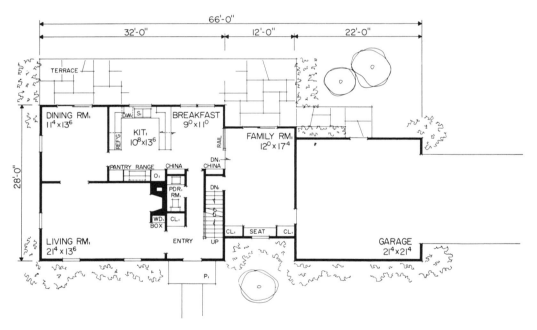

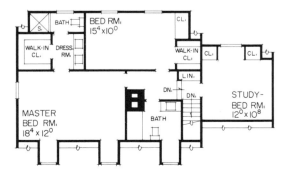

Fig. 4-15 Story-and-a-half plan. (Design 1870)

since the lower level does not contain vital services and can be completed as needs develop or budget allows.

Story-and-a-half When two full stories are not feasible and a level lot does not permit the convenient splitting of levels, the story-and-a-half design is often a good method of adding space to a fixed square foot area. The story-and-a-half plan shown in Fig. 4–15 utilizes a full first level to house the living and service areas and a partial second level containing the sleeping area. Since the slope of the roof reduces some eave-end outside wall headroom space, second-level dormers are usually added to provide additional space and light. Dormers are either individual, as shown in Fig. 4–15, or continuous (shed) as shown in Fig. 4–16. The obvious advantage of

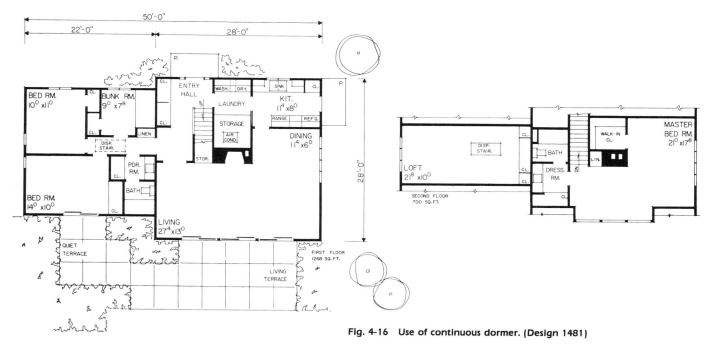

Fig. 4-16   Use of continuous dormer. (Design 1481)

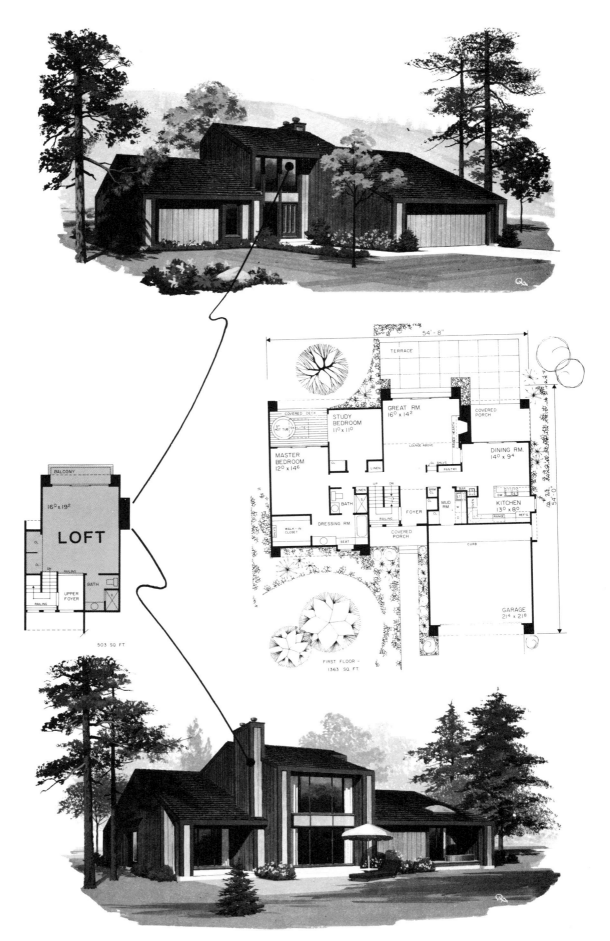

Fig. 4-17   Loft plan. (Design 2822)

continuous dormers is the additional space provided. Many colonial plans contain individual dormers in the front of the residence and shed dormers in the rear to maximize the amount of second-level space. The use of a story-and-a-half plan is also an excellent way of utilizing unfinished attic space, which would otherwise be wasted, for general storage, playroom, or hobby activities.

Lofts Another method of utilizing otherwise unused space is the addition of lofts. Lofts are a very effective means of adding living space without additional compartmentalization of an open plan or without adding to the width or length dimensions of the house. When combined with high cathedral ceilings, lofts can provide additional semiprivate living or sleeping space without expanding the house on the lot. If a solid inside balcony is used, the back of the loft cannot be seen from the lower level, but light and air circulation can be derived from the adjacent space. Some lofts must receive all of their natural light from adjacent rooms or may be designed to extend to another outside wall, as shown in the loft in Fig. 4–17.

Lofts often have the additional advantage of being optional; that is, they can be designed into the structure but not built initially. This is especially true in A-frame homes. For example, the house shown in Fig. 4–18 can be built and function effectively with only the first two levels. The third level, the loft shown on the right, can be added as needed to provide additional sleeping or recreation space.

Basement Plans

Building a house with a basement can add valuable living space much less expensively than adding the equivalent amount of space at ground level or as a second level. This is because part of the basement wall is needed for the foundation even if no basement is planned. Basements are the only way to expand living space without building out or up. Basements can initially be extended deep foundations and can be finished at a later time as budget and needs demand. Heated base-

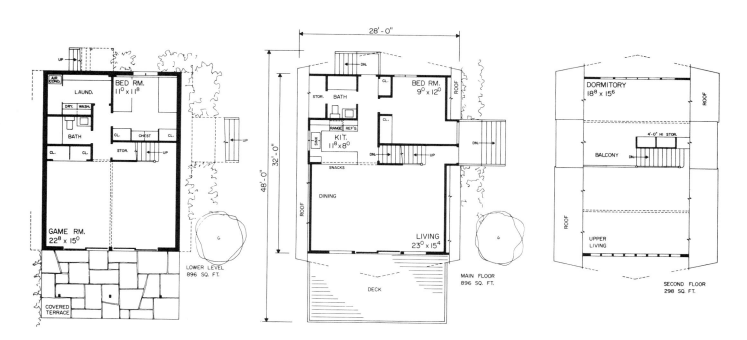

Fig. 4-18 A-frame with loft. (Design 1499)

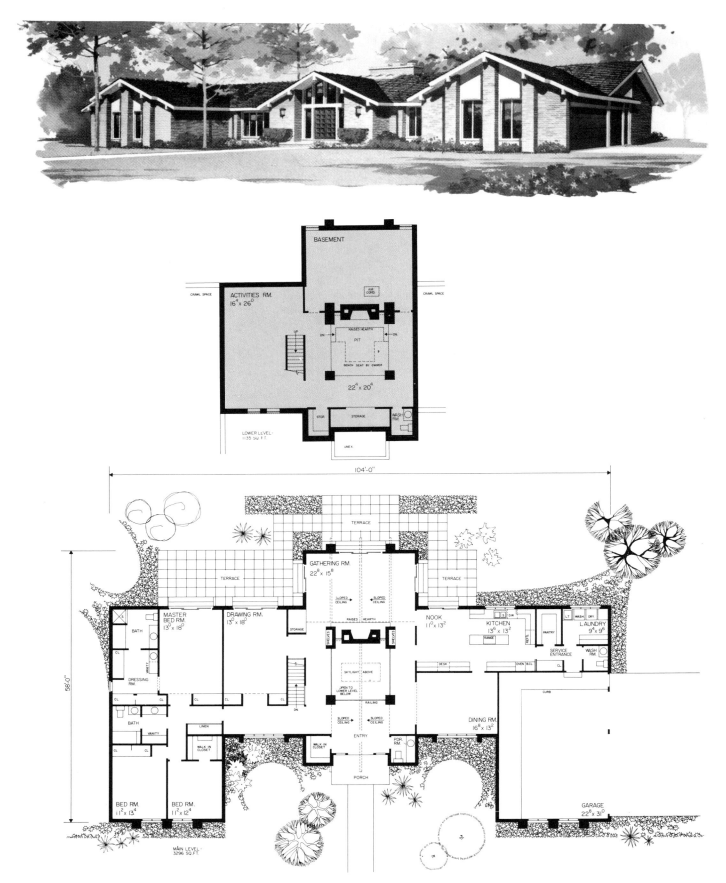

Fig. 4-19 Partial basement plan. (Design 2710)

ments have the additional value of helping to provide more stable heat for the entire house, since heat rises and first-level floors are kept warm from beneath. In larger homes, basements need not cover the entire area under the house but may be excavated only where desirable, as shown in the plan in Fig. 4–19. Basements must be carefully planned according to the methods used to design the alignment of first and second levels to ensure the alignment of stairwells, fireplaces, and end walls.

Basements do have some potentially serious problems which must be planned and compensat-ed for. Natural light is unavailable unless the foundation is built high enough to allow base-ment windows to be added. Often the addition of this much space to the exposed area of the foun-dation ruins the lines of the house and requires additional entry stairs to connect the ground level with the first-floor level. Basements must also be artificially vented and should be avoided in wet or poor drainage areas. For these reasons the plan for the basement should be developed at the time the design for the remainder of the house is prepared, even though it may not be developed and decorated at the same time. See Fig. 4-20.

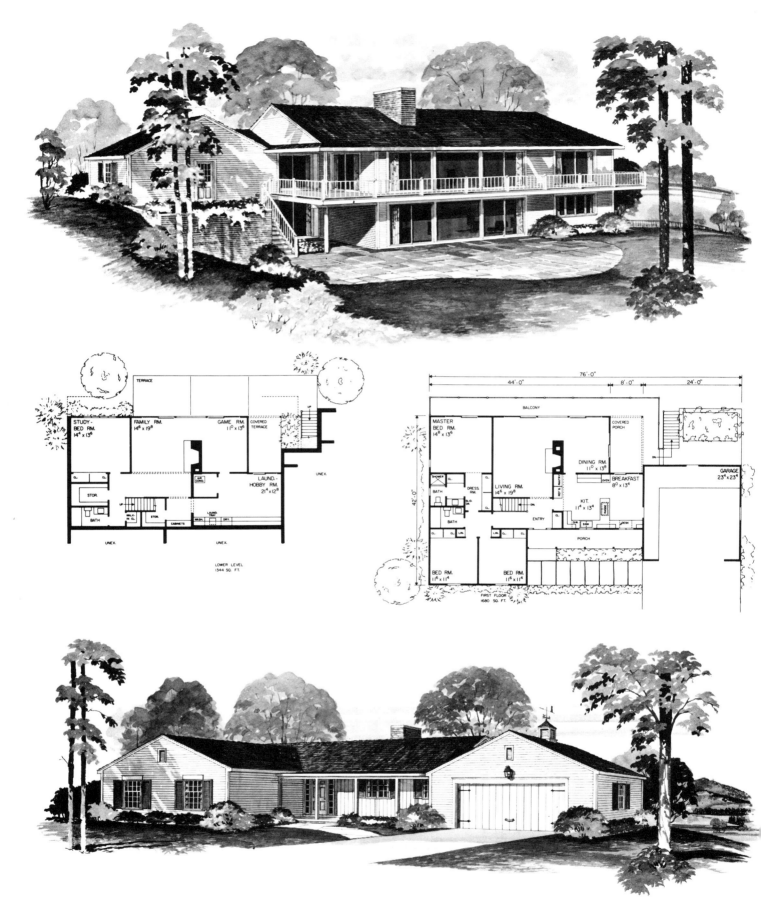

Fig. 4-20 Basement plan with one side open. (Design 1974)

CHAPTER 5

Guidelines for Room Planning

Determining the size, shape, and location of each room in a plan involves an analysis of room functions and the amount of space required for those functions. It also involves a careful study of storage facilities, door and window locations, traffic areas, and structural lighting. Space for appliances, fixtures, and furniture must also be given space consideration in room planning. Since the cost of a home is largely determined by the size and number of rooms, room sizes must be adjusted to conform to an acceptable price range.

Room Sizes

Even where no financial restrictions exist, room sizes are limited by the size of the building or area available for building. Furthermore, a room can actually be too large, as well as too small, to be functional for the purpose intended. Figures 5–1 and 5–2a and b show examples of small, medium, and large rooms designed into small, medium, and large homes. Figure 5–1 shows an extremely small home, 768 square feet. Rooms in small homes are, of course, equally small; however, in extremely small homes, such as this, the living area is usually disproportionately large. For example, the living room in Fig. 5–1 is almost as large as the living room shown in Fig. 5–2a. In the plan shown in Fig. 5–2a, which is 1648 square feet, not only are the rooms slightly larger but there are more rooms. Figure 5–2b shows an extremely large plan covering over 3000 square feet on the first floor and almost 2300 square feet on the top floor. In this plan the rooms are larger,

but the majority of the space is accomplished by the addition of more rooms. For example, this plan has a master bedroom suite plus three bedrooms on the upper level and one bedroom on the lower level, plus a study that can be converted into a bedroom if necessary. Since there are so many room size options, the occupants' real wants and needs must be analyzed to determine whether to combine some functions into a few larger rooms or plan for more rooms that are slightly smaller. Sometimes rooms may appear adequate in size on the plan until the human dimension is added.

It is often difficult to visualize the exact amount of room space that will be occupied by furniture or that should be allowed for traffic movement through a given room. One device that can be used as point of reference is a template of a human figure, as shown in Fig. 5–3. With this template you can observe and imagine yourself moving through each room to check the appropriateness of furniture placement and the adequacy of traffic allowances.

Room Functions

While the specific functions of each room are determined by the identification of individual wants and needs, as defined in Chapter 2, there are some rather common functions that are usually associated with each residential room. For example, the living room can be the entertainment center, the recreational center, the library, music room, television center, reception room, social

Fig. 5-1 Extremely small plan. (Design 1402)

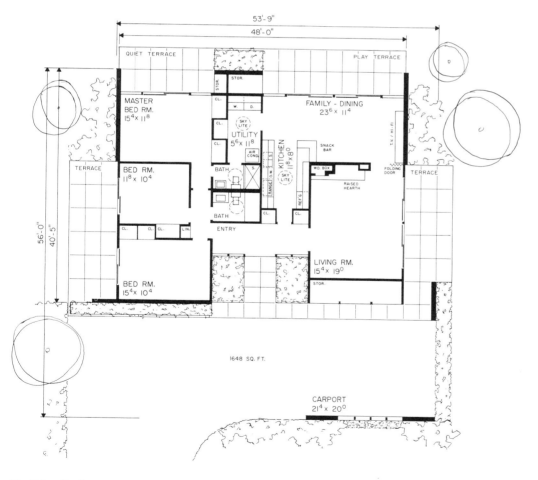

Fig. 5-2a Medium-size plan. (Design 3183)

Within the floor plan:

QUIET TERRACE

PLAY TERRACE

53'-9"

48'-0"

56'-0"

40'-5"

MASTER BED RM. 15⁴ x 11⁸

STOR.

STOR.

CL.

W. D.

FAMILY - DINING 23⁶ x 11⁴

CL.

UTILITY 5⁶ x 11⁸

SKY LITE

T.V./ HI-FI

CL.

AIR COND.

BATH

KITCHEN 11⁸ x 8⁰

SNACK BAR

TERRACE

BED RM. 11⁸ x 10⁴

RANGE D.W. S.

SKY LITE

WD. BOX

RAISED HEARTH

FOLDING DOOR

TERRACE

BATH

REF G.

CL.

CL. CL. CL. LIN.

ENTRY

BED RM. 15⁴ x 10⁴

LIVING RM. 15⁴ x 19⁰

STOR.

1648 SQ. FT.

CARPORT 21⁴ x 20⁰

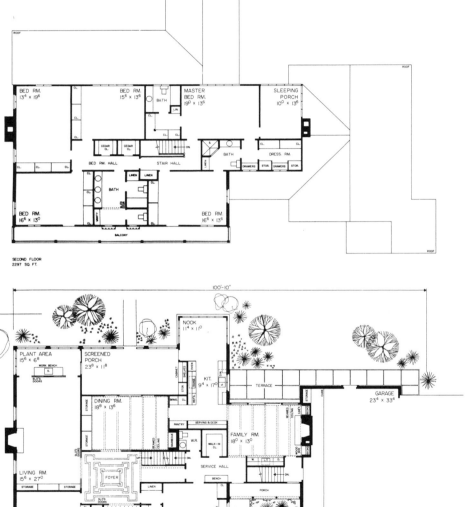

Fig. 5-2b   Large floor plan. (Design 2214)

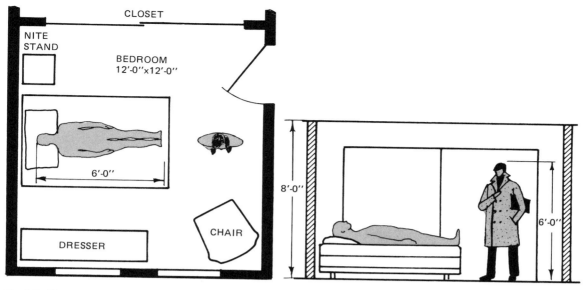

Fig. 5-3 Size comparisons.

room, study, and occasionally the dining center. But individual needs and wants determine which of these are needed or just wanted in the living room for each individual. The dining room is, of course, the place to gather in both casual and formal situations for breakfast, lunch, or dinner. Some may prefer a separate, formal dining area potentially capable of seating large numbers for dinner; others may prefer to have less formal facilities or to combine the dining function into a living/dining area. Often a family room performs many of the functions normally associated with the living room. However, the main purpose of the family room is to provide facilities for family-centered activities. If it is designed for the entire family—children and adults alike—it may include space for sewing, games, hobbies, and music room activities. In some cases the family room may be designed as a children's or young adults' activities room, thus segregating the adults from the children. In these circumstances sometimes the family room becomes more of a recreation room (game room or play room), and it must then, of course, include facilities for those activities. Often a den or study can be designed for many different purposes, depending on the living habits of the occupants. The den may function basically as a reading room, writing room, hobby room, or professional office. The den can also often double as a guest bedroom.

The preparation of food is the basic function of the kitchen. However, the kitchen may also be used as a dining area and laundry. The functions of a kitchen can be further broken down and organized under three subfunctional areas:·The storage and mixing center, in which the refrigerator is the major appliance; the preparation and

cleaning center, in which the sink is the major appliance; and the cooking center, which includes the range and oven. All of these may be connected with surface counters and wall cabinets. The utility room functions as an area for washing, drying, ironing, sewing, and storage of household cleaning equipment. It may also contain heating and air conditioning equipment, the hot water heater, and related equipment such as humidifiers and air purifiers. The major function of a garage is, of course, the storage of automobiles. But to most effectively utilize space, a garage may also function as a major source of storage or as a workshop, unless a separate workshop area is provided for maintenance and hobby work.

In the sleeping area the functions are rather obvious. However, in addition to using bedrooms for sleeping, some bedrooms may also provide facilities for writing, reading, sewing, relaxing, and even watching television. And some master bedroom suites may include a separate lounge. Likewise, in addition to the normal functions of the bathroom, facilities may also include areas for dressing, exercising, sunning, and laundering.

In larger homes the functions listed on needs and wants lists may be divided among very specialized single-function rooms, such as a sewing room, pool room, study, or media room, as shown in Fig. 5–4a. But in extremely small dwellings these functions may need to be combined into a very few number of rooms. Regardless, some compromises are usually necessary, and those compromises should be related first to the real needs and secondarily to the wants of the occupants. This often leads to the development of many combination rooms. For example, the garage may also function as a game or recreation room, or a bath may be designed and expanded to include exercise facilities, as shown in Fig. 5–4b.

Figure 5–5 shows a plan in which the shop and laundry areas could have also been planned as additional garage space or as a recreation room.

Fig. 5-4a Specialized function room.

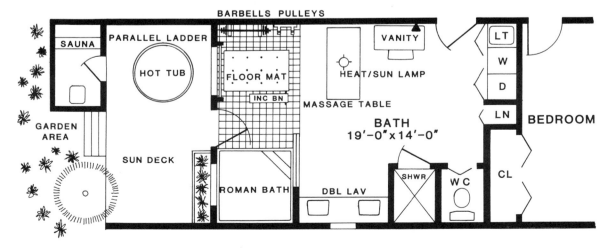

Fig. 5-4b Plan for unique needs.

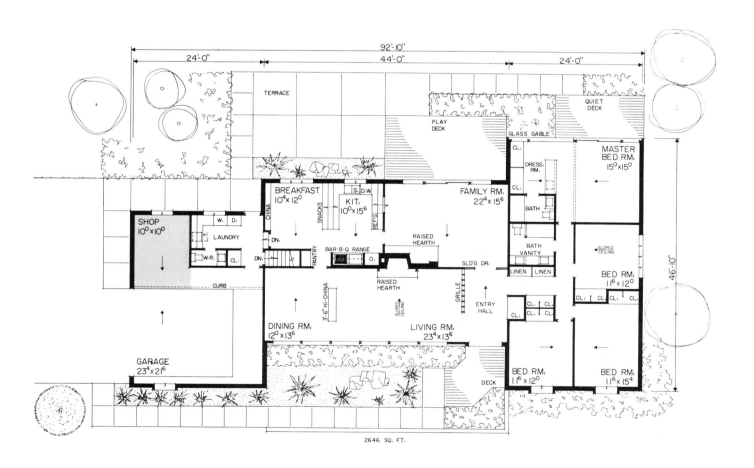

Fig. 5-5 Shop and laundry plan. (Design 1876)

Room Locations

In Chapter 2 the location of specific rooms was covered. Here examples of room locations in relation to other rooms or areas is presented. Figure 5–6a shows a classic example of the separation of the living area from the sleeping area on opposite sides of an entry hall. This is a most popular arrangement because of the separation and because of the natural alignment of the living room, dining room, kitchen, family room, and entry hall—which forms a circular living-area traffic pattern. In this plan the kitchen functions directly with the dining room and/or with the family room, which is part of the living area but effectively separated from the main living/dining room area. Figure 5–6b shows a family room which is also accessible from the kitchen or living room but is more isolated directly behind the garage. The disadvantage of this plan compared to the plan shown in Figure 5–6a is the need to use the living room as a traffic access to the family room, unless the garage or the rear terrace entrance is used. However, please note how the designer effectively eliminated an awkward offset between the living room and dining room by completely eliminating the lower right corner of the dining room, thus making the plan much more open.

Not only is the location of each room in relation to other rooms very important, but the position of the entrance foyer and halls is also extremely significant in separating rooms and providing logical access within a minimum amount of space. Figure 5–6c shows a plan with three entry-access options: the kitchen area to the right, the living area to the rear, and the sleeping area to the left. This is accomplished without the excessive use of space and without sacrificing the correct relationship between living room (gathering room), dining room, and kitchen. In this plan the front right bedroom is designed to function as an optional office which also has direct entry from the foyer. If this room is converted into a bedroom the entrance would then be positioned where the closet now exists. Notice how the fireplace in this plan separates the foyer and gathering room. It's also possible to design this fireplace as a two-way, see-through type, which enhances the open plan without sacrificing entry privacy.

Another effective location for an entry hall is shown in Fig. 5–6d. In this location the entry hall is flanked by the family room on the left and the sleeping area on the right, with direct access to the living/dining area at the rear. If a larger entry hall is desired, the front hall closet can be eliminated and another located on the inside of the family room. Here again, the circular relationship (see Fig. 5–6d) of the entry hall, living, dining, kitchen, and family room provides a most effective traffic pattern.

In more formal settings, such as shown in Fig. 5–6e, the dining room and living room may be designed with their own separate access from the entrance hall. However, in this case access to the family room must then be made either through the living room or from the kitchen. Since there is a service entrance provided through the garage and connected to the kitchen, this alternative may not be objectionable for those preferring a more

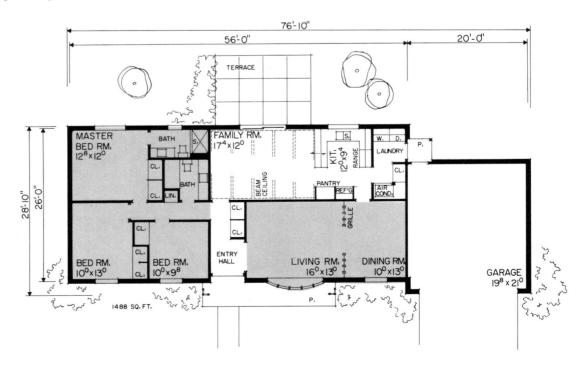

Fig. 5-6a Living-sleeping separation. (Design 1388)

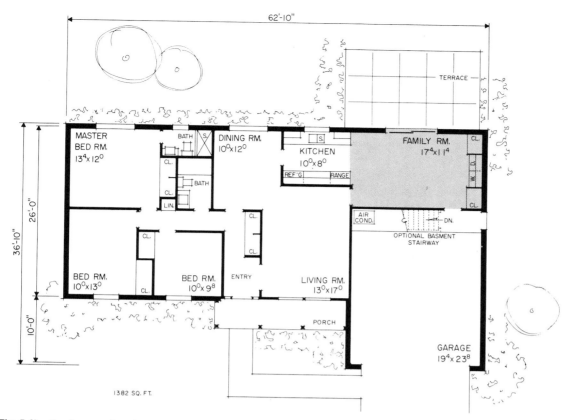

Fig. 5-6b Family room location. (Design 1305)

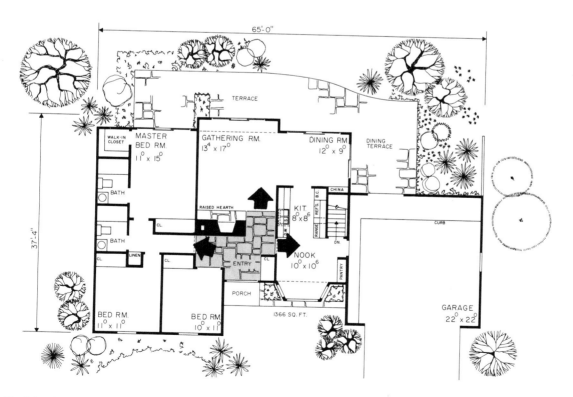

Fig. 5-6c Three entry access options. (Design 2505)

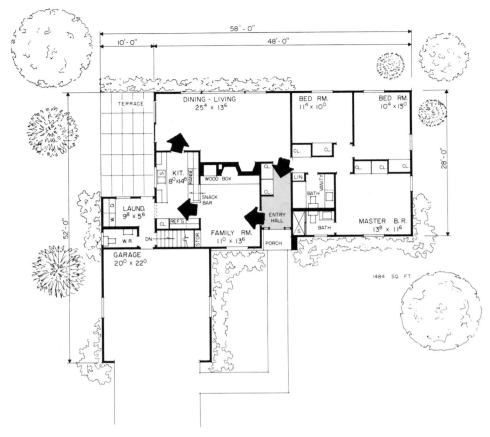

Fig. 5-6d Effective entry location. (Design 1094)

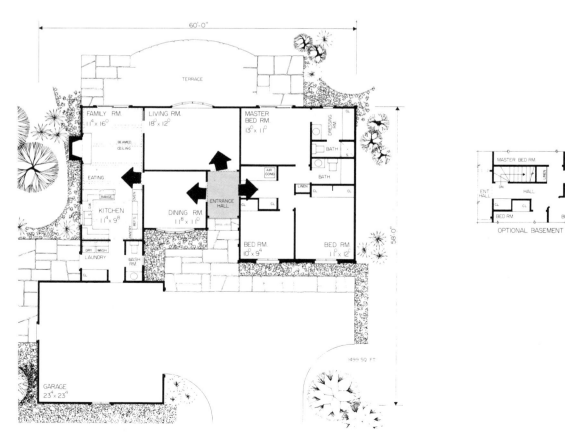

Fig. 5-6e Closed plan entry. (Design 2606)

formal, closed living-area plan. The plan shown in Fig. 5–6f is even more formal and closed, with the living room located to the left of the entrance hall and the dining room on the right. Also observe that the alignment of bedrooms across the back of the house is a very efficient use of rectangular space. Please note, however, that when rooms in an area are aligned as are these bedrooms, long access halls may often be necessary.

An unexpected and frequent solution to long hall problems is shown in Fig. 5–6g. In this case the open plan allows part of the living area to be used as traffic space without directly violating the functional internal space of the living room.

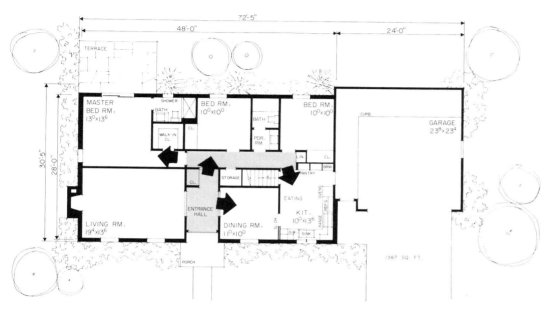

Fig. 5-6f Formal entry arrangement. (Design 1939)

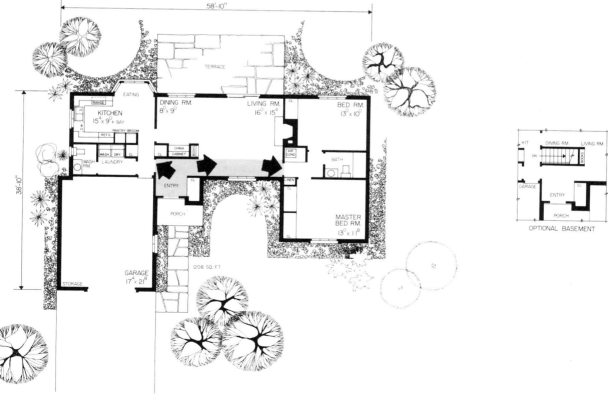

Fig. 5-6g Hall as part of living area. (Design 2607)

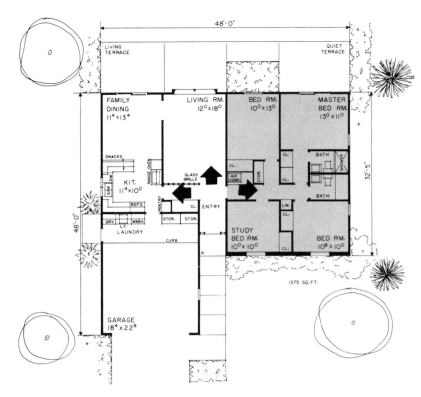

Fig. 5-6h **Fig. 5-6h Entry with area access. (Design 1944)**

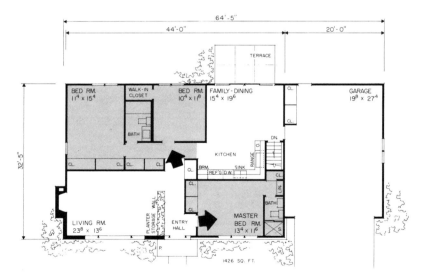

Fig. 5-6I Separation of master bedroom from other bedrooms. (Design 1025)

Thus, in this two-bedroom home a long hall *does* exist between the entry hall and the sleeping area, but since no wall exists between the hall and the living room a more open feeling is achieved. Direct access is also effectively provided between the entry hall and the service area without the use of any additional hall space.

Another very efficient location of the entry in relation to other rooms is shown in Fig. 5–6h. In this plan the rectangular clustering of the sleeping area provides a very effective use of space and also allows access to the study directly from the entry. Just a few steps are needed to gain access from the entry to either the sleeping area, living area, or kitchen and remainder of the service area. Although the clustering of rooms, such as the sleeping area arrangement shown in Fig. 5–6h, is usually very effective there are times when a separation may be more desirable. For example, if there's a need to separate the master bedroom suite from the children's bedrooms, then the solution shown in Fig. 5–6i is extremely effective on a one-level plan. In this plan the living room is also separated from the family room, which is an integral part of the kitchen. This clusters the family room with the children's bedrooms and the remainder of the service area and keeps the master bedroom directly related only to the living room and entry.

Room Shapes

Room shapes vary from plan to plan and from room to room, depending on the space available and the functional requirements for each room. However, some room shapes serve most needs better and are easier to furnish than others.

Living room shapes Living room shapes fall into several categories: rectangular, square, L-shaped, hexagonal or octagonal, round, or irregular. Rectangular-shaped living rooms accommodate furniture best because of the elongation of two walls. Dining rooms also benefit by rectangular shapes because the dining room table, which is usually rectangular, is normally positioned in the center of the room. Thus the rectangular space surrounding it is required, as shown in Fig. 5–7a. Figure 5–7b shows a square living room and dining room in a formal, closed plan. Square rooms, unless they are very large, usually create problems in furniture placement. In dining rooms, however, the additional space is often used for buffets or similar type dining furniture, leaving the remaining rectangular space for the dining room table and chairs. Octagonal rooms, hexagonal rooms (see Fig. 5–7c), or round rooms are most unique and require equally unique furniture placement. Usually rooms of this type are designed either with built-in furniture or with custom-made or preselected furniture. When shapes such as the hexagon, octagon, or circle are

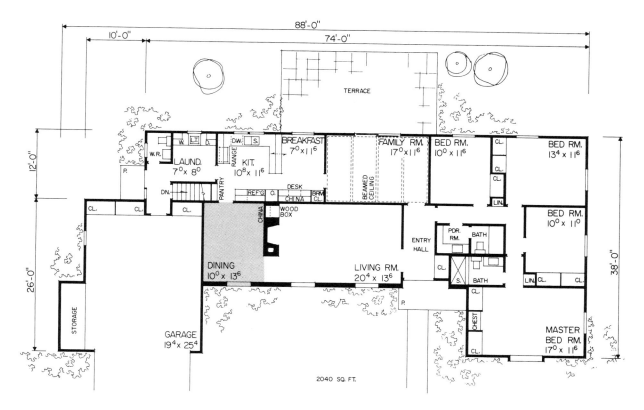

Fig. 5-7a   Rectangular dining room. (Design 1149)

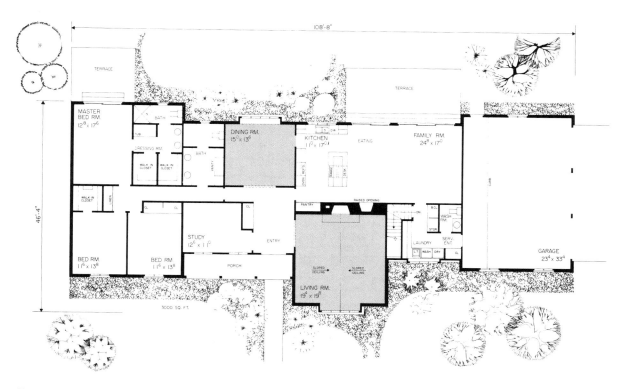

Fig. 5-7b   Square living and dining rooms. (Design 2767)

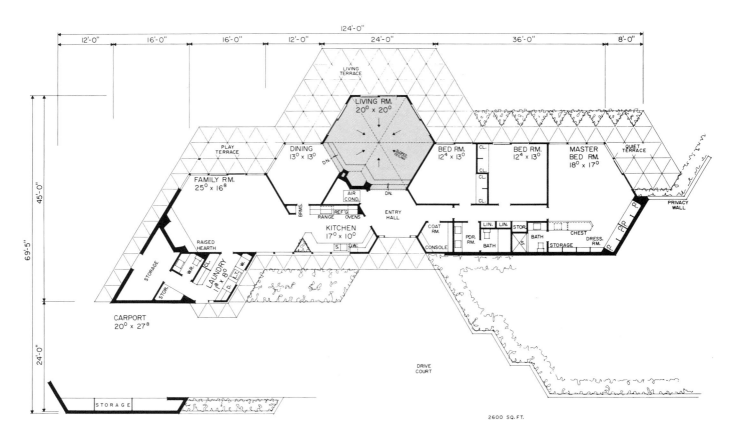

Fig. 5-7c Hexagonal living room. (Design 1792)

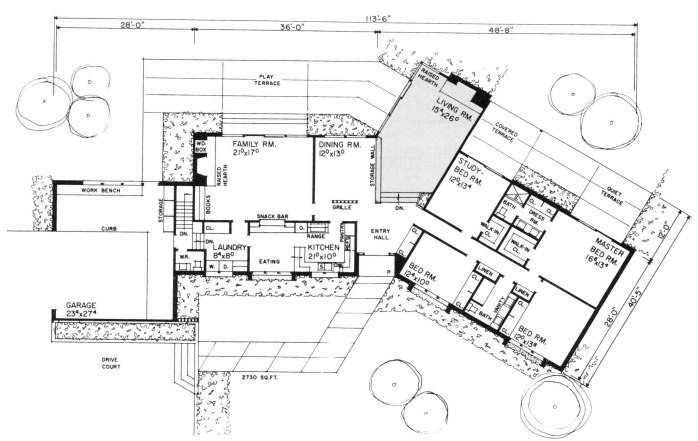

Fig. 5-7d Irregular shaped living room. (Design 1820)

used they are usually part of an overall house plan using those geometric shapes, as shown in Fig. 5–7c. This allows the angles of all rooms to be interrelated geometrically. Irregularly shaped living areas, such as the one shown in Fig. 5–7d, are usually the result of the intersection of angular wings or irregularly shaped structures. If preplanning of furniture placement and facilities is neglected, much angular space tends to be wasted.

L-shaped rooms, as shown in Fig. 5–7e, are quite popular for open-plan living areas, but nearly always involve a combination of the living/dining area and are rarely used for living rooms or dining rooms alone. Figure 5–7e shows a common application of the L-shaped living room with the dining room. The smaller portion of the L is usually the dining area and is connected to a kitchen or breakfast room.

Kitchen shapes The basic kitchen shapes are based on the position of the "work triangle." The work triangle is created by connecting the three basic centers of the kitchen: the storage and mixing center, the preparation and cleaning center, and the cooking center. If you draw a line connecting these three centers a triangle is formed. The perimeter of this triangle in an effi-

cient kitchen should not exceed 22 feet. Although the position of the three areas on the work triangle may vary greatly, the most efficient arrangements fall into the following categories:

U-shaped kitchens, as shown in Fig. 5–7f, are very efficient. The sink is usually located at the bottom of the U, and the range and refrigerator are usually at the opposite sides, although the position of the centers can be changed and the length of each leg of the U can be altered. Equal spacing of the centers usually results in the most efficient work triangle.

The peninsula kitchen is similar to the U kitchen. However, one end of the U is not enclosed with a wall and one of the centers is located on this unenclosed (peninsula) wall. The cooking center is most often located in this peninsula, and the peninsula is often used to join the kitchen to the dining room or family room. Figure 5–7g shows various arrangements of peninsula kitchens and the resulting work triangles.

The L-shaped kitchen has two continuous counters containing appliances and equipment on two adjoining walls. The work triangle is not in the traffic pattern. However, the remaining space is often used for other kitchen facilities, such as dining or laundry facilities. If the walls of

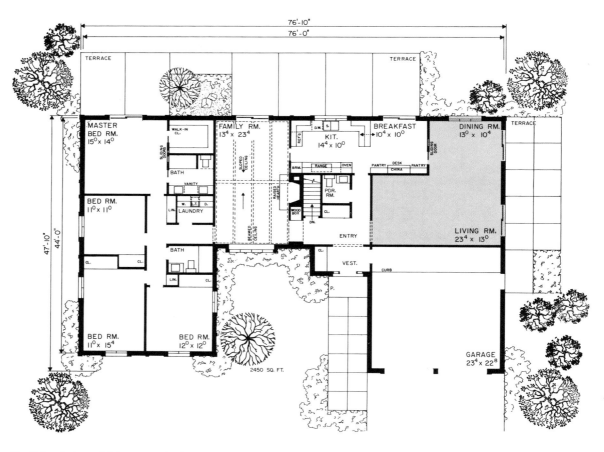

Fig. 5-7e   L-shaped living area. (Design 2142)

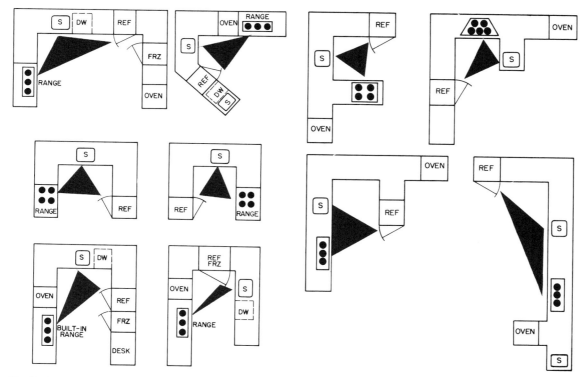

Fig. 5-7f   U-shaped kitchens.

Fig. 5-7g   Peninsula kitchens.

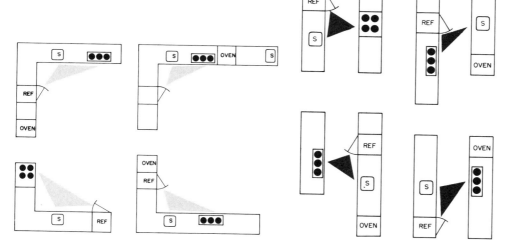

Fig. 5-7h   L-shaped kitchens.

Fig. 5-7i   Corridor kitchens.

an L-shaped kitchen are too long, the compact efficiency of the kitchen is destroyed. Figure 5–7h shows several L-shaped kitchens and the work triangles that result from these arrangements.

Corridor kitchens are shaped just as the name implies. They are kitchens with centers located on two walls and a corridor separating the centers. The two-wall corridor kitchens shown in Fig. 5–7i are very efficient arrangements for long, narrow rooms. A corridor kitchen is unsatisfac-

tory, however, if considerable traffic passes through the work triangle. Nevertheless, a corridor kitchen produces one of the most efficient work triangles of all arrangements, if correctly placed and if the corridor width is about four feet width.

A one-wall kitchen is an excellent plan for small apartments, cabins, or houses where little space is available. The work centers are located in an open line and produce a very efficient arrange-

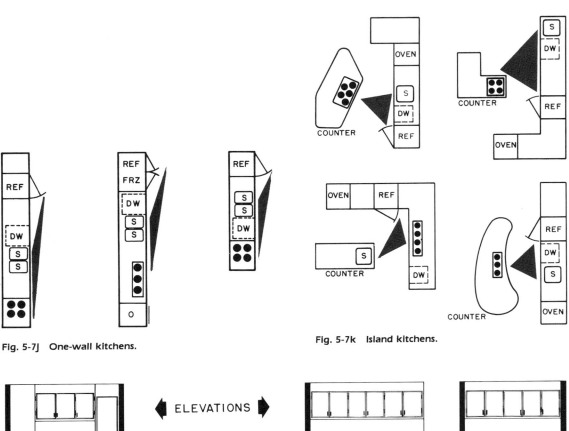

Fig. 5-7J One-wall kitchens.

Fig. 5-7k Island kitchens.

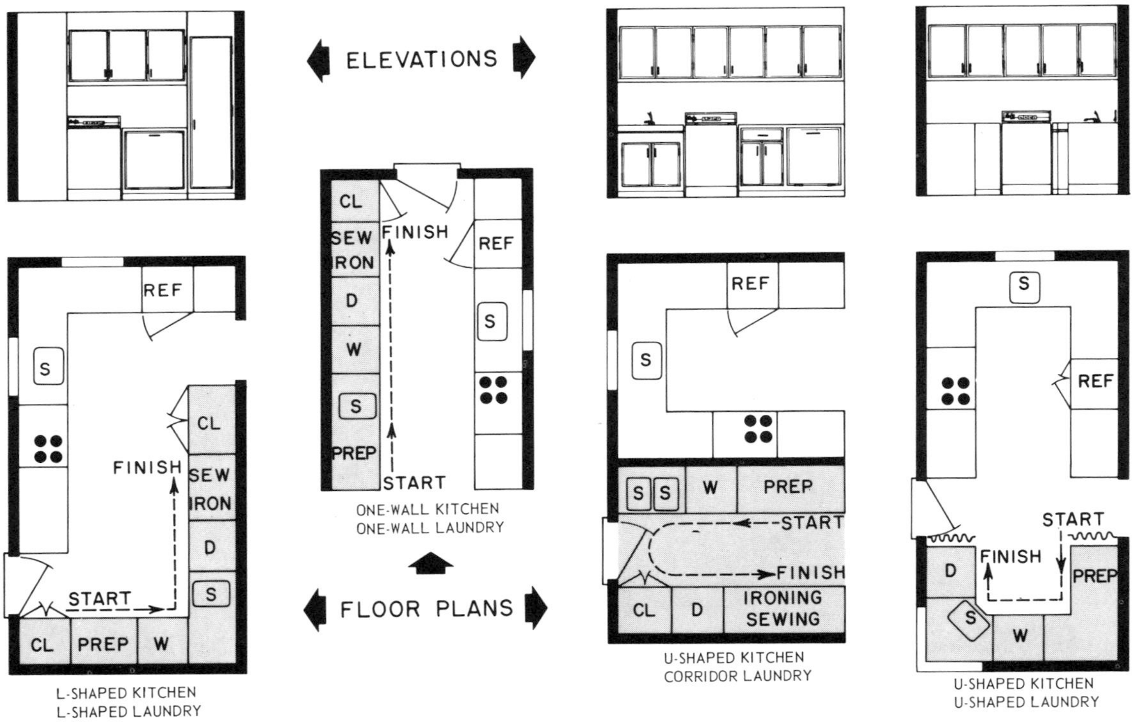

ELEVATIONS

ONE-WALL KITCHEN
ONE-WALL LAUNDRY

FLOOR PLANS

L-SHAPED KITCHEN
L-SHAPED LAUNDRY

U-SHAPED KITCHEN
CORRIDOR LAUNDRY

U-SHAPED KITCHEN
U-SHAPED LAUNDRY

Fig. 5-7l Laundry plans.

ment, as shown in Fig. 5–7j. However, in planning the one-wall kitchen the designer must be careful to avoid making the wall too long and must be sure to provide adequate storage facilities.

The island in an island kitchen serves as a separator for different parts of the kitchen. It usually has a range top or sink, or both, and is accessible on all sides. Other facilities that are sometimes located in the island are the mixing center, work table, buffet counter, or extra sink. Figure 5–7k shows several island kitchen arrangements.

A family kitchen is an open kitchen using any combination of the above basic plans. Its function is to provide a meeting place for the entire family, in addition to providing for the normal kitchen functions. Family kitchens are normally divided into two sections: one section is for food preparation, which includes the three work centers, and the other section includes a dining area. Family kitchens must obviously be rather large to accommodate these facilities. The average size of a family kitchen should be at least 225 square feet. Another popular trend dictated by increasing construction costs is the elimination of the separate family room in favor of the country-kitchen. This area combines the kitchen, breakfast room,

and family room. The result is a single spacious area that serves for the function of food preparation, informal dining, and sitting.

Utility room shapes The shape of utility rooms depends on the amount of space needed for heating, air conditioning and hot water heating, and laundry facilities. The laundry area, although only one part of the utility room, is the area most demanding yet flexible in size and shape. Ideally, to make the laundry work as easy as possible, the appliances and work spaces should be located in the order in which they are used. Such an arrangement will save time and effort. Since there are four steps in the process of laundering, the equipment needed for these steps should be grouped so that the laundry activities can proceed from one stage to another in an orderly and efficient manner, as shown in Fig. 5–7l. Please note how these plans sequence the various steps of (1) receiving and preparation, (2) washing, (3) drying, and (4) ironing and/or storage. Figure 5–7m shows several alternative sizes and shapes of laundry rooms exclusive of heating, ventilating, air conditioning, and hot water facilities. These, of course, may sometimes be located in the utility room with the laundry, or in a mechanical utility room separate from the laundry.

Garage shapes Garage shapes depend on the number of cars to be housed and the need for additional storage, hobby, or workshop facilities that may be planned into the garage. Figure 5–7n shows typical garage sizes for one- and two-car garages.

Bedroom and bath shapes The shape (and size) of a bedroom depends on the amount of furniture and type of furniture needed. A minimum-sized bedroom would accommodate a single bed, bed-

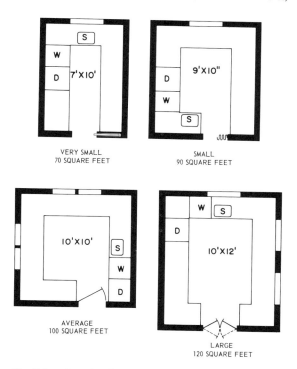

Fig. 5-7m   Laundry sizes.

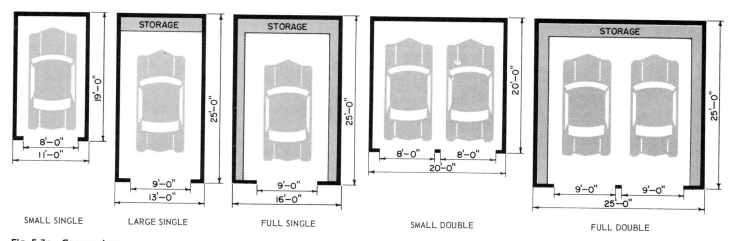

Fig. 5-7n   Garage sizes.

side table, and dresser. In contrast, a complete master bedroom suite might include twin beds or a double or kingsize bed, bedside stands, dressers, chest of drawers, lounge chairs, dressing areas, and adjacent master baths. Figure 5–7o shows several basic shapes of bedrooms: the L-shaped, square, and rectangular. The rectangular is the most popular. However, the L-shape does often exist in master bedroom suites to accommodate walk-in closets or extensions for the bath area, or a dressing room area as shown in Fig. 5–7p. Figure 5–7q shows a master bedroom suite with the bath and dressing areas clustered into a rectangle, allowing the remainder of the space to be unobstructed for the master bedroom furniture placement. Irregular shapes are rare in bedroom suites. However, Fig. 5–7r shows how an irregularly shaped sleeping area is integrated into an overall irregularly shaped plan. When irregular shapes such as the one shown in this plan are used, additional space is usually needed to compensate for the furniture, shapes, and angular walls. Just as in the living area, furniture for irregularly shaped bedrooms should be preplanned, custom-designed, or at least prepositioned with templates before the plan is finalized.

The shape and size of the bath is influenced by the spacing of the basic fixtures, the number of auxilliary functions requiring additional equipment, the arrangement or compartmentalization of areas, and the relationship to other rooms or halls. Figure 5–7s shows various bath shapes and arrangements of fixtures for various size baths. Figure 5–7r shows an effective positioning plan for the master bathroom, master bedroom dressing area, and bath in a back-to-back arrangement with the sleeping-area general bath. In Fig. 5–7q, the powder room, which is entered from the entry hall, and the sleeping-area general bath are back-to-back but are separated from the master bedroom/bath facilities, which are clustered to accommodate two adjoining dressing rooms. Both of these plans make effective use of common plumbing walls.

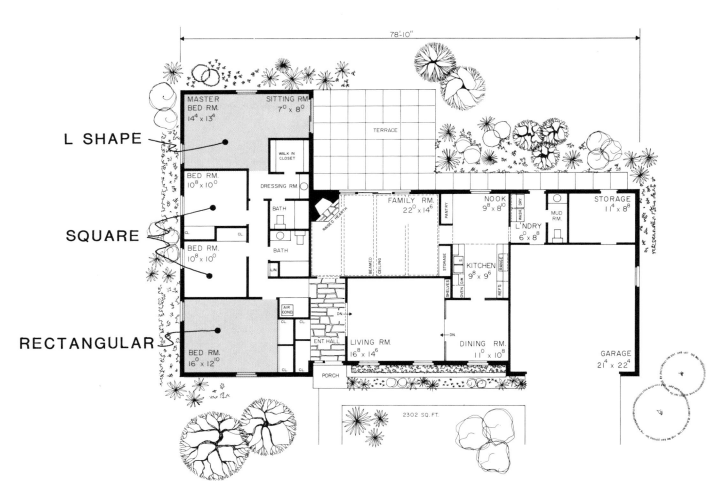

Fig. 5-7o   Bedroom shapes. (Design 2353)

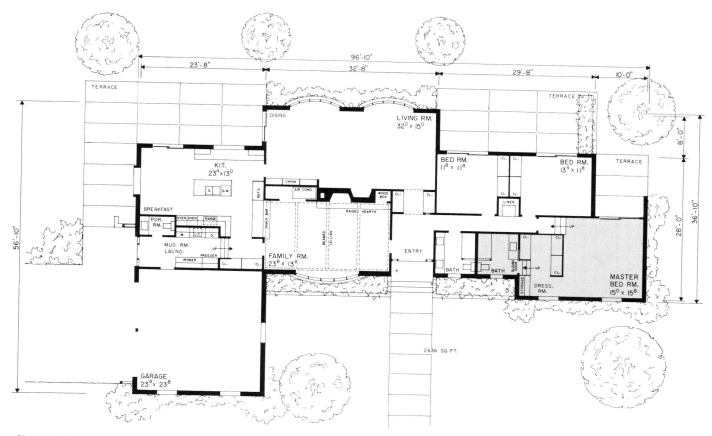

Fig. 5-7p   Master bedroom plan. (Design 1251)

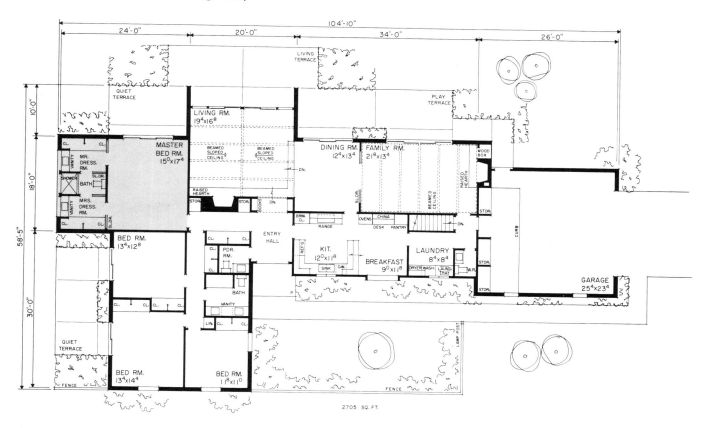

Fig. 5-7q   Master bedroom rectangular cluster. (Design 1952)

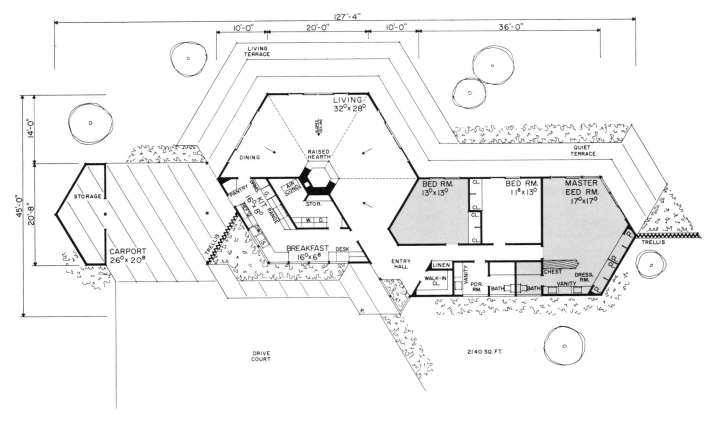

Fig. 5-7r Effective master bedroom positioning. (Design 1830)

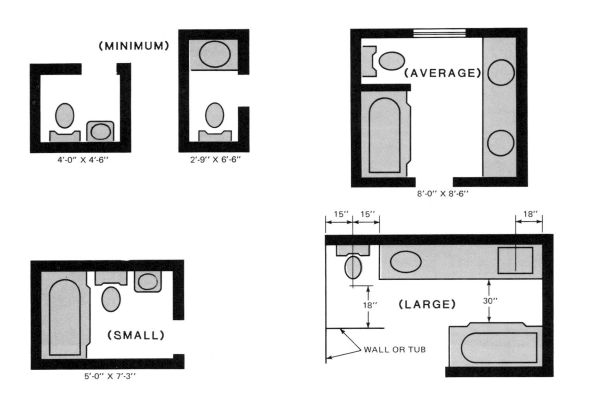

Fig. 5-7s Bath shapes.

Storage

Although there should be separate, general storage facilities planned into every house for both indoor and outdoor equipment and supplies, storage facilities must also be designed into every area and room as an integral part of the design process. Facilities and equipment used for storage within various rooms include closets, furniture, and built-in cabinets, as shown in Fig. 5–8a.

Closets Wardrobe closets, as shown in Fig. 5–8b, are shallow closets built into the wall. The minimum depth for a wardrobe closet is 24″. If the closet is more than 30″ it is inconvenient to reach into the back. Swinging or sliding doors should expose all parts of the closet to reach. A disadvantage of the wardrobe closet is the amount of wall space needed for the doors, which precludes furniture placement into that wall.

Walk-in closets are closets large enough to walk into. The area needed for this type of closet is equal to the amount of space needed to hang clothes plus space to walk and turn. Although some area is wasted in the passage, the use of the walk-in closet does provide more wall area for furniture placement since only one door is needed, as shown in Fig. 5–8c.

Wall closets are shallow closets positioned on a wall holding shelves and drawers. Wall closets are normally 18″ deep, since this size provides

access to all stored items without using an excessive amount of floor space. Figure 5–8d is an example of an effective wall storage closet. Protruding closets that create an offset in a room, as shown on the left, should be avoided. Often by filling the entire wall between two bedrooms with closet space, it is possible to design a square or rectangular room without the use of offsets. Doors and closets should be sufficiently wide to allow easy access. Swing-out doors have the advantage of providing extra storage space on the back of the door. However, space must be allowed for the swing of the door. For this reason sliding doors are usually preferred on all closets except very shallow linen closets.

Built-in storage facilities If carefully designed during the room planning process, extensive facilities for storage can be built into every room. The two illustrations in Fig. 5–8e show various built-in facilities for each room in a home that can be used for storage in addition to the normal closets, cabinets, and furniture. Built-in facilities usually utilize otherwise wasted space, such as the space under a bed, under a window seat, a room divider, over the hood of the car, and so forth. For example, built-in wall cabinets, as shown in Fig. 5–8f, when built from floor to ceiling, maximize the total amount of wall space rather than storage furniture placed on the wall which only covers part of the area. Often built-in

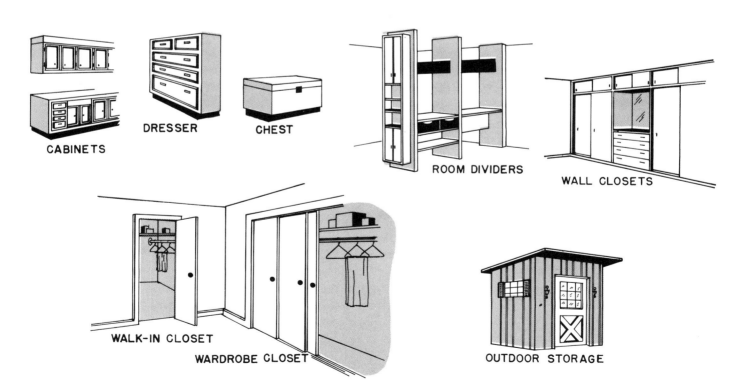

Fig. 5-8a Types of storage facilities.

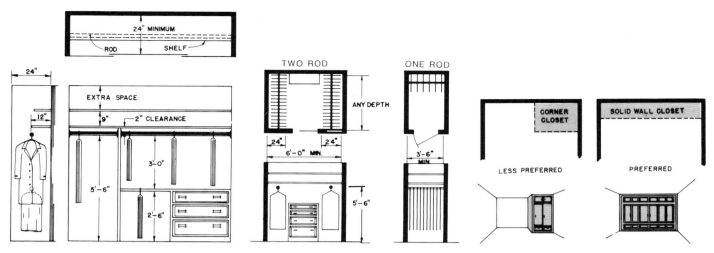

Fig. 5-8b Wardrobe closet dimensions.

Fig. 5-8c Walk-in closet dimensions.

Fig. 5-8d Wall storage closet.

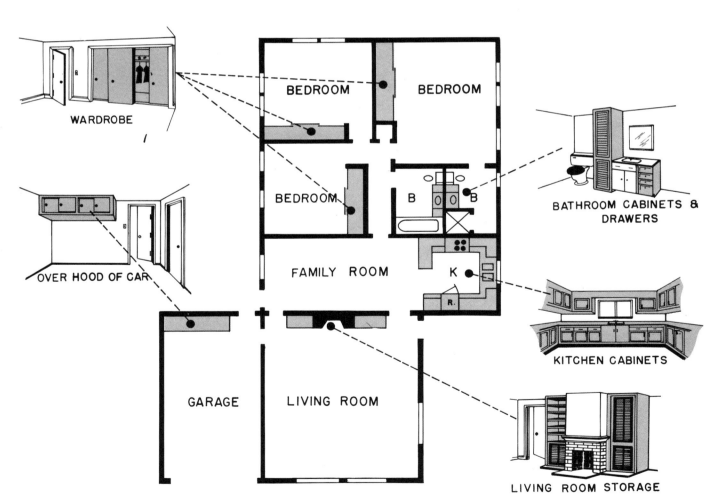

Fig. 5-8e Built-in storage facilities.

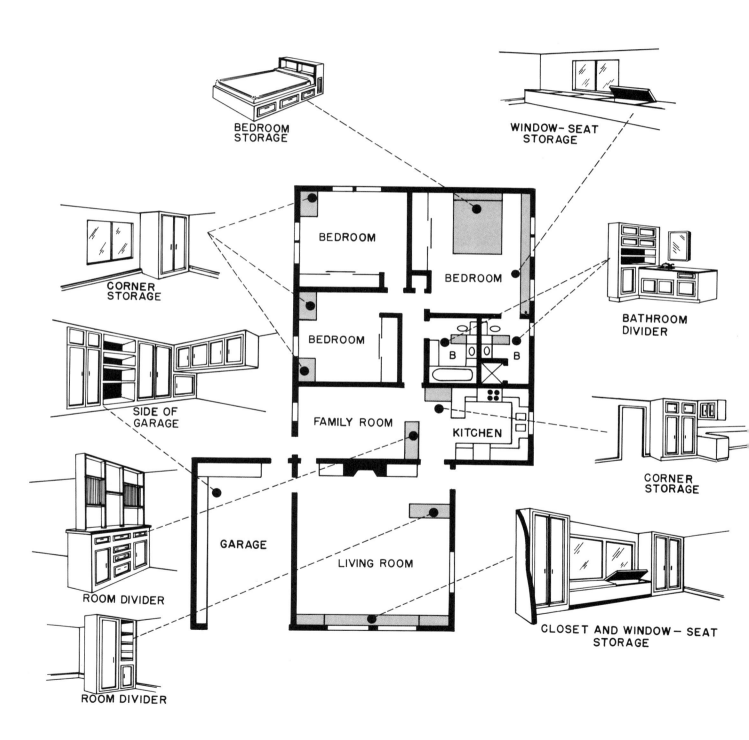

BEDROOM
STORAGE

WINDOW-SEAT
STORAGE

CORNER
STORAGE

BATHROOM
DIVIDER

SIDE OF
GARAGE

BEDROOM

BEDROOM

BEDROOM

B   B

FAMILY ROOM

KITCHEN

CORNER
STORAGE

ROOM DIVIDER

GARAGE

LIVING ROOM

CLOSET AND WINDOW—SEAT
STORAGE

ROOM DIVIDER

Fig. 5-8f Built-in wall cabinets.

Fig. 5-8g Built-in closets.

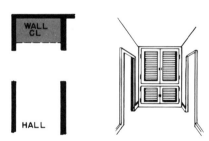

Fig. 5-8h Use of dead-end space.

storage facilities can be used to eliminate the need for conventional furniture. The storage design in Fig. 5–8g, for example, uses built-in closets and drawer storage, thus eliminating the need for chests of drawers or dressers. But the most effective use of built-in storage facilities are in dead-end spaces, as shown in Fig. 5–8h, where the built-in hall closet utilizes a normally wasted dead space in a hall. Other major built-in storage facilities, of course, include kitchen wall and base cabinets, bathroom cabinets, and bookshelves.

Furniture storage If storage is successfully planned in the design process there can be little need for furniture specifically devoted to storage purposes. However, chests of drawers and dressers in the bedroom are the usual exception. These pieces of furniture provide not only storage but working surfaces for articles.

Windows and Doors

Both window and doors are internal design features which must be considered in conjunction with the exterior and must be studied carefully in the process of room planning.

Windows Windows function to admit light and to provide ventilation and a view of the exterior. Obtaining uniform daylight throughout each room depends on the size and location of windows; the amount of reflection of light from the floors, walls, ceilings, and furnishings; and the compass direction of the window wall. Although

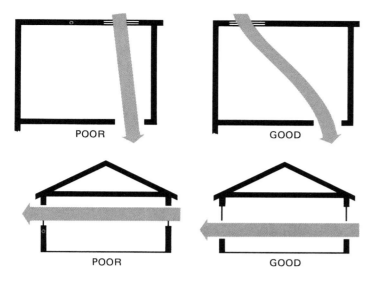

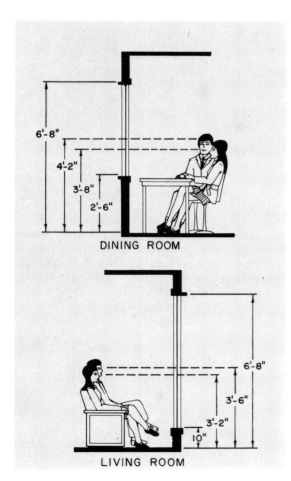

Fig. 5-9a Window location for air circulation.

Fig. 5-9b Window heights. (Small Homes Council)

most building codes recommend the glass area be not less than 10 percent of the room floor area, 20 percent is more desirable. On brighter days excess light can be controlled by blinds or drapes.

The effectiveness of good window ventilation depends on which windows are opened, their location, and how far they are opened. Most building codes recommend a minimum of 5 percent of the floor area for ventilation, but 10 percent is more desirable. To control the air movement coming into the home, double-hung, horizontal sliding, casement, and awning windows should be located where possible in the lower part of the wall. Windows should be located to provide the best possible air movement, as shown in Fig. 5–9a. (Note also the relationship of the door to the open windows in this illustration.) But remember, windows should also be located to take full advantage of desirable views. In rooms such as kitchens and bedrooms where the wall space is limited, the window sill height varies from 10″ to 3′6″, as shown in Fig. 5–9b. This provides wall space below the windows for cabinets and furniture arrangement, and at the same time provides an adequate view when people are either standing or sitting. In dining and living rooms, the view from the window should be observed from a sitting position. For adequate viewing the top of the sill should not be more than 2′6″ from the floor.

Doors Residential doors may be installed to swing, slide, or fold. The most popular door used in residential design is the swinging door. This type of door is hinged on one side and usually opens against a wall. In designing swinging doors in a residence, do not swing bedroom doors into halls. Exterior doors should be swung into the

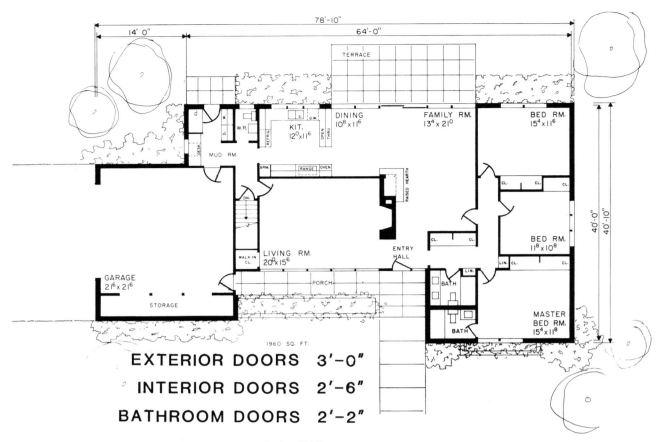

EXTERIOR DOORS 3'-0"

INTERIOR DOORS 2'-6"

BATHROOM DOORS 2'-2"

Fig. 5-10a   Doors swing into rooms. (Design 3219)

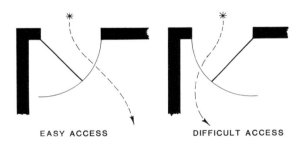

EASY ACCESS   DIFFICULT ACCESS

Fig. 5-10b   Swing door toward wall.

house, as shown in Fig. 5–10a. Doors should always be swung toward an adjacent wall for easy entrance as shown in Fig. 5–10b. For this reason doors should usually be located as close as possible to the wall next to the hinge, since the space behind a door swing is not practical for furniture location. Swing doors are usually preferred because they move with the person opening the door. And for that reason are usually used as the main access to the home and to the individual rooms.

Fireplaces

Fireplaces for residential use are designed in three types. Those constructed totally on the site, those using a manufactured firebox and flue systems, and freestanding units. Fireplaces vary greatly in size and shape. The firebox opening, the mantel (if any), the hearth position, the material treatment, and the color of the surrounding trim must all be considered in planning a room which includes a fireplace. But the most important fireplace consideration in room planning is the determination of the type of fireplace opening. A fireplace can be open from the front (Fig. 5–11a), open on two sides (Fig. 5–11b), three sides (Fig. 5–11c), see-through (Fig. 5–11d), or freestanding (Fig. 5–11e). The type of fireplace opening is directly related to the location designed for the fireplace. However, convenience, appearance, and draft availability internally and externally are also of prime consideration in fireplace location. Living rooms, recreation rooms, and family rooms are the most common fireplace locations, although dining rooms and bedrooms are also often frequent choices. Structural support for the fireplace is of paramount importance since great structural weight is involved. Therefore, fireplaces and chimneys must rest on a firm concrete footing specified by local building codes.

Each fireplace must have its own flue. If fireplaces are used on two levels, a common chimney can be used to contain several flues, as shown in

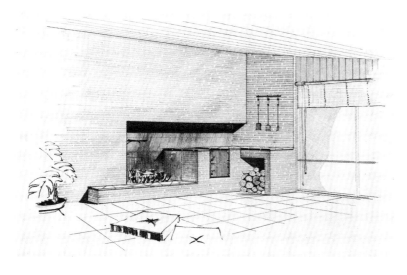

Fig. 5-11a One-sided fireplace.

Fig. 5-11b Two-sided fireplace.

Fig. 5-11c Three-sided fireplace.

Fig. 5-11d   See-through fireplace.

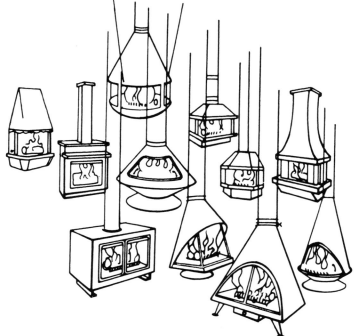

Fig. 5-11e   Freestanding fireplaces. (Majestic-American Standard)

Fig. 5-11f   Fireplace flue system. (Majestic-American Standard)

Fig. 5–11f. This type of alignment is illustrated in the plan shown in Fig. 5–11g. You will observe that this arrangement allows the lower-level fireplace to serve both the breakfast room and living room and is aligned with the fireplace in the master bedroom above. This chimney also contains the flue, which originates in the basement heating plant. Regardless of whether a fireplace is used above another, space must always be allotted for the passage of the chimney through all levels from the fireplace location to the roof. Figure 5–11h shows a plan which includes a fireplace in the kitchen, dining room, living room, and family room on the lower level. Observe how space was provided on the upper level for the passage of the chimney through these areas. This space must always be planned for in advance. A more common example of this practice is shown in the first level living room fireplace placed directly above the recreation room fireplace on the lower level, as shown in Fig. 5–11i. Thus, whenever possible fireplaces should be either aligned side by side or stacked vertically to elimi-

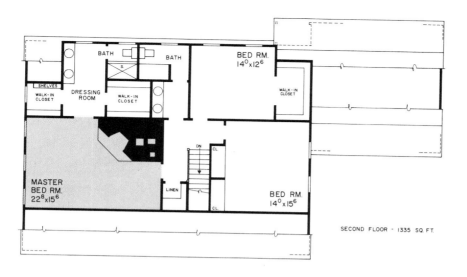

SECOND FLOOR - 1335 SQ. FT.

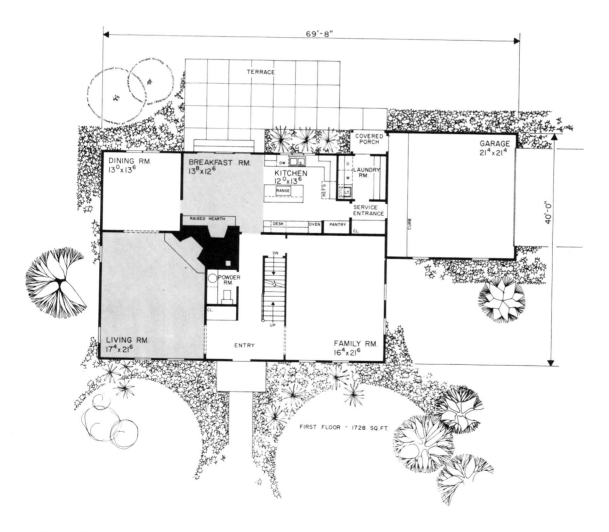

Fig. 5-11g   Alignment of fireplaces. (Design 2652)

Fig. 5-11h   Second level flue alignment. (Design 2638)

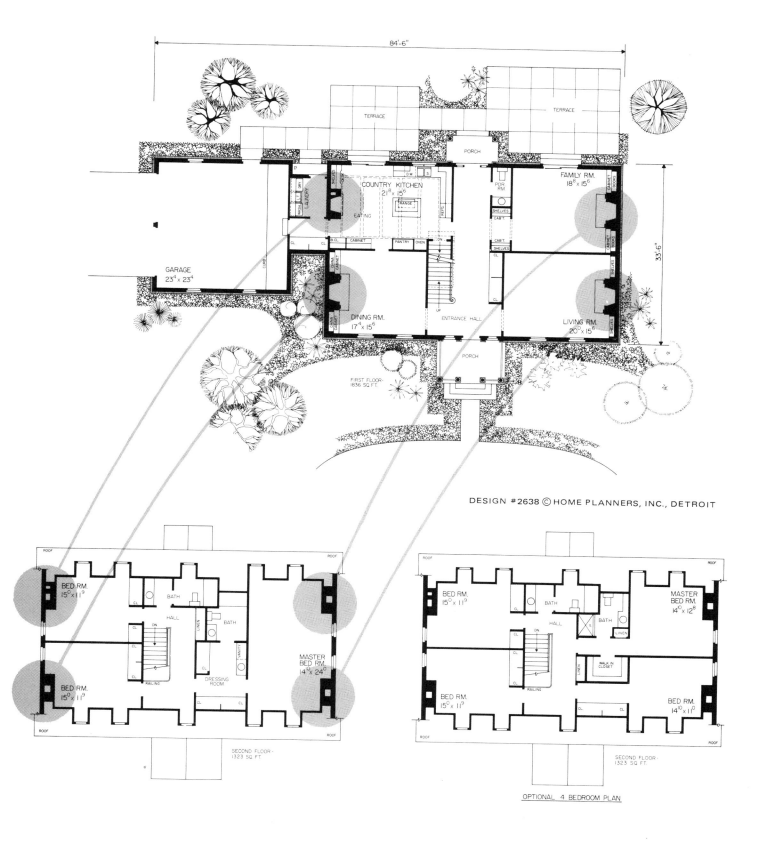

84'-6"

TERRACE

TERRACE

PORCH

P

D.W.

S

COUNTRY KITCHEN
21⁸ x 15⁶

PDR.
RM.

FAMILY RM.
18⁸ x 15⁶

CABINET
BOOKS

SHELVES

EATING

RANGE

REFG

SHELVES

GARAGE
23⁴ x 23⁴

LAUNDRY
WASH DRY

CL

CL

B.CL

CABINET

PANTRY

OVEN

DN

CAB'T

SHELVES

CABINET
BOOKS

CURB

CHINA CABINET

CAB'T

SHELVES

CL

33'-6"

DINING RM.
17⁴ x 15⁶

UP

ENTRANCE HALL

LIVING RM.
20⁰ x 15⁶

SHELVES

PORCH

FIRST FLOOR -
1836 SQ. FT.

DESIGN #2638 © HOME PLANNERS, INC., DETROIT

ROOF

ROOF

BED RM.
15⁰ x 11⁹

CL

BATH

HALL

LINEN

BATH

DN

VANITY

BED RM.
15⁰ x 11⁹

CL

CL

CL

RAILING

DRESSING ROOM

CL

MASTER BED RM.
14⁰ x 24⁰

ROOF

CL

CL

ROOF

SECOND FLOOR -
1323 SQ. FT.

ROOF

ROOF

BED RM.
15⁰ x 11⁹

CL

BATH

HALL

BATH

S

LINEN

MASTER BED RM.
14¹⁰ x 12⁸

DN

CL

LINEN

WALK IN CLOSET

BED RM.
15⁰ x 11⁹

CL

CL

RAILING

CL

CL

BED RM.
14¹⁰ x 11⁰

ROOF

ROOF

SECOND FLOOR -
1323 SQ. FT.

OPTIONAL 4 BEDROOM PLAN

Guidelines for Room Planning 121

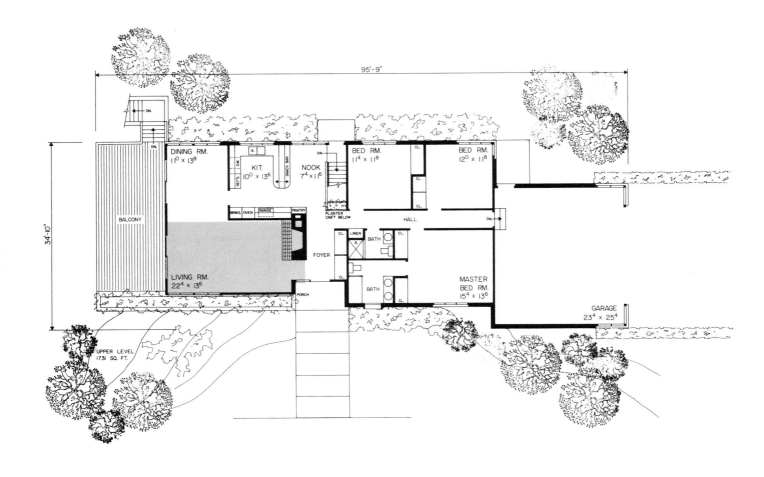

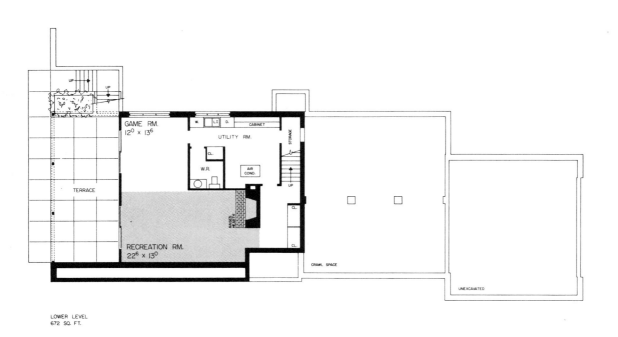

Fig. 5-11i Lower level flue alignment. (Design 2272)

nate the need for additional chimneys. Figure 5–11j shows a very effective use of one chimney with three fireplaces in which the lower-level family room fireplace is aligned with the living room and study fireplaces on the main level. But in this case the living room and study fireplaces are also stacked side by side so that one large chimney with three flues can serve all three fireplaces.

In addition to providing heat and atmosphere, fireplaces can also function in open plans as room dividers, as shown in Fig. 5–11k. Using a see-through fireplace such as this to separate the living room and study is very effective when total isolation is not required. Another common separation use for the see-through fireplace is between the living and dining room in an open plan.

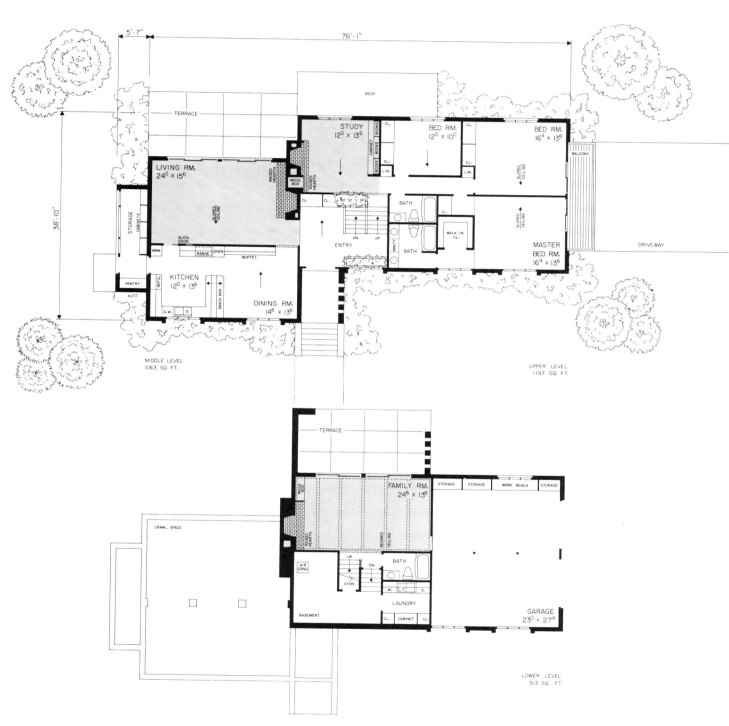

Fig. 5-11J Alignment of three fireplaces and flues. (Design 2267)

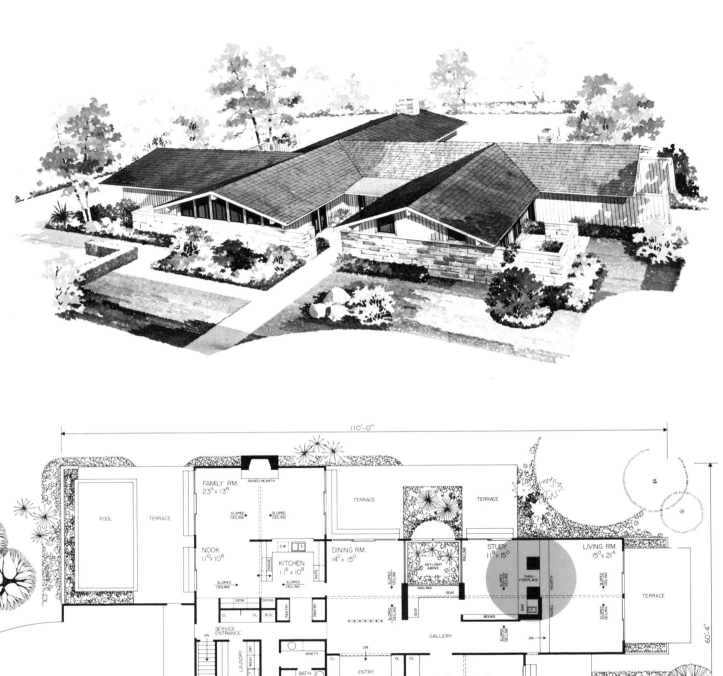

Fig. 5-11k Fireplace as room divider. (Design 2747)

Fixtures and Appliances

Since rooms are designed to fulfill specific functions, the furniture, fixtures, and appliances selected for each room also contribute to the total functioning of the room. Furniture can be rearranged or changed, but fixtures and appliances are a fixed and integral part of the room and their selection and location must be carefully designed accordingly.

Kitchen appliances Kitchen appliances must be positioned for utmost efficiency. Figure 5–12a shows a U-shaped kitchen, with access at the back of the U to the utility room and to the dining room. The back of the U also accommodates a snack bar which can be used either from the kitchen side or dining room side. In this U-shaped kitchen the sink is at the top of the U and the range and refrigerator are at the two ends. Please note that access can be gained from the dining area to the utility room through the kitchen, but this is through the back of the U and does not interfere with the functioning of the work triangle. The L-shaped kitchen shown in Fig. 5–12b

connects with the entry on one side and the dining area on the other and also includes a snack bar which can function from the open dining area in this extremely small plan. The appliances in this kitchen are placed on two walls, with the sink, dishwasher, and refrigerator aligned on the same wall and the sink on the other leg of the L, creating a slightly long but very effective work triangle.

Typical appliance placement for one-wall kitchens is shown in Fig. 5–12c. In this plan the oven-range, sink, and refrigerator are all aligned on a wall opposite a snack bar which adjoins the eating area of the family kitchen. Very small plans like this one with combination family/kitchen/dining facilities are very effective for one-wall kitchens. This type of one-wall appliance placement with a separator snack bar provides an alignment of the appliances using the minimum amount of space. The one-wall corridor kitchen as shown in Fig. 5–12d is almost a part of the dining room, since in this case the dining area is extremely informal and part of an open-plan living area. In this plan the three basic appliances form an equilateral work triangle. Figure 5–12e shows a

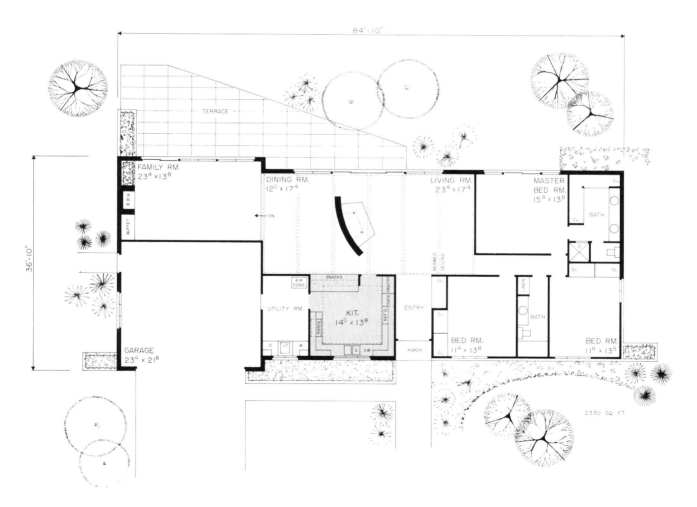

Fig. 5-12a U-shaped kitchen plan. (Design 2303)

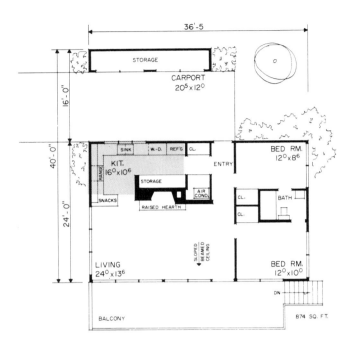

Fig. 5-12b L-shaped kitchen plan. (Design 2405)

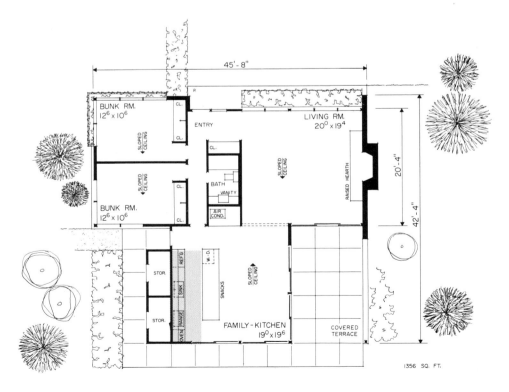

Fig. 5-12c One-wall kitchen plan. (Design 2411)

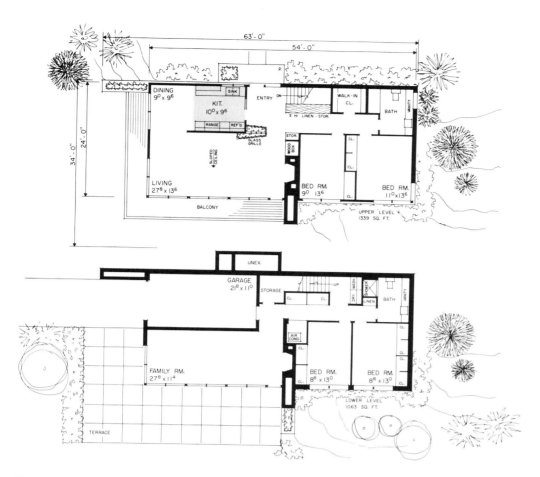

Fig. 5-12d   Open kitchen-dining plan. (Design 2403)

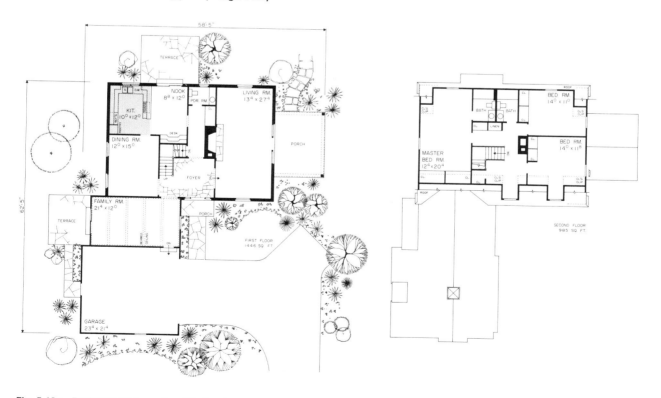

Fig. 5-12e   Peninsula kitchen plan. (Design 2313)

peninsula kitchen, which is actually an adaptation of the U, with the wall between the kitchen and the nook area completely open except for the range peninsula. In this plan access to the kitchen from the rear entrance is directly through the nook, but the kitchen is also in good proximity to the dining room. The appliances are placed similar to the location found in most U-shaped plans.

Figure 5–12f is an example of an island kitchen using a range island adjacent to a nook area. Access from the kitchen to the dining room is through the nook area, so furniture placement in the nook area must be carefully planned. Note that in this arrangement the kitchen not only interfaces with the nook and dining room but also includes a snack bar ledge which services the family room.

Laundry appliances Laundry appliances and fixtures—washer, dryer, laundry tubs, and storage

—can be located in the kitchen, in the utility room, in the garage, or in a separate laundry room. But regardless of the location the dryer must be vented to the outside and the noise level of the washer and dryer in operation considered in locating the laundry facilities away from the living or sleeping area of the home. This is accomplished in Fig. 5–12g by locating the laundry with a hobby room on the lower level of the one-story plan. However, in Fig. 5–12h, the laundry is located on the same level but as far as possible from the living area. The positioning of the laundry room in this location, next to the garage and separated from the remainder of the house by the service entrance, is very effective in baffling any laundry noise, odors, or humidity from the remainder of the house. This location also provides easy access from the kitchen and garage, which creates a very efficient service area traffic pattern. Since all laundry appliances create

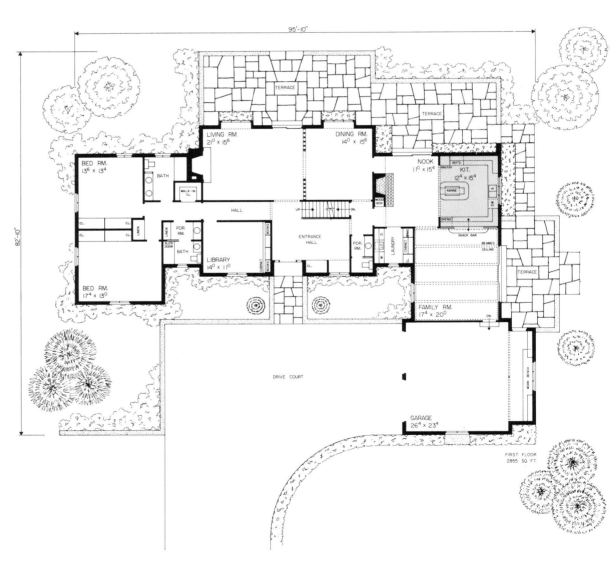

Fig. 5-12f Range island plan. (Design 2245)

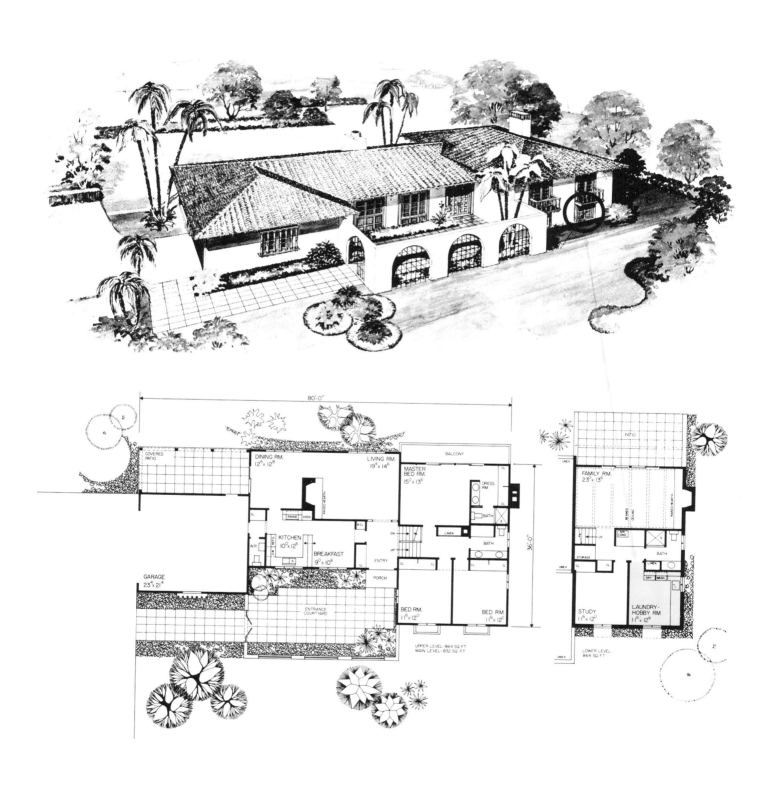

Fig. 5-12g Laundry plan. (Design 2143)

Fig. 5-12h   Laundry and garage with service entrance. (Design 2301)

BED RM.
12²×13¹⁰

SITTING RM.
11⁸×10⁴

BATH

BED RM.
12²×13¹⁰

LINEN

DN.

WALK-IN CL.

CL.

RAILING

WALK-IN CL.

CL.

CL.

LINEN

BATH

WALK-IN CL.

BED RM.
19²×13¹⁰

DRESS'G.

MASTER
BED RM.
19²×13¹⁰

Second Floor
1815 SQ. FT.

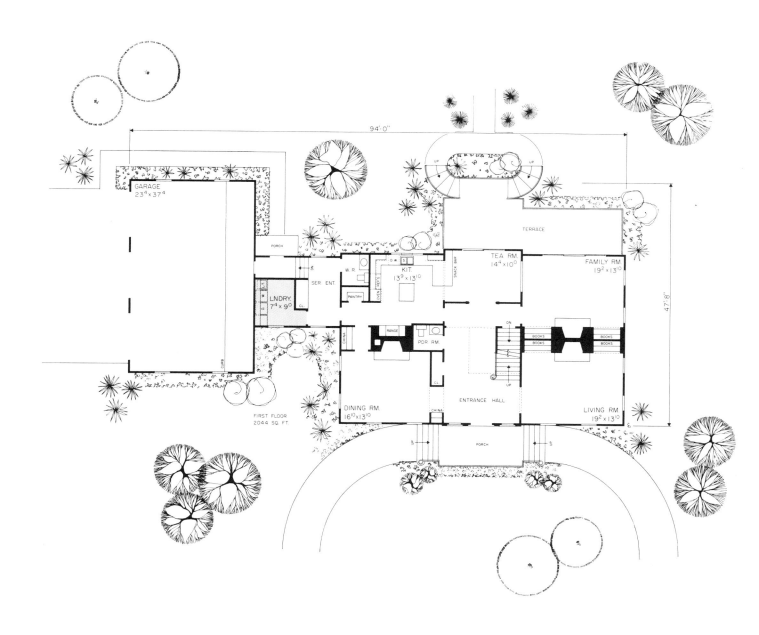

94'-0"

GARAGE
23⁴×37⁴

PORCH

TERRACE

CURB

SER. ENT.

W.R.

LNDRY.
7⁴×9⁰

PANTRY

KIT.
13⁹×13¹⁰

SNACK BAR

TEA RM.
14⁴×10⁰

FAMILY RM.
19²×13¹⁰

47'-8"

CHINA

RANGE

PDR. RM.

DN.

BOOKS

BOOKS

BOOKS

BOOKS

CL.

UP

FIRST FLOOR
2044 SQ. FT.

DINING RM.
16¹⁰×13¹⁰

CHINA

ENTRANCE HALL

LIVING RM.
19²×13¹⁰

PORCH

both humidity and some excessive noise their location away from the living area and the sleeping area is always advisable. However if the appliances are used only during the day, proximity to the sleeping area is often not critical.

Bath appliances and fixtures The three basic fixtures included in most bathrooms are a lavatory, water closet, and tub or shower. The efficiency of the bath is greatly dependent upon the effectiveness of the arrangement of these three fixtures. Mirrors should be located a distance from the tub to minimize fogging. Sinks should be well lighted and free from traffic. The water closet needs a minimum of 15″ from the center to the side wall or other fixtures, as shown in Fig. 5–12*i*. Tubs and showers are available in a great variety of sizes and shapes. Square, rectangular, or sunken-pool tubs allow flexibility in fixture arrangement. Typical sizes for bathroom fixtures are shown in Fig. 5–12*j*, but remember, although most bath fixtures are not the same size, the location, spacing, and number of fixtures greatly affects the size of the bath.

In locating bath fixtures, or any plumbing fixtures, try to locate them to share a plumbing wall.

A plumbing wall is an internal partition used to house plumbing lines. The location of plumbing fixtures back to back on a plumbing wall greatly reduces the length of plumbing lines and also provides easy access for problem troubleshooting. Both of these factors greatly reduce costs. Figure 5–12*k* shows bath and kitchen plumbing fixtures located on a common plumbing wall. Figure 5–12*l* shows several plumbing walls which contain adjacent bath piping and kitchen water lines. When plumbing lines extend vertically through several floors, the position of plumbing walls must be planned to align vertically. For example, a plumbing wall for a first-level bath in a multi-level house must be located to provide a vertical upward path for a vent stack. Likewise, a second-level bath should be located to provide vertical access for plumbing lines with a minimum of horizontal piping. In addition, a second-level bath must be provided with an extra-wide (6″) rough frame vertical wall in which the soil stack can be placed. Note the convenient location of the bath fixtures in Fig. 5–12*m*, which provides horizontal alignment for all bath water lines, soil stack, and vent stacks. However, if plastic pipe is used a standard 4″ stud wall can be erected.

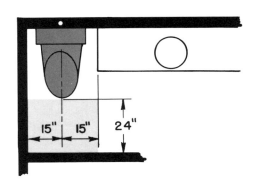

Fig. 5-12i Water closet spacing.

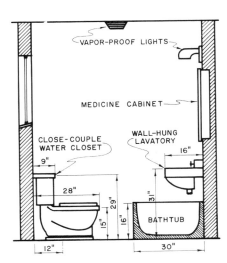

Fig. 5-12J Bath fixture sizes.

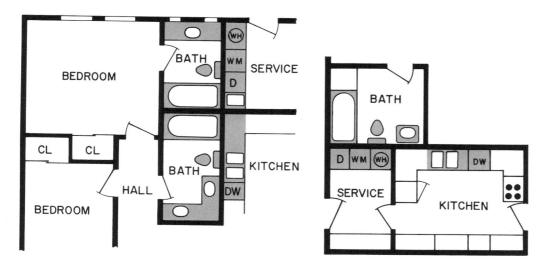

Fig. 5-12k   Efficient fixture location.

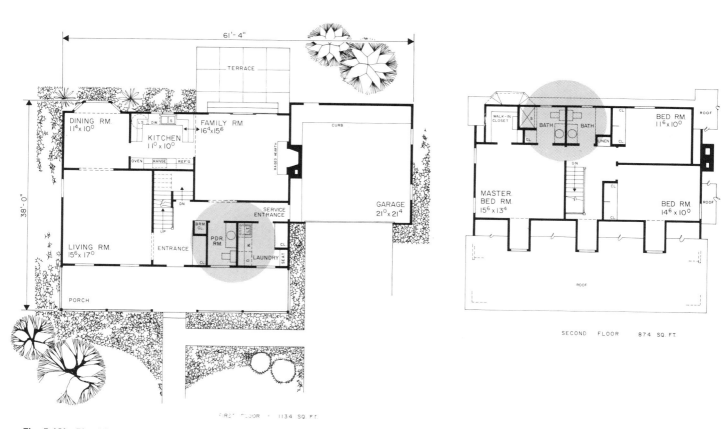

Fig. 5-12l   Plumbing wall alignments. (Design 2776)

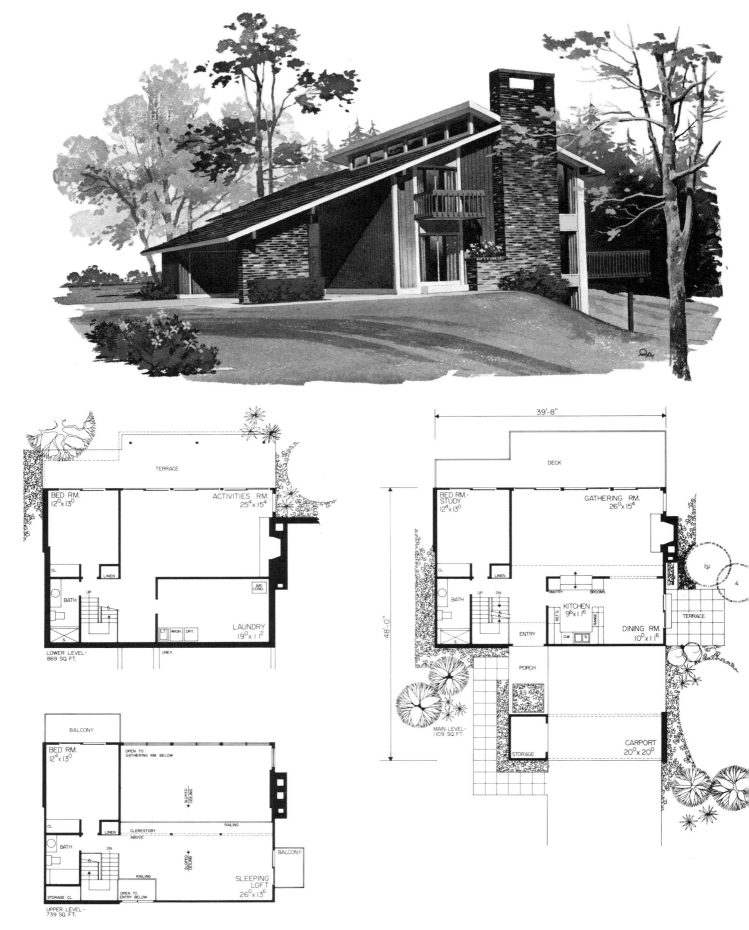

TERRACE

BED RM.
12^0 x 13^0

ACTIVITIES RM.
25^4 x 15^4

CL.

LINEN

AIR
COND.

BATH

UP

LAUNDRY
19^0 x 11^2

LT. WASH. DRY.

LOWER LEVEL-
869 SQ. FT.

UNEX.

BALCONY

BED RM.
12^4 x 13^0

OPEN TO
GATHERING RM. BELOW

CL.

LINEN CLERESTORY
ABOVE

RAILING

SLOPED CEILING

BATH

DN.

SLOPED CEILING

BALCONY

RAILING

SLEEPING
LOFT
26^0 x 13^6

STORAGE CL.

OPEN TO
ENTRY BELOW

UPPER LEVEL-
739 SQ. FT.

39'-8"

DECK

BED RM.-
STUDY
12^4 x 13^0

GATHERING RM.
26^0 x 15^4

CL.

LINEN

BATH

UP DN.

PANTRY BROOMS

48'-0"

REF'G.

KITCHEN
9^6 x 11^6

RANGE

ENTRY

D.W.

TERRACE

DINING RM.
10^0 x 11^6

PORCH

MAIN LEVEL-
1109 SQ. FT.

STORAGE

CARPORT
20^0 x 20^0

Fig 5-12m Vertical alignment of stack walls. (Design 2548)

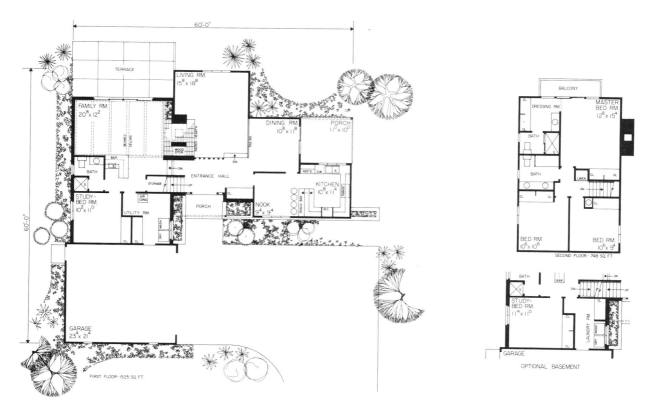

Fig 5-12m   continued. (Design 2379)

Traffic Patterns

External traffic

Entrances Entrances are divided into several different types: the main entrance, the service entrance, and special-purpose entrances. Figure 5–13a shows examples of each of these three types. The entrance is composed of an outside waiting area (porch, marquee, lanai), a separation (door), and an inside waiting area (foyer, entrance hall). Entrances provide for and control the flow of traffic into and out of a building. Different types of entrances have different functions.

The main entrance provides access to the house, through which all major traffic radiates. The main entrance should be readily identifiable by a stranger. It should provide shelter to anyone awaiting entrance. For example, the porch in Fig. 5–13a provides shelter for the main entrance. Some provision should be made in the main entrance wall for the viewing of callers from the inside. This can be accomplished through the use of side panels, lights (panes) in the door, or windows which face the side of the entrance, as shown in Fig. 5–13a. The main entrance should also be planned to create a desirable first impression. A direct view of other areas of the house from the foyer should be baffled but not sealed off. This result is often accomplished by placing the access to the other rooms at the rear or to one side of the entrance foyer.

The entrance foyer should include a closet for

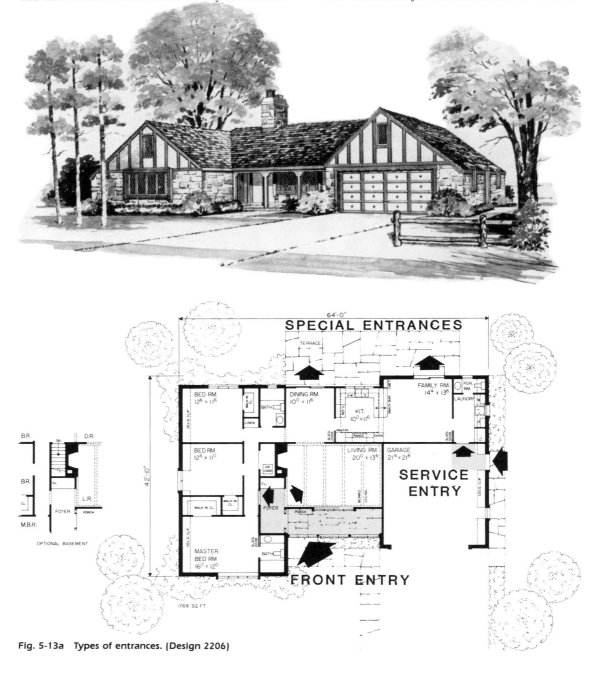

Fig. 5-13a   Types of entrances. (Design 2206)

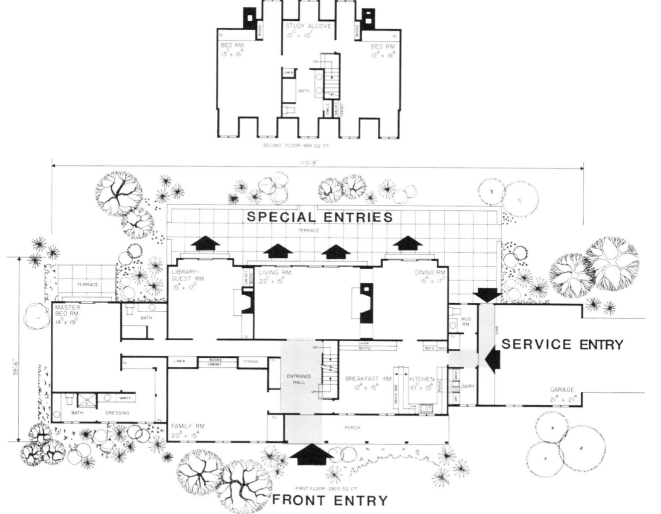

SPECIAL ENTRIES

SERVICE ENTRY

FRONT ENTRY

Fig. 5-13b   Entrance alternatives. (Design 2342)

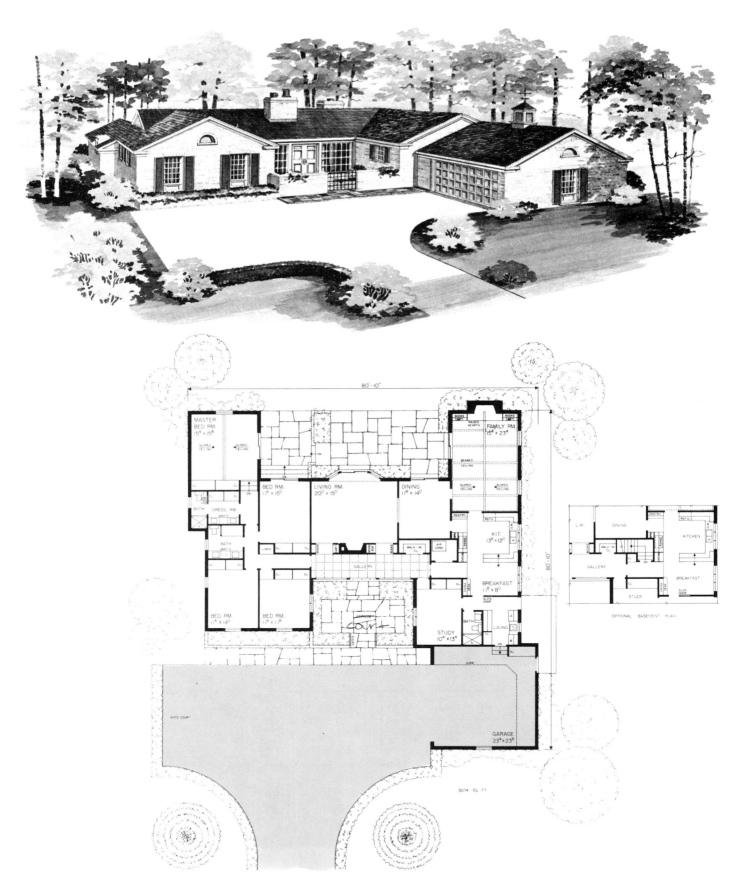

Fig. 5-14a Spacious driveway system. (Design 2183)

the storage of outside clothing and bad-weather gear. This foyer closet should have the capacity to accommodate both family and guests and be at least 24″ deep. The foyer closet shown in Fig. 5–13a is located at a convenient distance from the entrance door and utilizes an otherwise dead space at the end of the foyer.

The service entrance provides access to the house through which supplies can be delivered to the service areas without going through other parts of the house. It should also provide access to parts of the service area (garage, laundry, workshop) for which the main entrance is inappropriate and inconvenient. Notice how the service entrance in Fig. 5–13b provides access from the garage and also connects both the laundry and mud room with the kitchen.

Special-purpose entrances and exits do not provide for public access to the house. Instead, they provide for movement from the inside living areas of the house to the outside living areas. For example, a sliding door from the living area to the patio is a special-purpose entrance. It is not an entrance through which street, drive, or sidewalk traffic would have access.

Driveways Driveways must be carefully planned to ensure an effective exterior traffic flow of both people and cars. A driveway can be planned for purposes other than providing access to the garage and temporary parking space for guests. Although aprons are designed to provide space for turning the car in order to eliminate backing out onto a main street, by adding a wider space to a driveway apron a hard smooth surface can be provided for car washing and children's games. The driveway should be accessible from the main entrance and should also provide easy access to the service area of the home. Sufficient space in the driveway should also be provided for parking of guests cars. Figure 5–14a shows a driveway which provides all of these features: access to main entrance, rear entry, laundry entry, parking and turning space, and a solid play surface.

Driveways should be designed at least several feet wider than the track of the car (approximately 9′). However, slightly wider driveways are desirable. Figure 5–14b shows different driveway sizes and configurations for access, parking, and turning.

When space is not available for aprons, straight-line driveways accessed directly either from the front or from the side should be planned. Figure 5–14c shows a driveway designed for a front entrance garage. Notice how the driveway provides access to the front entrance and to the service entrance without total visibility to the service entrance from the front. If the lot and house position allow a driveway access from the side, it is often desirable for aesthetic reasons. Figure 5–14d shows a side entry driveway with access to the main entrance and direct connection to the rear patio and to the laundry service entrance.

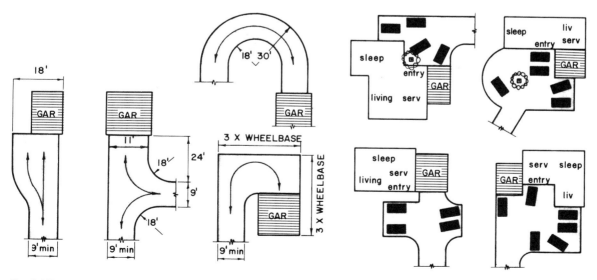

Fig. 5-14b Apron arrangements.

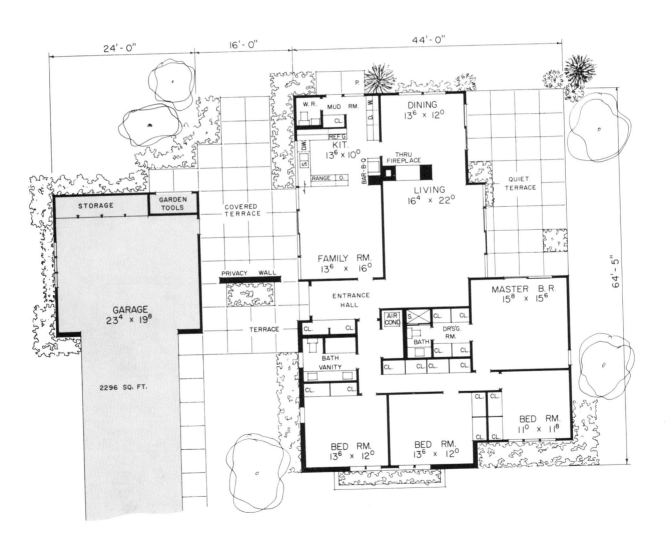

Fig. 5-14c   Front entry garage and drive. (Design 3157)

DESIGN #2751 © HOME PLANNERS, INC., DETROIT

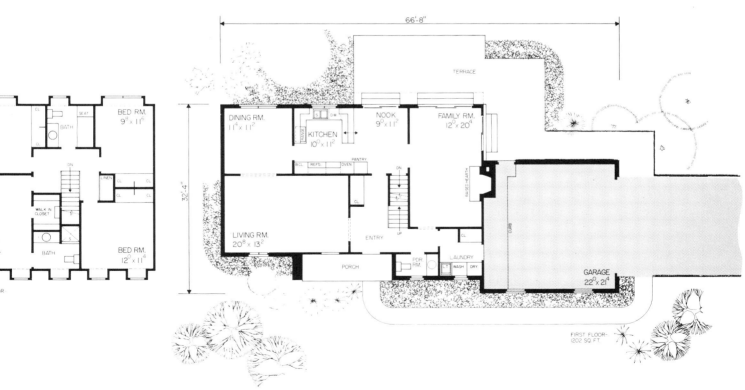

Side entry garage and drive. (Design 2751)

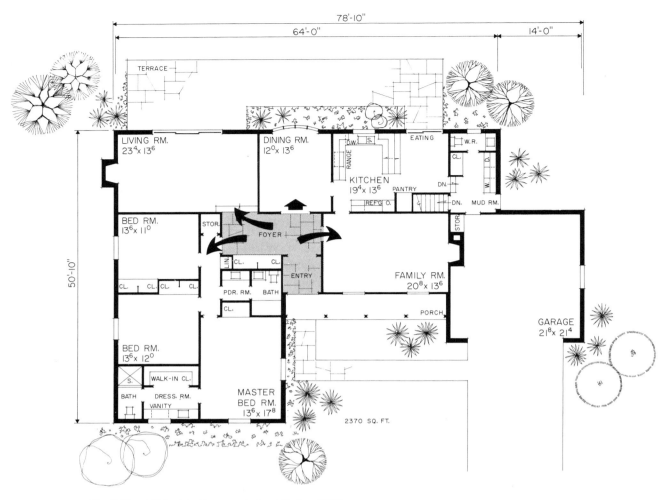

Fig. 5-14e   Efficient traffic control plan. (Design 1786)

Internal Traffic

Circulation   The traffic areas of the house provide passage from one room or area to another. The main traffic areas of a residence include the halls, entrance foyers, stairs, lanais, and areas of rooms that are part of the traffic pattern. Traffic patterns of a residence should be carefully considered in the design of room layouts, with a minimum amount of space devoted to traffic areas. Extremely long halls and corridors should be avoided because they are difficult to light and provide no usable living space. Traffic patterns that require passage through one room to get to another should also be avoided, especially in the sleeping area.

The traffic pattern shown in the plan in Fig. 5–14e is efficient and functional. It contains a minimum amount of wasted hall space without creating a boxed-in appearance. It provides access to each of the areas without passing through other areas. The arrows clearly show that the sleeping area, living area, and service area are accessible from the entrance without passage through other areas. The service entrance provides access to the kitchen from the garage and other parts of the service area.

One method of determining the effectiveness of the traffic pattern of a house is to imagine yourself moving through the house by placing your pencil on the floor plan and tracing your route through the house as you perform daily routines. If you trace through a whole day's activities, including those of other members of the household, you will be able to see graphically where the heaviest traffic occurs and whether the traffic areas have been planned effectively. Figure 5–14f shows a well-designed traffic pattern. Notice the easy flow from one area to another with a minimum amount of changes in direction.

Halls   Halls are the highways and streets of the home. They provide a controlled path which connects the various areas of the house. Hall space should be kept to a minimum and eliminate the passage of traffic through rooms. Figure 5–14g shows how long, wasteful hall space can be

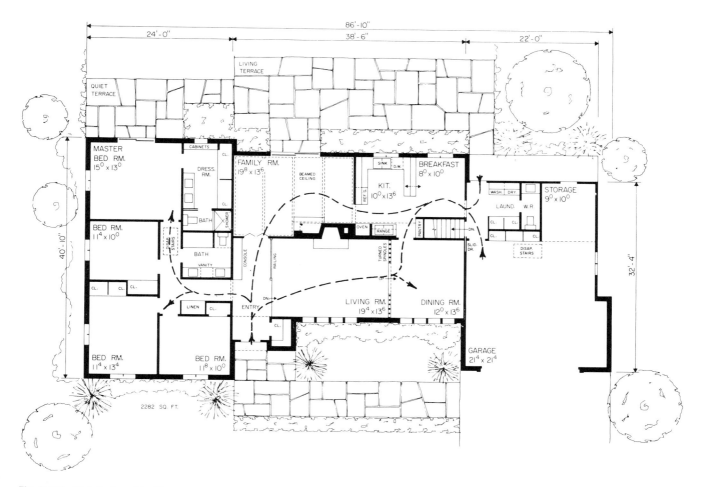

Fig. 5-14f   Well-designed traffic pattern. (Design 1989)

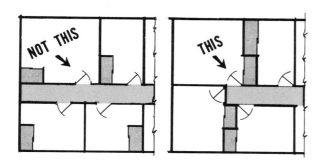

Fig. 5-14g   Hall design dos and don'ts.

shortened to provide more room or storage space. Long, dark, tunnel-like halls should be avoided. Halls should be well lighted, light in color and texture, and planned to be consistent with the decor of the entire house. The hall shown in Fig. 5–14h is extremely long; however, the negative effect is minimized by the use of a glass partition between the hall and the family room. This plan also contains an excessively long hall in the sleeping area. The plan shown in Fig. 5–14i, conversely, contains a minimum amount of hall space in relation to the size of the house. Notice that the living and service areas are directly accessible from the foyer, and the sleeping area

hall provides maximum privacy for four bedrooms with a minimum of traffic space. Another method of channeling hall traffic without the use of solid walls is with the use of dividers. Planters, half-walls, louvered walls, and even furniture can be used as dividers. Separations using partial dividers, such as this type, enables both the hall and the living room to share ventilation, light, and heat.

Another method of designing halls and corridors as an integral part of the area design is with the use of movable partitions like the Japanese scheme of placing these partitions between the living area and a hall. In some Japanese homes

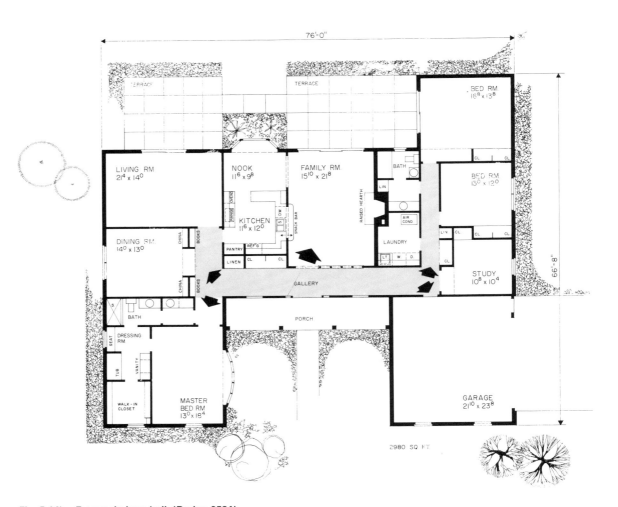

Fig. 5-14h Extremely long hall. (Design 2784)

this hall actually becomes a lanai when the partition between the living area and the hall is closed and the outside wall is opened.

Stairs Stairs are inclined hallways. They provide access from one level to another. Stairs may lead directly from one area to another without a change of direction. They may turn 90° by means of a landing, or they may turn 180° through the use of several landings. Figure 5–14j shows the basic types of stairs and the amount of space utilized by each type.

With the use of newer, stronger building materials and new building techniques there is no longer any reason for enclosing stairs in walls that restrict light and ventilation. Stairs can now be supported by many different devices. Center-supported stairs therefore do not need side walls or other supports. Even when vertical supports are necessary or desirable it is not mandatory to completely close in the wall. The combination of open-stair assemblies with windows provides the maximum amount of light, especially when the windows in the open area extend through several levels.

There are many variables to consider in designing stairs. The tread width, the rise height, the width of the stair opening, and the headroom all help to determine the total design and length of

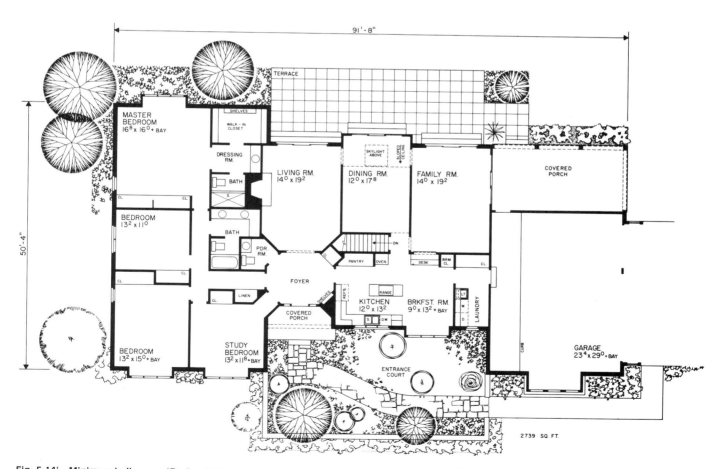

Fig. 5-14i   Minimum hall space. (Design 285)

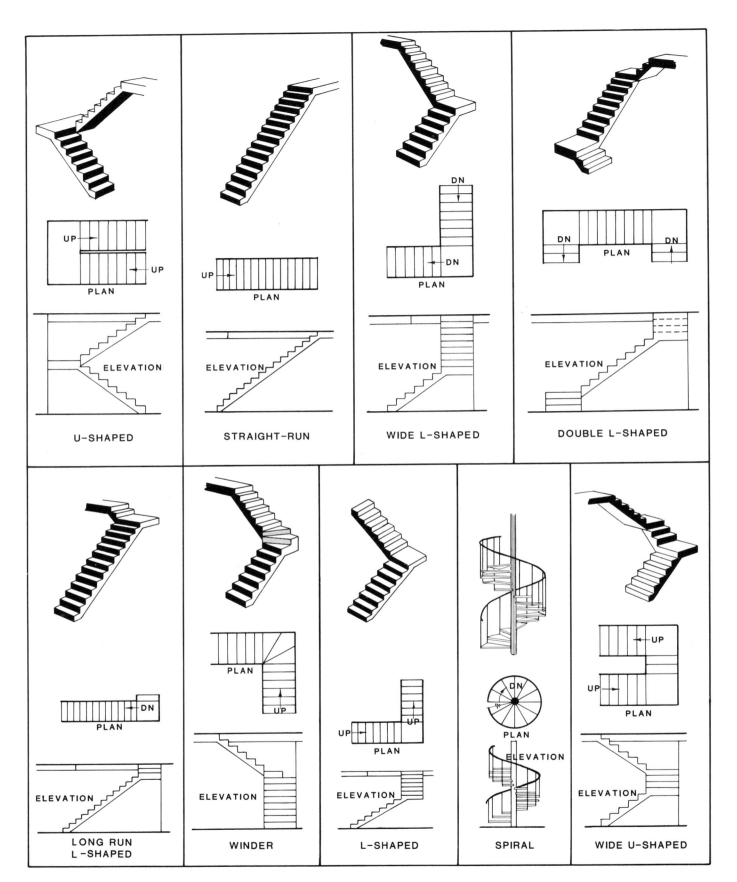

Fig. 5-14J Types of stairs.

the stairwell. These must be controlled to provide a comfortable and safe stair system.

The tread is the horizontal part of the stair, the part upon which you walk. The average width of the tread is 10″. The riser is the vertical part of the stair. The average riser height is 7¼″. The correct relationship of tread to riser size is critical. Figure 5–14k shows the importance of correct tread and riser design.

The overall width of the stairs is the length or distance across the treads. A minimum of 3′ should be allowed for the total stair width. However, a width of 3′–6″ or even 4′–0″ is preferred (see Fig. 5–14l).

Headroom is the vertical distance between the top of each tread and the top of the stairwell ceiling. A minimum headroom distance of 6′–8″ should be allowed, as shown in Fig. 5–14m. However, distances of 7′–0″ are more desirable.

Landings are horizontal surfaces in a stair system which allow turns in the stair direction. On long, straight stair assemblies, landings are designed to provide a rest area or break in the monotonous rhythmic pattern of the stairs. Landing dimensions must provide sufficient space to turn the specified angle, and more clearance must be allowed when a door must open onto a landing, as shown in Fig. 5–14n.

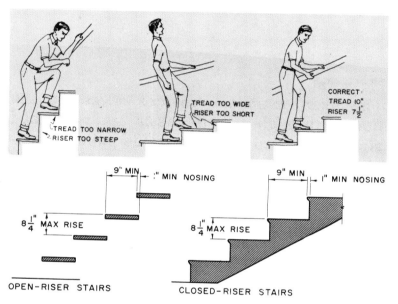

Fig. 5-14k   Tread and riser design.

Fig. 5-14m   Minimum headroom.

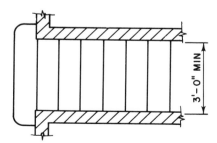

Fig. 5-14l   Stair widths.

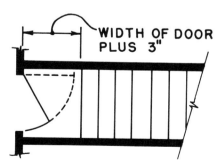

Fig. 5-14n   Landing-door swing clearance.

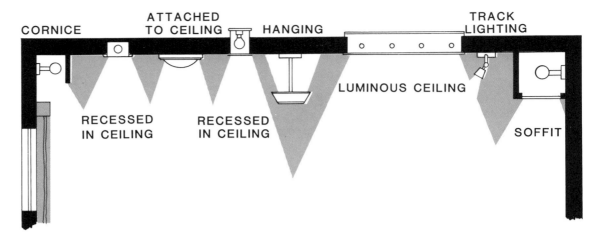

CORNICE ATTACHED TO CEILING HANGING TRACK LIGHTING

LUMINOUS CEILING

RECESSED IN CEILING RECESSED IN CEILING SOFFIT

Fig. 5-14o Types of structural ceiling fixtures.

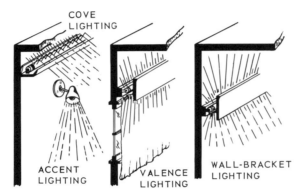

COVE LIGHTING

ACCENT LIGHTING VALENCE LIGHTING WALL-BRACKET LIGHTING

Fig. 5-14p Types of structural wall fixtures.

Lighting

No room is completely designed until the electrical and lighting requirements are satisfied. Effective lighting in a home is provided by three methods. General lighting spreads an even, low-level light throughout a room. Specific (local) lighting directs light to a defined area used for a specific visual task. Decorative lighting makes use of lights to develop different moods and to accent objects of interest.

General lighting is achieved by direct or indirect methods of light dispersement. General lighting can be produced by many portable lamps, ceiling fixtures, or long lengths of light on the walls. In the living and sleeping areas, the intensity of general lighting should be low; however, a higher level of general lighting should be used in the service area and bathrooms. In addition to artificial general light sources, skylights can be used to admit light during the day. If the skylight is covered with translucent panels, it can contain an artificial light source, usually fluorescent, for nightime use. Specific (local) lighting for a partic-

ular visual task is directed into the area in which the task will be done. The specific light in a room will add to the general lighting level. Decorative lighting is used for atmosphere and interest when activities do not require much light. Bright lights are stimulating; low levels of lighting are quieting. Decorative lighting strives for unusual effects. Some of these can be obtained with candlelight, lights behind draperies, lights under planters, lights in the bottoms of ponds, lights controlled with a dimmer switch, and different types of cover materials over floor lights and spotlights.

Lighting fixtures Planning for portable lighting requires careful consideration for the location of convenient outlets. Thus, even though the actual fixture need not be part of the floor plan, the location of outlets must be included. Permanent lighting fixtures, however, must be integrally designed into the plan since these fixtures become a structural part of the house. Structural lighting fixtures are designed for either wall or ceiling mounting. Types of structural ceiling fixtures are shown in Fig. 5–14o. Types of structural wall fixtures include valance, wall bracket, and cornice fixtures and are shown in Fig. 5–14p.

A valance is a covering over a long source of light over a window. Its light illuminates the wall and draperies for the spacious effect that daylight gives a room. A wall bracket defuses the light of a valance. It gives an upward and downward wash of light difficult to obtain on an inner wall. A cornice is attached to the wall and can be used with or without drapes. All light from this fixture is directed downward to give an impression of height to the room. Cove lighting is a continual light source on a wall, near the ceiling that directs indirect light upward to the ceiling.

In addition to the types of positions of lighting facilities, the planner must consider the best type of lighting dispersement for each room. There are four types of lighting dispersement: direct, indirect, semidirect, and diffused. Direct light shines directly on an object without obstruction from the light source. Indirect light is reflected from large surfaces. Semidirect light shines down mainly as direct light, but a small portion of it is directed upward as indirect light. Diffused light is spread evenly in all directions.

Reflectance of light must also be carefully considered by the home planner since all objects absorb and reflect light. Some white surfaces reflect as much as 94 percent of the light received. Some black surfaces reflect only 2 percent of the light received. The remainder of the light is absorbed. The proper amount of reflectance is obtained by the selection of color and type of finish for each surface. The amounts of reflectance that are recommended are from 60 to 90 percent for the ceiling, from 35 to 60 percent for the walls, and from 15 to 35 percent for the floor. All surfaces in a room will act as a secondary source of light when light is reflected. But excessive reflection causes glare. However, glare can be eliminated from a secondary source of light by designing a dull or matte finish on surfaces or by avoiding strong beams of light and strong contrasts of light. Eliminating excessive glare is essential in designing adequate and effective lighting.

Illumination planning The following general guidelines should be observed when planning the lighting of each room.

The kitchen requires a high level of general lighting from ceiling fixtures. Specific lighting for all work areas—range, sink, tables, and counters —is also recommended.

The bathroom requires a high level of general lighting from ceiling fixtures. The shower and water closet, if compartmented, should have a recessed, vaporproof light. Mirrors should have lights on two sides to provide direct local lighting for shaving, general grooming, and makeup application.

The living room requires a low level of general lighting but should have specific lighting for reading and other visual tasks. Decorative lighting should also be used to create the desired atmosphere.

The dining area requires a low level of general lighting, with local lighting over the dining table. The entrance and foyer require a high level of general and decorative lighting. Traffic areas require a high level of general lighting for safety. Reading and desk areas require a high level of general light and specific light that is diffused and glareless. There should be no shadows. A mark of a poorly designed general lighting system is excessive shadow.

The bedroom requires a low level of general lighting but should have specific lighting for reading in bed and on both sides of the dressing table mirror. The dressing area requires a high level of general lighting. Children's bedrooms require a high level of general lighting, and bedroom closets should have a fixture placed high at the front of the closet.

Television viewing requires a very low level of general lighting. Television should not be viewed in total darkness because the strong contrast of a dark room and the bright screen is tiring to the eyes.

Outdoor lighting is accomplished by placement of waterproof floodlights and spotlights. Extensive outdoor lighting will provide convenience, beauty, and safety. Areas which could be illuminated include the landscaping, game areas, barbecue area, patio, garden, front of picture window, pools, and driveways (see Fig. 5-15). Outdoor lights should not shine directly on windows. Lights near the windows should be placed above the windows to eliminate the glare. Ground lights should be shielded by bushes to keep them from shining into the windows or into the eyes of approaching guests or neighbors. In fact, lights aimed at a person's direct view should be avoided. Lights should be directed on objects, not on people, for maximum soft effect.

Fig. 5-15 Effective use of outdoor lighting.

CHAPTER 6

Design Skills

The Architect's Scale

When a drawing of an object is prepared to exactly the same size as the actual object, the drawing scale is full-size (1:1). However, architectural structures are obviously too large to be drawn full size. They must, therefore, be reduced in scale to fit on sheets of paper. Many different drawing scales are possible (see Fig. 6–1), but ⅛″ = 1′–0″ or ¼″ = 1′–0″ are the most commonly used scales for architectural drawings. The size of the drawing is determined by the scale used, as shown in Fig. 6–2. In this illustration the different wall thicknesses at different scales are shown.

The main function of the architect's scale is to enable the designer to draw a building at a convenient size and to enable the builder to think in relation to the actual size of the structure. When a drawing is prepared to a reduced scale, 1′ (12″) may actually be drawn ¼″ long (see Fig. 6–3). Thus ¼″ on the drawing equals one actual foot of the building. On the reduced scale, the builder does not think of this ¼″ line as representing ¼″ but thinks of it as being 1′ long. On the architect's scale, two scales are located on each face. One scale reads from left to right. The other scale, which is twice as large, reads from right to left (see Fig. 6–4). For example, the ¼ scale, and half of this, the ⅛ scale, are placed on the same face. Similarly, the ¾ scale and the ⅜ scale are placed on the same face but are read from different directions. If the scale is read from the wrong direction, the measurement could be wrong, since the second row of numbers reads from the oppo-

site side of the scale at half scale, or twice the value.

The architect's scale is most commonly used to measure distances where the divisions of the scale equal 1′ or 1″. For example, in the ¼″ scale shown in Fig. 6–3, ¼″ can equal either 1″ or 1′. Since buildings are very large, most major architectural drawings use a scale which relates the parts of the scale to a foot. Thus a scale of ¼″ = 1′–0″ is a very common architect scale.

In reading an architect's scale, observe that the section at the end of the scale is not part of the numerical scale. When measuring with the scale, start with the zero line, not with the outside end line of the fully divided section. Always start with the number of feet or inches you wish to measure and then add the additional inches or fractional part of one inch in the subdivided area. Figure 6–5 shows this principle applied to measuring several walls using a ¼″ = 1′–0″ scale. Notice the dimensioned distance of 8′–0″ extends from the 8 to the 0 on the scale and the 6″ wall is shown as ½′ (6″) on the subdivided foot on the end of the scale.

When the scale of a drawing changes, the length of each line increases or decreases and the width of various areas also increases or decreases. The actual appearance of a typical corner wall at a scale of ¹⁄₁₆″ = 1′–0″, ⅛″ = 1′–0″, ¼″ = 1′–0″, and ½″ = 1′–0″ is shown in Fig. 6–2. You can see that the wall drawn to the scale of ¹⁄₁₆″ = 1′–0″ is relatively small and that a great amount of detail would be impossible. The ½″ = 1′–0″ wall would probably cover too large an area on a drawing if

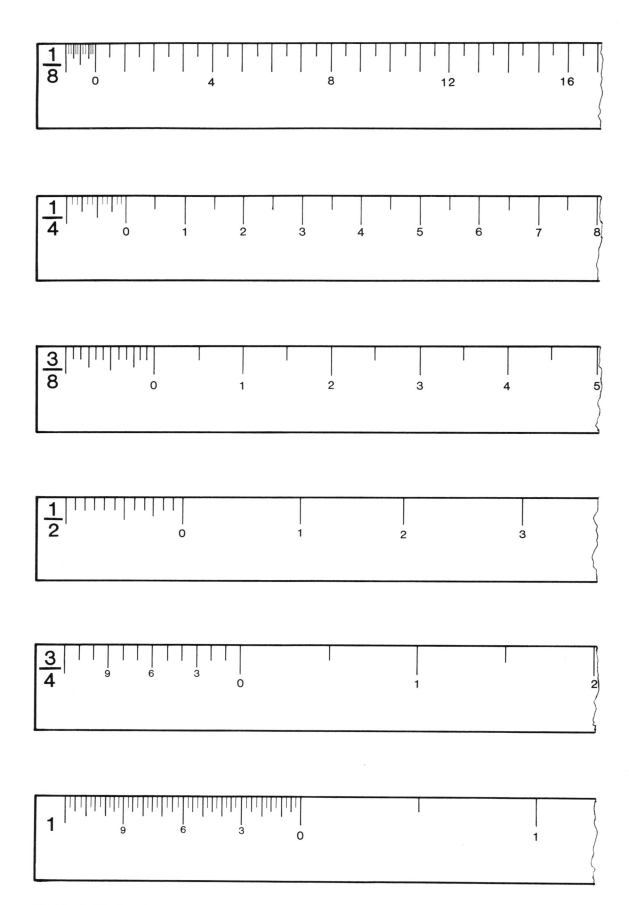

Fig. 6-1 Architect's scales.

Fig. 6-2   Effect of scale on wall size.

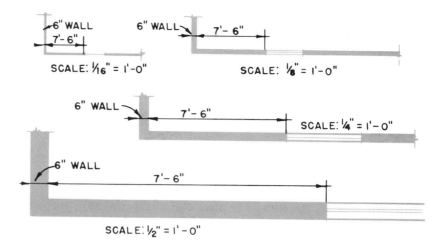

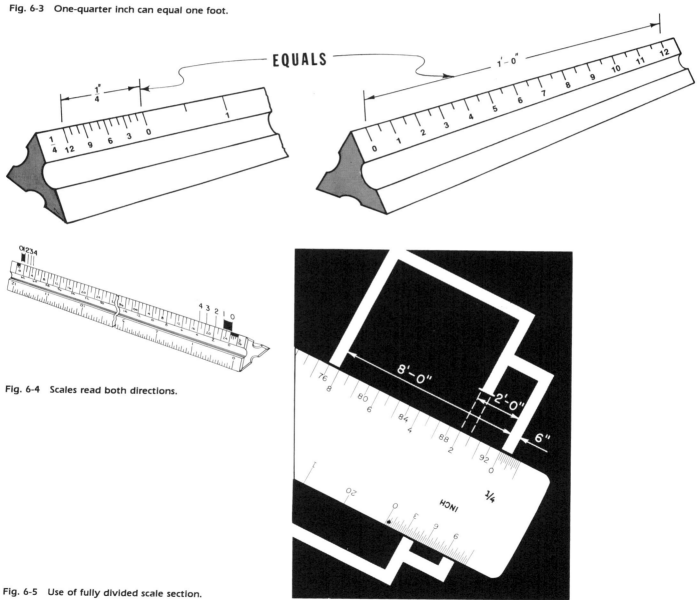

Fig. 6-3   One-quarter inch can equal one foot.

Fig. 6-4   Scales read both directions.

Fig. 6-5   Use of fully divided scale section.

the building is very large. Therefore, the ¼″ = 1′–0″ and ⅛″ = 1′–0″ scales are the most popular for most basic architectural drawings, except for details.

Figure 6–6 shows the comparative distances used to measure 1′–9″ as it appears on various architect's scales. The solid bar on top of each of these scales represents 1′–9″. The same comparison would exist if the scales were related to 1″ rather than 1′. In this case, a distance of 1¾″ would have produced the same line length as 1′–9″ on the floor representation. Figure 6–7 shows the distance 5′–6″ on the 1″ = 1′–0″, ½″ = 1′–0″, ¼″ = 1′–0″ and ⅛″ = 1′–0″ scales.

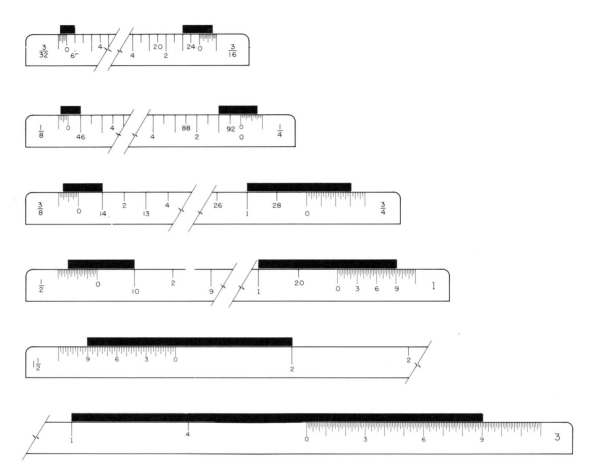

Fig. 6-6 One foot nine inches shown on different scales.

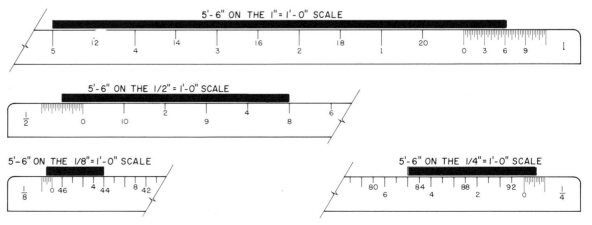

Fig. 6-7 Five feet six inches shown on different scales.

Dimensioning

Floor plan dimensions show the builder the width and length of the building. They show the location of doors, windows, stairs, and fireplaces. They show the width and length of each room, closet, and hall. There are several kinds of dimensions found on floor plans, as shown in Fig. 6–8.

Overall dimensions show the total length of a building. Subdimensions show the length of subdivisions of a building, and positioning dimensions show the position of features such as doors, windows, and fixtures. Figure 6–9 shows several methods of dimensioning a floor plan, depending on the amount of detail desired.

Some floor plans which are not used for con-

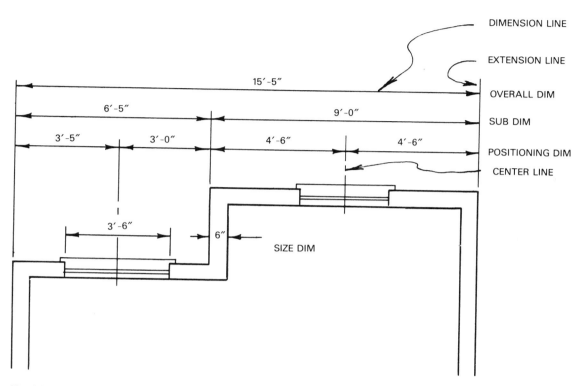

Fig. 6-8   Types of architectural dimensions.

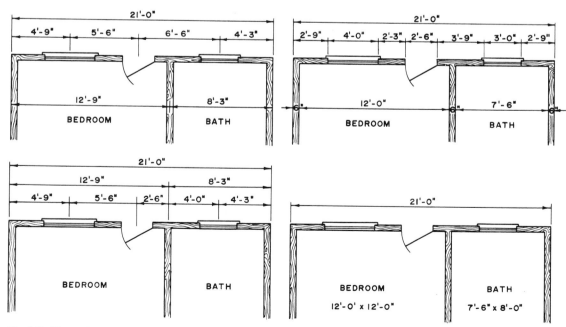

Fig. 6-9   Floor-plan dimensioning methods.

struction purposes (abbreviated plans) include only bare-minimum dimensions. The plans shown thus far in this book are of this type. If a floor plan is not to be used for construction purposes, many of the detail dimensions are unnecessary and clutter the floor plan, making reading of the plan difficult. For this reason, abbreviated plans show only overall dimensions and sizes of rooms. Dimensions are not positioned on dimension lines, and the limited dimensions shown are sufficient to summarize the relative sizes of the building and its rooms. But these dimensions are not sufficient for building purposes, only for general interpretation.

A floor plan must be completely dimensioned to ensure that the building will be constructed precisely as designed. Precise detail dimensions convey the exact wishes of the designer to the builder, thus the contractor is given little tolerance in interpreting the size and position of the various features of the plan. Dimensions show the size of materials and exactly where they are to be located. Dimensions show the builder the width, height, and length of the building and subdivisions of the building. They show the location of doors, windows, stairs, fireplace, and planter.

The number of dimensions included on an architectural plan depends largely on how much freedom of interpretation the designer wants to give to the builder. If complete dimensions are shown on a plan, the builder cannot deviate greatly from the original design. However, if only a few dimensions are shown then the builder must determine the sizes of many areas, fixtures, and details. When this occurs the builder must provide the dimensions and is placed in the position of designer.

Sketching

The home planner must be able to record ideas clearly through the use of floor plan sketches, and these sketches should be sufficiently accurate to be understood by another. Anyone reading another's sketch should be able to interpret it without asking questions. This means a good technical sketch should graphically show the shape and size of the house through lines and dimensions. However, notes can be added to a sketch to clarify design features which cannot be drawn or dimensioned conveniently.

All sketches, regardless of their complexity, are based on only a few types of lines and geometric shapes. Lines are either straight or curved. Straight lines are either horizontal, vertical, or angular. Curved lines are either circles, arcs, or combinations of both. The most common geometric shapes used in architectural sketches include the square, rectangle, triangle, and circle.

Good sketching lines are made with short, light strokes using a soft pencil such as F, B, or HB. First, lines should be drawn very lightly, then darkened when you are satisfied with the location of each line.

In sketching straight lines, hold the pencil with a firm but relaxed grip about 1 inch from the point. Then move the pencil in short strokes as you sketch. Don't push the pencil.

In sketching horizontal lines, as shown in Fig. 6–10, mark the beginning and end of the line with a point, then sight between the points as you move your hand and connect the two parts with short, even strokes. Do not attempt to draw a single continuous straight line in one move, because your hand will tend to move in an arc created by your stationary elbow.

Vertical lines are drawn by placing points at each end and connecting the points by pulling the pencil toward you in short, even strokes, as shown in Fig. 6–11. Diagonal lines, as shown in Fig. 6–12, are drawn in a similar manner by rotating the paper to create either a vertical or horizontal plane for sketching.

Sketching arcs and circles should be done by first locating the center of the arc or circle. Then measure the distance from the center to the circumference on each axis line. For a smooth circle, draw additional lines on a 45°, 30°, and 60° axes and mark the same distance from the center to the circumference. Then connect these lines with short, even strokes, as shown in Fig. 6–13.

Cross-section (grid or graph) paper, as shown in Figs. 6–14 and 6–15, can be used to ensure that sketched lines are parallel or perpendicular.

Fig. 6-10   Sketching horizontal lines.

Fig. 6-11   Sketching vertical lines.

Fig. 6-12   Sketching diagonal lines.

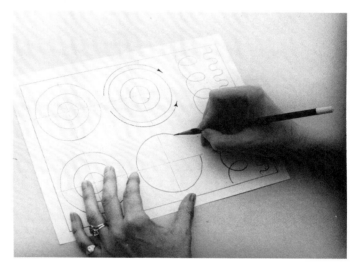

Fig. 6-13   Sketching arcs and circles.

Fig. 6-14   Floor plan sketch on cross section paper.

Fig. 6-15   Elevation sketch on cross section paper.

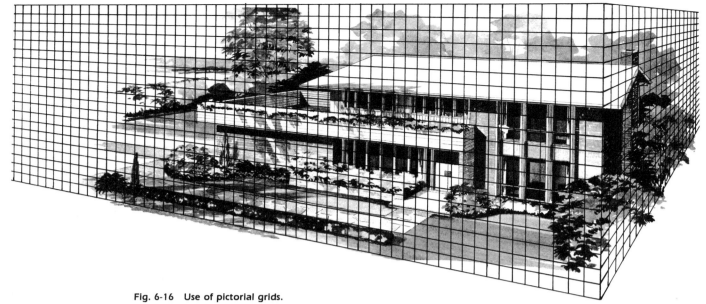

Fig. 6-16 Use of pictorial grids.

Cross-section paper printed with lines spaced to the scale desired can eliminate the need for the use of an architect's scale on most preliminary architectural sketches. For example, if the lines on cross-section paper are spaced at ¼″ (4 lines per inch) intervals, then each square equals 1 square foot at ¼″ = 1′–0″ scale. Likewise, cross-section paper with lines spaced ⅛″ apart can be used to produce sketches at a scale of ⅛″ = 1′–0″. Special grid paper is also available for the preparation of pictorial sketches, such as that shown in Fig. 6–16.

Residential Design Practices

Part 1 covered the basic principles of residential design, which provided the foundations for the creation of effective functional architectural plans. Part 2 deals with the practical methods of developing effective architectural plans to satisfy individual needs and wants as related to lifestyle, taste, and financial considerations. Included in this part are the logical steps suggested to effectively select and alter our architectural plan to meet individual needs and wants.

CHAPTER 7

Plan Selection

Remember, as covered in Chapter 2, that all of the individual *needs* and as many as possible *wants* should be satisfied in the development of an architectural plan. But this must of course be done within the framework of budgetary restrictions.

Satisfying Basic Needs and Wants

Evolving an architectural plan from raw data concerning individual wants and needs as they relate to one's lifestyle and architectural taste is naturally the ideal way to ensure a good match between these personal requirements and the final architectural plan. For example, the residence shown in Fig. 7–1 was developed for a family that felt they needed a separate bedroom for each of three children; a guest lavatory; a quiet study; a master bedroom suite complete with bathtub, shower, and exercise facilities; a two-car garage; a living and dining room sized appropriately to seat ten; and a living area fireplace. The plan also provided for many of their wants, which include Early American style, two-level plan, basement, large entry, and a large family kitchen. Several of the wants, such as a pool and tennis court, gave way to others, at least for the present, because of the initial costs involved. Likewise, the plan shown in Fig. 7–2 provides for the vacation house needs of a family by including a boat dock, master bedroom, two children's bedrooms, open lake-view living area, and carport.

There are circumstances when the architectural style may almost dominate and seem to surpass the actual needs and wants as a basic criterion for the selection of an architectural plan. In this case, needs must still be addressed, but functional wants may actually give way to architectural style wants. When this happens the architectural style actually becomes a need. For example, the Spanish style of architecture shown in Fig. 7–3 could dominate the selection and design of the plan but should not result in the sacrificing of any real needs. In cases such as this, the arrangement of facilities can usually be adjusted to provide for the required needs without giving up significant wants.

Although this design process is the most ideal way to create the best possible functional design, very few home planners can or do design a home completely "from scratch." Most draw on knowledge of similar plans or parts of plans which consciously or subconsciously are altered to meet the unique architectural needs of the present.

Short-Cutting Process

The total design sequence, involving the formal identification of needs and wants and the logical development of the appropriate architectural plan, should always be pursued in the design process. But there are methods of short-cutting this process. One very effective method of short-cutting the design process is to carefully and logically select a professionally prepared home

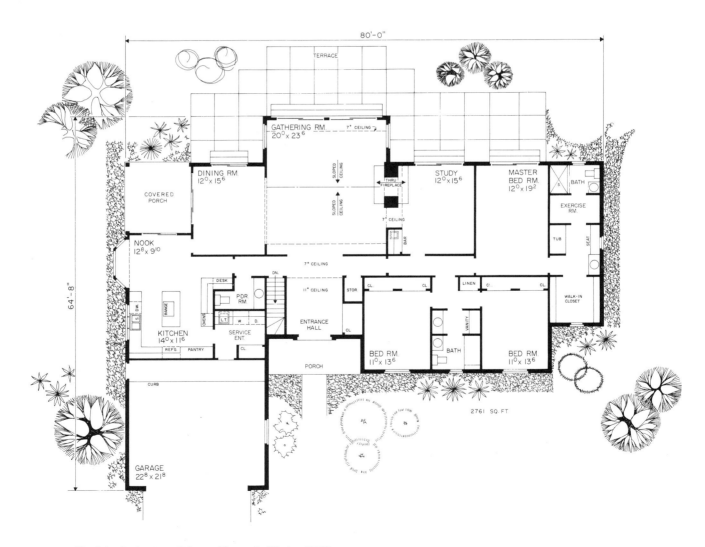

Fig. 7-1 A plan to satisfy specific needs. (Design 2778)

Labels within the floor plan:

TERRACE

GATHERING RM.
$20^0 \times 23^6$
7' CEILING

DINING RM.
$12^0 \times 15^6$

STUDY
$12^0 \times 15^6$

MASTER
BED RM.
$12^0 \times 19^2$

BATH

EXERCISE
RM.

COVERED
PORCH

SLOPED
CEILING

THRU
FIREPLACE

SLOPED
CEILING

7' CEILING

TUB

SEAT

NOOK
$12^8 \times 9^{10}$

BAR

7' CEILING

WALK-IN
CLOSET

DESK

DN.

11' CEILING

STOR.

CL.

CL.

LINEN

CL.

CL.

PDR.
RM.

RANGE

OVENS

LT

W. D.

SERVICE
ENT.

ENTRANCE
HALL

CL.

VANITY

BATH

KITCHEN
$14^0 \times 11^6$

REFG.

PANTRY

CL.

BED RM.
$11^0 \times 13^6$

BED RM.
$11^0 \times 13^6$

PORCH

CURB

2761 SQ. FT.

GARAGE
$22^8 \times 21^8$

80'-0"

64'-8"

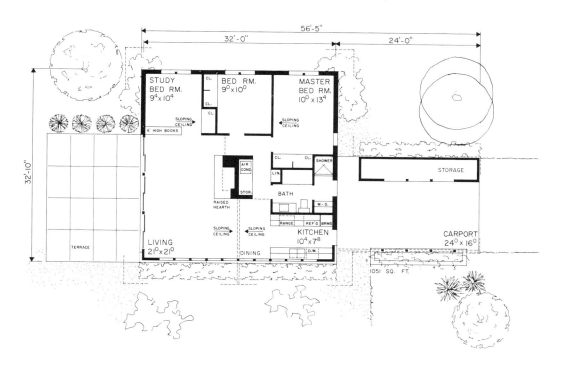

Fig. 7-2 A plan to satisfy vacation house needs. (Design 2416)

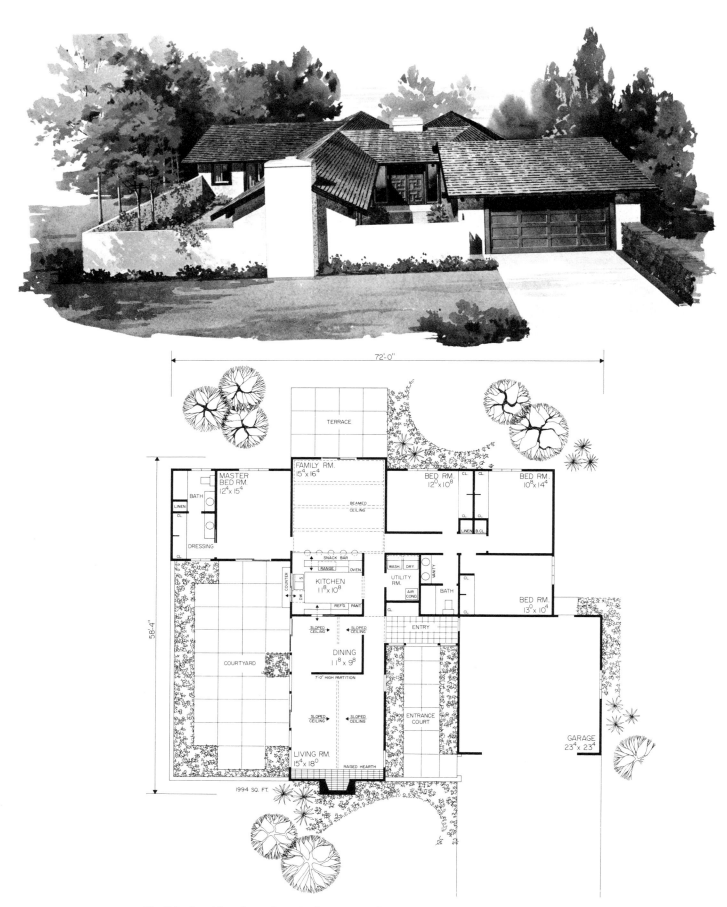

Fig. 7-3 Spanish style can be a dominant need. (Design 2386)

plan which satisfies all listed needs and as many wants as possible. Once this is done, sizes can be changed, styles adjusted, and configurations altered either to adjust for specific needs or to accommodate the maximum number of wants. The task is to maximize the strengths of the plan while making only minor adjustments in altering the design to provide for *all* needs and as many wants as possible. If major surgery on the plan is necessary to adjust for basic needs, then probably the wrong plan has been chosen.

The process of selecting the correct plan—the plan which satisfies *all* needs (or can be easily adjusted to do so) and can be altered, without major realignments, to accommodate most wants —is critical to creating the right plan for each individual. Thus, time spent in analyzing wants and needs and in carefully selecting the plan which comes the closest to satisfying these will save enormous amounts of time in later adjustments to the plan. For, keep in mind, there are some plan alterations which can be made easily, some which are very difficult, and some which are just about impossible. Many plans are totally ruined by making inappropriate changes that could have been avoided by the selection of a different plan. Steps in short-cutting the design process involves the identification of needs and wants as described above and compromising some wants within the availability of resources. In other words: the objective is to get as much as possible for the available money while satisfying all absolute needs. This, of course, involves a careful assessment, not only of wants and needs, but of your financial circumstances.

Financial Considerations

Although the clear identification of lifestyle wants and needs can provide a logical design path for the home planner, none of this is practical without carefully considering the financial costs involved. Without knowing the potential costs, any architectural plan is only a dream. But by matching wants and needs with a realistic assessment of the cost of satisfying those wants and needs, the dream can become a reality.

Many factors influence the total cost of the house: site cost, labor costs, materials specified, and the size of the structure. The location of the site is extremely important. An identical house built on an identical lot can vary many thousand dollars in cost, depending on whether it is located in a city, in a suburb, or in the country. Labor costs also vary greatly from one part of the country to another and from urban to rural locations in the same geographic area. Normally, labor costs are lower in rural areas. The third important variable contributing to the difference in housing costs is the cost of materials. Material costs vary greatly, depending upon whether materials are native to the region or must be imported. For

example, in some areas brick is a relatively inexpensive building material. In other parts of the country, a brick home may be one of the most expensive. Climate also has an important effect on the cost of building. In moderate climates many costs can be reduced by installing smaller heating plants and frost-deep foundations. In other climates, air conditioning is almost mandatory.

The most accurate method of estimating the cost of a house involves adding the total cost of all the materials to the hourly rate for labor, multiplied by the anticipated number of hours it will take to build the home. Then the cost of the lot, landscaping, and various architect's, surveyors', and legal fees are added. However, two quicker methods for estimating the cost of a house are the square foot method and cubic foot method. These methods are not as accurate as itemizing the cost of all materials, labor, and other items; however, they do provide a quick, rough estimate for speculative purposes.

In general, the cost of the average home ranges from $60 to $80 per square foot of floor space, depending on the geographical location and type of material used. Each local office of the Federal Housing Administration can supply current estimating information applicable to the locale.

Figure 7–4 shows the computation of the cost of a one-level house at $60 per square foot. This house is 30′ × 40′ or 1200 square feet. At $60 per square foot the house is estimated to cost approximately $72,000, using the square foot method.

Using the cubic foot method of estimating, this house would cost $73,440. This estimate is determined by the cubic space (14,400 cubic feet) multiplied by the cost of cubic construction ($5.10), as shown in Fig. 7–4. The cubic foot method is a more accurate method for multilevel structures.

The square foot and cubic foot methods are at best rough estimates, but they are very fast to calculate. However, the actual final cost of a building depends on the quality (unit cost) and quantity of the building materials used, plus the cost of financing and the cost of real estate. Figure 7–5 shows a breakdown of the square foot building costs by category, which provides a more accurate method of calculating costs.

Other costs, in addition to the cost of the home and financing, must also be considered. These include service charges, title search, insurance costs, and transfer taxes. These are called "closing costs." The lawyer's, architect's, and surveyor's fees are sometimes included in the closing costs. Lawyers' fees range between $150 and $400, and surveys cost between $100 and $500. Architects usually work on a 7 percent commission basis— 10 percent if they supervise construction in addition to designing the structure.

But even after analyzing the design and construction costs for a home, the prospective home builder cannot determine the financial feasibility

ROOF TOP
MID-ATTIC (12'-0")
CEILING LINE
FLOOR LINE

30'

40'

Square Foot Method

Construction cost: $60 per square foot
Square footage: 30' × 40" = 1200 square feet
Cost: 1200 × $60 = $72,000

Cubic Foot Method

Construction cost: $5.82 per cubic foot
Cubic volume: floor area (square feet) × height
Cubic volume: 1200 × 12 = 14,400 cubic feet
Total cost: cubic volume × cost per cubic foot
Total costs: $1400 × $5.10 = $73,440

Fig. 7-4 Methods of estimating costs.

Use the following "cost estimating" procedure to plan the cost of a home

1. _____ sq. ft. $70/sq. ft. = $_____
2. Basement—add $8.00/sq. ft. $_____
3. Extra bath (over one) add $5,000. $_____
4. Extra half-bath—add $3,000. $_____
5. One-car garage—add $3,000. $_____
6. Two-car garage—add $4,500. $_____
7. Covered porches—add $10.00/sq. ft. $_____
8. Each fireplace—add $2,000. $_____
9. Veneer masonry exterior—add
   $5.00/sq. ft. $_____
10. Finished attic—add $10.00/sq. ft. $_____
11. Cost of a lot in your community. $_____
12. Add 5% to 10% of item #1 for ir-
    regular design, hillside lot, special
    construction features. $_____
13. Cost of second story level $40.00/
    sq. ft. $_____
14. Cost of converting attic area to liv-
    ing space $15.00/sq. ft. $_____
15. Total estimated cost of home (with-
    in 10%) $_____

Fig. 7-5 Cost estimating procedure.

of the venture until the costs of financing are carefully considered.

Since most household budgets are established on a monthly basis, the monthly payments needed to purchase and maintain a residence are more significant than the total cost of the home. Monthly payments are broken into the four categories mentioned before: principal, interest, taxes, and insurance (PITI). Figure 7–6 shows the average amortizations for 10-year, 20-year, and 30-year loans.

The prospective home buyer and builder should consider the following factors before selecting a particular institution for a mortgage: the interest rate, the number of years needed to repay, prepayment penalties, total amount of monthly payment, conditions of approval, placement fees, amount of down payment required, service fees, and closing fees. Typical closing costs on a home would include lawyers' fees, transfer taxes, escrow deposit, insurance, and survey fees.

If the home buyer considers the purchase or the building of a home as an investment, he or she should take steps to ensure maximum return on investment. If the home buyer purchases a home that costs considerably less than he or she can afford, the buyer may not be investing adequately. On the other hand, if the home buyer attempts to buy a home that is more expensive than he or she can afford, the payments will become a drain on the family budget and undue sacrifices will have to be made in order to compensate.

Family budgets vary greatly, and a house that may be a burden for one person to purchase may be quite suitable for another, even if the two owners are earning the same relative salary. In general, the cost of the house should not exceed three times the annual income.

Methods of Controlling Costs In review, some construction methods and material utilization that may greatly affect the ultimate cost of the home are listed as follows:

1. Square or rectangular homes are less expensive to build than irregularly shaped homes.
2. It is less expensive to build on a flat lot than on a sloping or hillside lot.
3. The use of locally manufactured or produced materials cuts costs greatly.
4. Using stock materials and stock sizes of components takes advantage of mass-production cost reductions.
5. The use of materials that can be quickly installed cuts labor costs. Prefabricating large sections or panels eliminates much time on the site.
6. The use of prefinished materials saves significant labor costs.
7. The use of prehung doors cuts considerable time.
8. Designing the home with a minimum amount of hall space increases the usable square footage and provides more living space for the cost.
9. The use of prefabricated fireboxes for fireplaces cuts installation and foundation costs.
10. Investigating existing building codes before beginning construction eliminates unnecessary changes as construction proceeds.
11. Refraining from changing the design or any aspect of the plan after construction begins helps hold down cost escalation.
12. Minimizing special jobs or custom-built items keeps cost from increasing.
13. Designing the house for short plumbing lines saves on materials.
14. Proper insulation saves heating and cooling costs.
15. Utilizing passive solar features, such as correct orientation, reduces future maintenance costs.

Checklist for Plan Selection

Before finalizing a home plan, or even selecting a plan as a basis for revision, the following check-

PRINCIPAL, INTEREST, TAXES, AND INSURANCE COSTS FOR A $50,000 LOAN AT 13 PERCENT INTEREST

10-year loan-$50,000 amortization-$746.56			
Payment breakdown	First payment	5th-year payment	Last payment
Principal	$204.91	$386.94	$738.61
Interest	541.65	359.62	7.95
Taxes (varies)	200.00	200.00	200.00
Insurance (varies)	50.00	50.00	50.00
Total Monthly Payments	$996.56	$996.56	$996.56

Note: Total interest for 10 years is $39,582.87

20-year loan-$50,000 amortization-$585.79			
Payment breakdown	First payment	10th-year payment	Last payment
Principal	$ 44.14	$159.10	$579.71
Interest	541.65	426.69	6.08
Taxes (varies)	200.00	200.00	200.00
Insurance (varies)	50.00	50.00	50.00
Total Monthly Payments	$835.79	$835.79	$835.79

Note: Total interest for 20 years is $90,571.20

30-year loan-$50,000 amortization-$553.10			
Payment breakdown	First payment	15th-year payment	Last payment
Principal	$ 11.45	$ 78.78	$547.91
Interest	541.65	474.32	5.19
Taxes (varies)	200.00	200.00	200.00
Insurance (varies)	50.00	50.00	50.00
Total Monthly Payments	$803.10	$803.10	$803.10

Note: Total interest for 30 years is $149,047.31

Fig. 7-6 Breakdowns of monthly payments.

lists should be carefully reviewed to ensure that you have considered all of the important factors in evaluating a plan or potential plan. A review of this checklist, compared to any plan and your needs and wants list, should highlight any deficiencies and serve to eliminate the plan or validate the appropriateness of it.

CHECKLIST FOR PLAN SELECTION

The Neighborhood

1. _____ Reasonable weather conditions
2. No excess
   _____ a. wind
   _____ b. smog or fog
   _____ c. odors
   _____ d. soot or dust
3. _____ The area is residential
4. There are no
   _____ a. factories
   _____ b. dumps
   _____ c. highways
   _____ d. railroads
   _____ e. airports
   _____ f. apartments
   _____ g. commercial buildings
5. _____ City-maintained streets
6. No hazards in the area
   _____ a. quarries
   _____ b. storage tanks
   _____ c. power stations
   _____ d. unprotected swimming pools
7. Reasonably close to
   _____ a. work
   _____ b. schools
   _____ c. churches
   _____ d. hospital
   _____ e. shopping
   _____ f. recreation
   _____ g. public transportation
   _____ h. library
   _____ i. police protection
   _____ j. fire protection
   _____ k. parks
   _____ l. cultural activities
8. _____ Streets are curved
9. _____ Traffic is slow
10. _____ Intersections are at right angles
11. _____ Street lighting
12. _____ Light traffic
13. _____ Visitor parking
14. _____ Good design in street
15. _____ Paved streets and curbs
16. _____ Area is not deteriorating
17. _____ Desirable expansion
18. _____ Has some open spaces
19. _____ Numerous and healthy trees
20. _____ Pleasant-looking homes
21. _____ Space between homes
22. _____ Water drains off
23. _____ Near sewerage line
24. _____ Storm sewers nearby
25. _____ Mail delivery
26. _____ Garbage pickup
27. _____ Trash pickup
28. _____ No city assessments

The Lot

1. _____ Title is clear
2. _____ No judgments against the seller
3. _____ No restrictions as to the use of the land or the deed
4. _____ No unpaid taxes or assessments
5. _____ Minimum of 70 feet of frontage
6. _____ House does not crowd the lot
7. _____ Possible to build on

8. _____ Few future assessments (sewers, lights, and so forth)
9. _____ Good top soil and soil percolation
10. _____ Good view
11. _____ No low spots to hold water
12. _____ Water drains off land away from the house
13. _____ No fill
14. _____ No water runoff from higher ground
15. _____ If cut or graded there is substantial retaining wall
16. _____ Permanent boundary markers
17. _____ Utilities available at property line
18. _____ Utility hook up is reasonable
19. _____ Utility rates are reasonable
20. _____ Taxes are reasonable
21. _____ Water supply is adequate
22. _____ Regular, simply shaped lot
23. _____ Trees
24. _____ Do not have to cut trees
25. _____ Privacy for outside activities
26. _____ Attractive front yard
27. _____ Front and rear yards are adequate
28. _____ Front yard is not divided up by walks and driveway
29. _____ Outdoor walks have stairs grouped

The Floor Plan

1. _____ Designed by licensed architect
2. _____ Supervised by reputable contractor
3. _____ Built by skilled builders
4. Orientation
   _____ a. sun
   _____ b. view
   _____ c. noise
   _____ d. breeze
   _____ e. contour of land
5. _____ Entry
6. _____ Planned for exterior expansion
7. Planned for interior expansion
   _____ a. attic
   _____ b. garage
   _____ c. basement
8. _____ Simple but functional plan
9. _____ Indoor recreation area
10. _____ Wall space for furniture in each room
11. Well-designed hall
    _____ a. leads to all areas
    _____ b. no congestions
    _____ c. no wasted space
    _____ d. 3' minimum width
12. _____ Easy to clean
13. _____ Easy to keep orderly
14. _____ Plan meets family's needs
15. _____ All rooms have direct emergency escape
16. Doorways functional
    _____ a. no unnecessary doors
    _____ b. wide enough for moving furniture through
    _____ c. can see visitors through locked front door
    _____ d. do not swing out into halls
    _____ e. swing open against a blank wall
    _____ f. do not bump other subjects
    _____ g. exteriors doors are solid
17. Windows are functional
    _____ a. not too small
    _____ b. enough but not too many
    _____ c. glare-free
    _____ d. roof overhang protection where needed
    _____ e. large ones have the best view

_____ *f.* easy to clean

_____ *g.* no interference with furniture placement

_____ *h.* over kitchen sink

_____ *i.* open easily

18. _____ No fancy gadgets

19. _____ Room sizes are adequate

20. _____ Well-designed stairs

_____ *a.* treads are 9″ minimum

_____ *b.* risers are 8″ maximum

_____ *c.* 36″ minimum width

_____ *d.* 3′ minimum landings

_____ *e.* attractive

_____ *f.* easily reached

21. _____ Overall plan "fits" family requirements

22. _____ Good traffic patterns

23. _____ Noisy areas separated from quiet areas

24. _____ Rooms have adequate wall space for furniture

25. _____ Halls are 3′6″ minimum

The Living Area

1. _____ Minimum space 12′ × 16′

2. _____ Front door traffic does not enter

3. _____ Not in a traffic pattern

4. _____ Windows on two sides

5. _____ Has a view

6. _____ Storage for books and music materials

7. _____ Can read from all sitting areas at night

8. _____ Decorative lighting

9. _____ Whole family plus guests can be seated

10. _____ Desk area

11. _____ Fireplace

12. _____ Wood storage

13. _____ No street noises

14. _____ Privacy from street

15. _____ Cheerful and pleasant decor

16. _____ Acoustical ceiling

17. _____ Cannot see or hear bathroom

18. _____ Powder room

19. _____ Comfortable for conversation

20. Dining room

_____ *a.* used enough to justify

_____ *b.* minimum of 3′ clearance around table

_____ *c.* can be opened or closed to kitchen and patio

_____ *d.* can be opened or closed to living room

_____ *e.* electrical outlets for table appliances

21. Family room

_____ *a.* minimum space 10′ × 12′

_____ *b.* room for family activities

_____ *c.* room for noisy activities

_____ *d.* room for messy activities

_____ *e.* activities will not disturb sleeping area

_____ *f.* finish materials are easy to clean and durable

_____ *g.* room for expansion

_____ *h.* separate from living room

_____ *i.* near kitchen

_____ *j.* fireplace

_____ *k.* adequate storage

22. _____ Dead-end circulation

23. _____ Adequate furniture arrangements

The Entry

1. _____ The entry is a focal point

2. _____ The outside is inviting

3. _____ The landing has a minimum depth of 5′

4. _____ Protected from the weather

5. _____ Has an approach walk

6. _____ Well planted

7. _____ Coat closet

8. _____ Leads to living, sleeping, and service areas

9. _____ Floor material attractive and easy to clean

10. _____ Decorative lighting

11. _____ Space for table

12. _____ Space to hang mirror

13. _____ Does not have direct view into any room

The Bedrooms

1. _____ Adequate number of bedrooms

2. _____ Adequate size—10′ × 12′ minimum

3. _____ Open into a hall

4. _____ Living space

5. _____ Children's bedroom has study and play area

6. _____ Oriented to north side

7. In quiet area

_____ *a.* soundproofing

_____ *b.* acoustical ceiling

_____ *c.* insulation in walls

_____ *d.* thermal glass

_____ *e.* double doors

_____ *f.* closet walls

8. _____ Privacy

9. _____ 4′ minimum wardrobe rod space per person

10. Master bedroom

_____ *a.* bath

_____ *b.* dressing area

_____ *c.* full-length mirror

_____ *d.* 12′ × 12′ minimum

11. Adequate windows

_____ *a.* natural light

_____ *b.* cross-ventilation

_____ *c.* windows on two walls

12. _____ Room for overnight guests

13. _____ Bathroom nearby

14. _____ Wall space for bed, nightstands, and dresser

15. _____ Quiet reading area

The Bathroom

1. _____ Well designed

2. _____ Plumbing lines are grouped

3. _____ Fixtures have space around them for proper use

4. _____ Doors do not interfere with fixtures

5. _____ Noises are insulated from other rooms

6. _____ Convenient to bedrooms

7. _____ Convenient for guests

8. _____ Ventilation

9. _____ Heating

10. _____ Attractive fixtures

11. _____ No windows over tub or shower

12. _____ Wall area around tub and shower

13. _____ Light fixtures are water tight

14. _____ Large medicine cabinet

15. _____ Children cannot open medicine cabinet

16. _____ No bathroom tie-ups

17. _____ Good lighting

18. _____ Accessible electrical outlets

19. _____ No electric appliance or switch near water supply

20. _____ Towel and linen storage

21. _____ Dirty clothes hamper

22. _____ Steamproof mirrors

23. _____ Wall and floor materials are waterproof

24. _____ All finishes are easy to maintain

25. _____ Curtain and towel rods securely fastened

26. _____ Grab bar by tub

27. _____ Mixing faucets

28. _____ Bath in service area

29. _____ No public view into open bathroom door

30. _____ Clean-up area for outdoor jobs and children's play

The Kitchen

1. _____ Centrally located
2. _____ The family can eat informally in the kitchen
3. _____ At least 20' of cabinet space
   _____ a. counter space on each side of major appliances
   _____ b. minimum of 8' counter work area
   _____ c. round storage in corners
   _____ d. no shelf is higher than 72"
   _____ e. floor cabinets 24" deep and 36" high
   _____ f. wall cabinets 15" deep
   _____ g. 15" clearance between wall and floor cabinets
4. _____ Major appliances in efficient order
   _____ a. service entry
   _____ b. refrigerator
   _____ c. sink
   _____ d. stove
   _____ e. dining area
5. _____ Work triangle is formed between appliances
   _____ a. between 12' and 20'
   _____ b. no traffic through the work triangle
   _____ c. refrigerator opens into the work triangle
   _____ d. at least six electric outlets in work triangle
   _____ e. no door between appliances
6. _____ No space between appliances and counters
7. _____ Window over sink
8. _____ No wasted space in kitchen
9. _____ Can close off kitchen from dining area
10. _____ Snack bar in kitchen
11. _____ Kitchen drawers are divided
12. _____ Built-in chopping block
13. _____ Writing and telephone desk
14. _____ Indoor play area visible from kitchen
15. _____ Outdoor play area visible from kitchen
16. _____ Exhaust fan
17. _____ Natural light
18. _____ Good lighting for each work area
19. _____ Convenient access to service area and garage
20. _____ Cheerful decor
21. _____ Durable surfaces
22. _____ Dishwasher
23. _____ Disposal
24. _____ Built-in appliances
25. _____ Bathroom nearby
26. _____ Room for freezer
27. _____ Pantry storage

The Utility Room

1. _____ Adequate laundry area
2. _____ Well-lighted work areas
3. _____ 240-volt outlet
4. _____ Gas outlet
5. _____ Sorting area
6. _____ Ironing area
7. _____ Drip-drying area
8. _____ Sewing and mending area
9. _____ On least desirable side of lot
10. _____ Exit to outdoor service area
11. _____ Exit near garage
12. _____ Sufficient cabinet space
13. _____ Bathroom in area
14. _____ Accessible from kitchen
15. _____ Adequate space for washer and dryer
16. _____ Laundry tray
17. _____ Outdoor exit is protected from the weather
18. _____ Window

Working Areas

1. _____ Home repair area
2. _____ Work area for hobbies
3. _____ Storage for paints and tools
4. _____ Garbage storage and collection
5. _____ Incinerator area
6. _____ Refuse area
7. _____ Delivery area
8. _____ Near parking
9. _____ 240-volt outlet for power tools

STORAGE

1. _____ General storage space for each person
2. _____ 4' of rod space for each person
3. _____ Closet doors are sealed to keep out dust
4. _____ Minimum wardrobe closet size is 40" × 22"
5. _____ Cedar closet storage for seasonal clothing
6. _____ Bulk storage area for seasonal paraphernalia
7. _____ Closets are lighted
8. _____ Walk-in closets have adequate turnaround area
9. Storage for:
   _____ a. linen and towels
   _____ b. cleaning materials
   _____ c. foods
   _____ d. bedding
   _____ e. outdoor furniture
   _____ f. sports equipment
   _____ g. toys—indoor
   _____ h. toys—outdoors
   _____ i. bicycles
   _____ j. luggage
   _____ k. out-of-season clothes
   _____ l. storm windows and doors
   _____ m. garden tools
   _____ n. tools and paints
   _____ o. hats
   _____ p. shoes
   _____ q. belts
   _____ r. ties
   _____ s. bridge tables and chairs
   _____ t. camping equipment
   _____ u. china
   _____ v. silver
   _____ w. minor appliances
   _____ x. books
10. _____ Closets are ventilated
11. _____ No mildew in closets
12. _____ Closets do not project into room
13. _____ Toothbrush holders in bathrooms
14. _____ Soap holders in bathrooms
15. _____ Adequate built-in storage
16. _____ Drawers cannot pull out of cabinet
17. _____ Drawers slide easily
18. _____ Drawers have divided partitions
19. _____ Adult storage areas easy to reach
20. _____ Children storage areas easy to reach
21. _____ Guest storage near entry
22. _____ Heavy storage areas have reinforced floors
23. _____ Sides of closets easy to reach
24. _____ Tops of closets easy to reach
25. _____ No wasted spaces around stored articles
26. _____ Sloping roof or stairs does not render closet useless
27. _____ Entry closet

The Exterior

1. _____ The design looks "right" for the lot
2. _____ Design varies from other homes nearby
3. _____ Design fits with unity on its site

4. _____ Definite style architecture—not mixed
5. _____ Simple, honest design
6. _____ Garage design goes with the house
7. _____ Attractive on all four sides
8. _____ Colors in good taste
9. _____ Finish materials in good taste
10. _____ Has charm and warmth
11. _____ Materials are consistent on all sides
12. _____ No false building effects
13. _____ Well-designed roof lines—not chopped up
14. _____ Window tops line up
15. _____ Bathroom windows are not obvious
16. _____ Does not look like a box
17. _____ Easy maintenance of finish materials
18. _____ Windows are protected from pedestrian view
19. _____ Attractive roof covering
20. _____ Gutters on roof
21. _____ Downspouts that drain into storm sewer
22. _____ Glass area protected with overhang or trees
23. _____ Dry around the house
24. _____ Several waterproof electric outlets
25. _____ Hose bib on each side
26. _____ Style will look good in the future

Outdoor Service Area

1. _____ Clothes hanging area
2. _____ Garbage storage
3. _____ Can storage
4. _____ On least desirable side of site
5. _____ Next to indoor service area
6. _____ Near garage
7. _____ Delivery area for trucks
8. _____ Fenced off from rest of site

Outdoor Living Area

1. _____ Area for dining
2. _____ Area for games
3. _____ Area for lounging
4. _____ Area for gardening
5. _____ Fenced for privacy
6. _____ Partly shaded
7. _____ Concrete deck at convenient places
8. _____ Garden walks
9. _____ Easy access to house
10. _____ Paved area for bikes and wagons
11. _____ Easy maintenance

Landscaping

1. _____ Planting at foundation ties
2. _____ Garden area
3. _____ Well-located trees
4. _____ Healthy trees
5. _____ Plants of slow-growing variety
6. _____ Landscaping professionally advised
7. _____ Pipes free of tree roots
8. _____ Garden walks
9. _____ Easy maintenance
10. _____ Extras as trellis or gazebo

Construction

1. _____ Sound construction
2. _____ All work complies to code
3. _____ Efficient contractor and supervision
4. _____ Honest builders
5. _____ Skilled builders
6. _____ Constructed to plans
7. Floors are well constructed
   _____ a. resilient
   _____ b. subfloor diagonal to joints
   _____ c. flat and even
   _____ d. slab is not cold
   _____ e. floor joists rest on 2″ of sill—minimum
   _____ f. girder lengths are joined under points of support
8. Foundation is well constructed
   _____ a. level
   _____ b. sill protected from termites
   _____ c. vapor barrier
   _____ d. no cracks
   _____ e. no water seepage
   _____ f. no dryrot in sills
   _____ g. garage slab drains
   _____ h. waterproofed
   _____ i. walls are 8″ thick
   _____ j. no water marks on basement walls
   _____ k. basement height 7′6″ minimum
   _____ l. sills bolted to foundation
   _____ m. adequate vents
9. Walls are well constructed
   _____ a. plumb
   _____ b. no waves
   _____ c. insulation
   _____ d. flashing at all exterior joints
   _____ e. solid sheathing
   _____ f. siding is neat and tight
   _____ g. drywall joints are invisible
10. Windows are properly installed
    _____ a. move freely
    _____ b. weatherstripped
    _____ c. caulked and sealed
    _____ d. good-quality glass
11. Doors properly hung
    _____ a. move freely
    _____ b. exterior doors weatherstripped
    _____ c. exterior doors are solid-core
    _____ d. interior doors are hollow-core
12. Roof is well constructed
    _____ a. rafters are straight
    _____ b. all corners are flashed
    _____ c. adequate vents in attic
    _____ d. no leaks
    _____ e. building paper under shingles
13. _____ Tile work is tight
14. _____ Hot water lines are insulated
15. _____ Mortar joints are neat
16. _____ Mortar joints do not form shelf to hold water
17. _____ Ceiling is 8′0″ minimum
18. _____ No exposed pipes
19. _____ No exposed wires
20. _____ Tight joints at cabinets and appliances
21. _____ Stairs have railings
22. _____ Neat trim application
23. _____ Builder responsible for new home flaws

The Fireplace

1. _____ There is a fireplace
2. _____ Wood storage near the fireplace
3. _____ Draws smoke
4. _____ Hearth in front (minimum 10″ on sides; 20″ in front)
5. _____ Does not project out into the room
6. _____ Has a clean-out
7. _____ Chimney top 2′ higher than roof ridge
8. _____ Chimney does not lean
9. _____ No leaks around chimney in roof
10. _____ No wood touches the chimney
11. _____ 2″ minimum air space between framing members and masonry
12. _____ No loose mortar
13. _____ Has a damper

14. _____ Space for furniture opposite fireplace
15. _____ Doors minimum of 6' from fireplace
16. _____ Windows minimum of 3' from fireplace
17. _____ On a long wall
18. _____ Install "heatilator"
19. _____ Install glass doors to minimize heat loss

EQUIPMENT

1. _____ All equipment listed in specifications and plans
2. _____ All new equipment has warranty
3. _____ All equipment is up to code standards
4. _____ All equipment is functional and not a fad
5. _____ Owner's choice of equipment meets builders allowance
6. _____ Public system for utilities
7. _____ Private well is deep; adequate and healthy water
8. Electrical equipment is adequate
   _____ a. inspected and guaranteed
   _____ b. 240 voltage
   _____ c. 120 voltage
   _____ d. sufficient electric outlets
   _____ e. sufficient electric circuits—minimum of six
   _____ f. circuit breakers
   _____ g. television aerial outlet
   _____ h. telephone outlets
   _____ i. outlets in convenient places
9. Adequate lighting
   _____ a. all rooms have general lighting
   _____ b. all rooms have specific lighting for specific tasks
   _____ c. silent switches
   _____ d. some decorative lighting
   _____ e. light at front door
   _____ f. outdoor lighting
10. Plumbing equipment is adequate
   _____ a. inspected and guaranteed
   _____ b. adequate water pressure
   _____ c. hot water heater—50-gallon minimum
   _____ d. shut-off valves at fixtures
   _____ e. satisfactory city sewer or septic tank
   _____ f. septic tank disposal field is adequate
   _____ g. septic tank is large enough for house (1000 gallons for three-bedroom house, plus 250 gallons for each additional bedroom)
   _____ h. water softener for hard water
   _____ i. siphon vertex or siphon reverse-trap water closet
   _____ j. clean-out plugs at all corners of waste lines
   _____ k. water lines will not rust
   _____ l. water pipes do not hammer
   _____ m. waste lines drain freely
   _____ n. cast iron with vitreous enamel bathtub
11. _____ Good ventilation through house and attic
12. Heating and cooling systems are adequate
   _____ a. insulation in roof, ceiling, walls
   _____ b. air conditioning system
   _____ c. heating and cooling outlets under windows
   _____ d. air purifier
   _____ e. thermostatic control
   _____ f. walls are clean over heat outlets
   _____ g. comfortable in hot or cold weather
   _____ h. automatic humidifier
   _____ i. furnace blower is belt-driven
   _____ j. quiet-heating plant
   _____ k. ducts are tight

13. Windows are of good quality
   _____ a. storm windows
   _____ b. secure locks
   _____ c. screened
   _____ d. double glazed in extreme weather (thermal)
   _____ e. glass is ripple-free
   _____ f. safety or safe thickness of glass
   _____ g. moisture-free
   _____ h. frost-free
14. Doors are of good quality
   _____ a. secure locks on exterior doors
   _____ b. attractive hardware
   _____ c. hardware is solid brass or bronze
15. _____ All meters easily accessible to meter readers
16. _____ Fire extinguisher in house and garage
17. _____ Acoustical ceiling
18. _____ Facilities to lock mail box
19. _____ Facilities to receive large packages
20. _____ Gas or electric incinerator
21. Adequate small hardware
   _____ a. soap dishes
   _____ b. toilet-paper holders
   _____ c. toothbrush holders
   _____ d. towel holders
   _____ e. bathtub grab bars
   _____ f. door and drawer pulls

The Garage

1. _____ Same style as the house
2. _____ Fits with the house
3. _____ Single garage 12' × 22' minimum
4. _____ Double garage 22' × 22' minimum
5. _____ Larger than minimum size if used for storage or workshop
6. _____ Protected passage to house
7. _____ Doors are safe
8. _____ Access to overhead storage

Financial Checklist

1. _____ Do you understand conveyancing fees (closing costs)?
2. _____ Is the house a good investment?
3. _____ Is the total cost approximately three times your annual income?
4. _____ Have you shopped for the best loan?
5. _____ Do you have a constant payment plan (sliding principal and interest)?
6. _____ Is there a prepayment penalty?
7. _____ Will a week's salary cover the total housing expense for one month?
8. _____ Are all the costs itemized in the contract?
9. Do you understand the following closing costs?
   _____ a. title search
   _____ b. lawyer
   _____ c. plot survey
   _____ d. insurance, fire, and public liability
   _____ e. mortgage tax
   _____ f. recording mortgage
   _____ g. recording deed
   _____ h. bank's commitment fee
   _____ i. state and county taxes
   _____ j. state and government revenue stamps
   _____ k. title insurance (protects lender)
   _____ l. homeowner's policy (protects owner)
   _____ m. transferring ownership
   _____ n. mortgage service charge
   _____ o. appraisal
   _____ p. notarizing documents
   _____ q. attendant fee (paying off previous mortgage)

_____ r. personal credit check
10. _____ Do you have extra cash to cover unforseen expenses?
11. Can you afford to pay the following?
  _____ a. closing costs
  _____ b. old assessments or bonds
  _____ c. new assessments or bonds
  _____ d. downpayment
  _____ e. immediate repairs
  _____ f. immediate purchases (furniture, appliances, landscape, tools, fences, carpets, drapes, patio)
  _____ g. adequate insurance
  _____ h. mortgage payments
  _____ i. general maintenance
  _____ j. utilities (water, heat, electricity, phone, gas, trash pickup)
  _____ k. special design features wanted

  _____ l. extras not covered in plans and contract
  _____ m. prepayment of interest and taxes for first month of transition
  _____ n. moving
  _____ o. gardener
  _____ p. travel to work
  _____ q. interest on construction loan
  _____ r. advances to contractors
12. Who will pay for the following?
  _____ a. supervision costs of architect or contractor
  _____ b. inspection fees
  _____ c. increased costs during building
  _____ d. building permits
  _____ e. difficulties in excavation
  _____ f. dry wells
  _____ g. extra features the building inspector insists upon

CHAPTER 8

Altering Plans

Once you are satisfied you have selected the architectural plan that most nearly fills your life-style needs, you are ready to begin to alter the plan to fit it exactly to all of your needs and as many of your wants as possible. In the altering process, too much emphasis cannot be placed on the need to control what changes can practically be made to a plan and what changes are impractical and should be avoided. Therefore, proceed carefully and logically in making changes, following the guidelines presented here. If you find yourself starting from the beginning or making major changes that require several other levels of changes to adjust for the first change, you probably are on the wrong track. At this point go back and find a plan that fills your needs better or that satisfies more of your wants. Or make another reassessment of your lifestyle needs and wants.

Methods of Making Changes

In making alterations to an existing plan, first attach a transparent overlay sheet of paper over the drawing. Then mark two corners with a + so the overlay sheet may be removed and replaced again in the same position if necessary. Next begin to make changes directly on the overlay sheet (See Fig. 8–1). Don't mark the original drawing. First add new walls, doors, windows, and facilities to be deleted, as shown in Fig. 8–2. After you have decided the changes made on the overlay are final, then either "white out" the deleted portions or continue to trace the remain-

der of the plan on the overlay. If you want to try several different design change options, remove the tracing paper overlay and begin with a new sheet. Use a different overlay sheet for each different option. After experimenting with as many as you feel necessary, study each overlay and look for combinations that may solve any lingering problems. Keep in mind that professional designers will use many, many overlays to solve a redesign problem, so don't be impatient. Often part of a design change from option 1 can be combined with a part of option 6 to provide the ideal solution. Do not hurry this step. Even when you think you have an ideal solution, put it aside and try a completely different approach. Then go back and compare. If you reach an impasse, put the drawing aside for a few days. Then take a fresh look at the problem. Problems that seem to defy solution one day may appear perfectly clear on another day.

Types of Design Alterations

Practically all design changes involve either room size, location, or shape changes, and this often also results in moving or changing doors, windows, and traffic areas. The remainder of the changes usually involve adding living space when none existed before or utilizing previously unused space for living, such as the basement or attic. But, regardless of the type of design change involved, the same basic guidelines as presented here should be followed. Study the design chang-

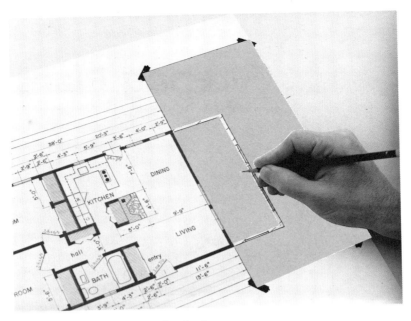

Fig. 8-1 Make changes on overlay sheet.

Altering room sizes Rooms are increased or altered in size to accommodate more furniture, appliances, facilities, and traffic areas, or simply to provide a greater feeling of space. Since it is often difficult to determine the ideal room size for each home, the use of furniture templates is a great help. Arranging and rearranging furniture in a room is heavy work. It is much easier to arrange furniture by the use of templates (See Fig. 8–3). Furniture templates are thin pieces of paper, cardboard, plastic, or metal which represent the width and length of pieces of furniture. They are used to determine exactly how much floor space each piece of furniture will occupy. One template is made for each piece of furniture on the furniture list. Templates are always prepared to the scale that is used for the floor plan drawing of the house. The scale most frequently used on floor plans is ¼″ = 1′–0″. Scales of ³⁄₁₆″ = 1′–0″ and ⅛″ = 1′–0″ are sometimes used. Templates show only the width and length of furniture and the floor space covered. Figure 8–4 shows common furniture sizes which can be used as a guide in constructing furniture templates. Wall-hung furniture or any projection from furniture, even though it does not touch the floor, should be included as a template because the floor space under this furniture is not usable for any other purpose. Furniture templates are placed in the arrangement that will best fit the living pattern anticipated for the room. Space must be allowed for free flow of traffic and for opening and closing doors, drawers, and windows. Figure 8–5 shows furniture templates placed on a floor plan. After a furniture arrangement has been established, the room dimensions can be finalized.

Common room sizes Determining what room sizes are desirable is only one aspect of room planning. Since the cost of the home is largely determined by the size and number of rooms, room sizes must be adjusted to conform to the acceptable price range. Figure 8–6 reviews sizes for each room in large, medium, and small dwellings. These dimensions represent only average widths and lengths. For a more complete listing of room sizes, review Chapter 5. To recheck the appropriateness of the size of each room, go through the procedure outlined in Chapter 5. This involves not only checking the space required for furniture by the use of templates but also includes the use of a scaled human template (See Fig. 8–7) to check the availability of space for other functions, such as traffic movement.

The experienced architect and home planner does not always go through the procedure of cutting out furniture templates and arranging them into patterns to arrive at room sizes. But the architect uses templates frequently to recheck designs. Until you are completely familiar with furniture dimensions and the sizes of building materials, the use of the procedures outlined here is recommended.

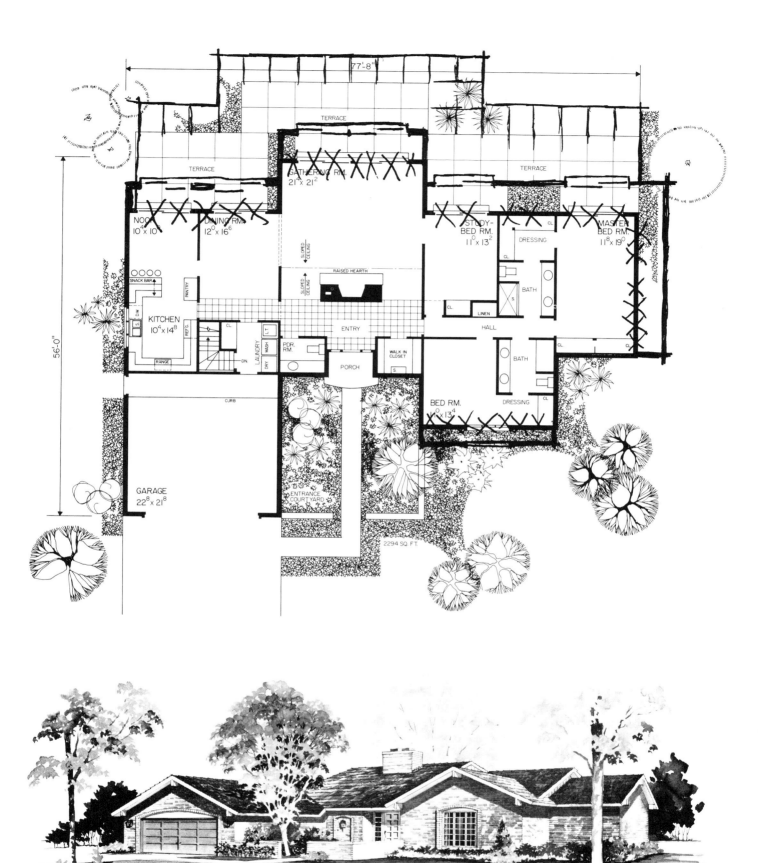

Fig. 8-2 Add new walls; cross out old. (Design 2594)

Living-area furniture and fixture templates
Scale ¼"=1'-0"

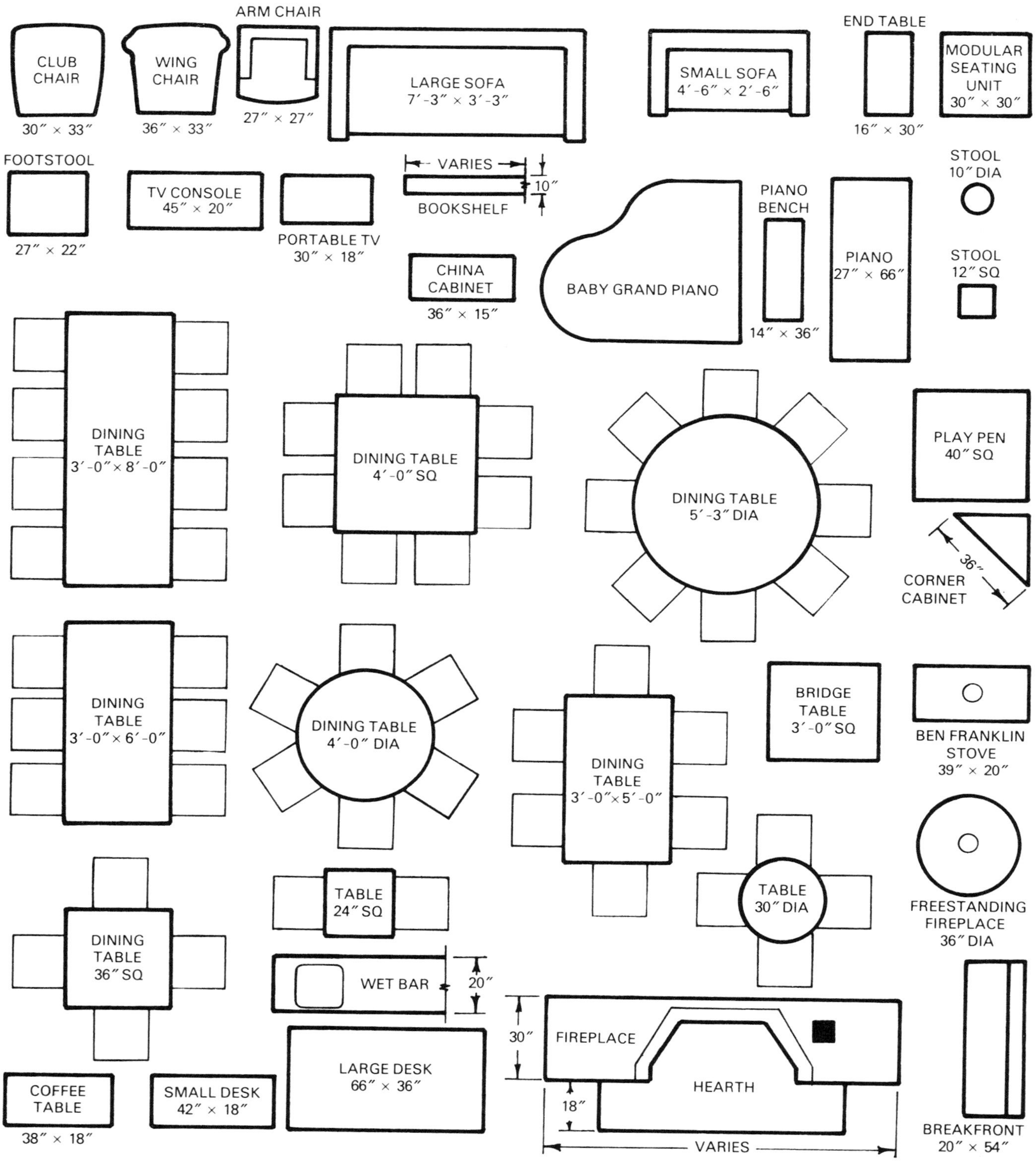

CLUB CHAIR
30" × 33"

WING CHAIR
36" × 33"

ARM CHAIR
27" × 27"

LARGE SOFA
7'-3" × 3'-3"

SMALL SOFA
4'-6" × 2'-6"

END TABLE
16" × 30"

MODULAR SEATING UNIT
30" × 30"

FOOTSTOOL
27" × 22"

TV CONSOLE
45" × 20"

PORTABLE TV
30" × 18"

VARIES
10"
BOOKSHELF

PIANO BENCH
14" × 36"

PIANO
27" × 66"

BABY GRAND PIANO

STOOL
10" DIA

STOOL
12" SQ

CHINA CABINET
36" × 15"

DINING TABLE
3'-0" × 8'-0"

DINING TABLE
4'-0" SQ

DINING TABLE
5'-3" DIA

PLAY PEN
40" SQ

CORNER CABINET
36"

DINING TABLE
3'-0" × 6'-0"

DINING TABLE
4'-0" DIA

DINING TABLE
3'-0" × 5'-0"

BRIDGE TABLE
3'-0" SQ

BEN FRANKLIN STOVE
39" × 20"

TABLE
30" DIA

FREESTANDING FIREPLACE
36" DIA

DINING TABLE
36" SQ

TABLE
24" SQ

WET BAR
20"

FIREPLACE
30"
HEARTH
18"
VARIES

COFFEE TABLE
38" × 18"

SMALL DESK
42" × 18"

LARGE DESK
66" × 36"

BREAKFRONT
20" × 54"

Fig. 8-3 Furniture templates.

Sleeping and service-area furniture templates
Scale ¼″=1′-0″

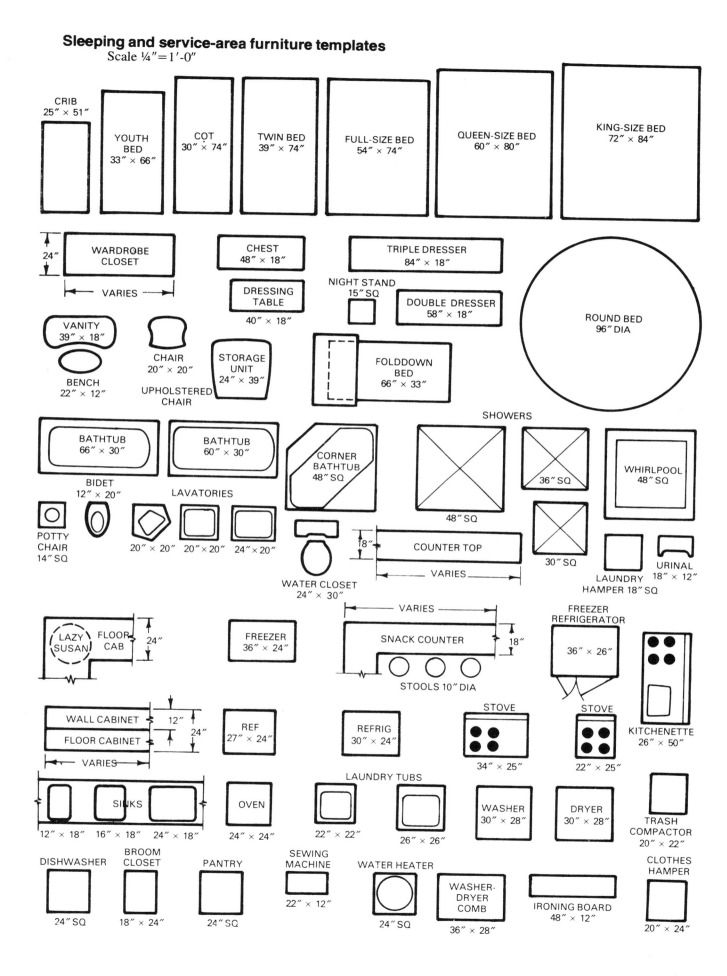

CRIB
25″ × 51″

YOUTH BED
33″ × 66″

COT
30″ × 74″

TWIN BED
39″ × 74″

FULL-SIZE BED
54″ × 74″

QUEEN-SIZE BED
60″ × 80″

KING-SIZE BED
72″ × 84″

24″

WARDROBE CLOSET

VARIES

CHEST
48″ × 18″

TRIPLE DRESSER
84″ × 18″

NIGHT STAND
15″ SQ

DRESSING TABLE
40″ × 18″

DOUBLE DRESSER
58″ × 18″

ROUND BED
96″ DIA

VANITY
39″ × 18″

CHAIR
20″ × 20″

STORAGE UNIT
24″ × 39″

FOLDDOWN BED
66″ × 33″

BENCH
22″ × 12″

UPHOLSTERED CHAIR

BATHTUB
66″ × 30″

BATHTUB
60″ × 30″

CORNER BATHTUB
48″ SQ

SHOWERS

36″ SQ

WHIRLPOOL
48″ SQ

BIDET
12″ × 20″

LAVATORIES

48″ SQ

30″ SQ

POTTY CHAIR
14″ SQ

20″ × 20″   20″ × 20″   24″ × 20″

18″

COUNTER TOP

VARIES

LAUNDRY HAMPER 18″ SQ

URINAL
18″ × 12″

WATER CLOSET
24″ × 30″

LAZY SUSAN

FLOOR CAB

24″

FREEZER
36″ × 24″

VARIES

SNACK COUNTER

18″

STOOLS 10″ DIA

FREEZER REFRIGERATOR
36″ × 26″

WALL CABINET   12″

FLOOR CABINET   24″

VARIES

REF
27″ × 24″

REFRIG
30″ × 24″

STOVE
34″ × 25″

STOVE
22″ × 25″

KITCHENETTE
26″ × 50″

SINKS

12″ × 18″   16″ × 18″   24″ × 18″

OVEN
24″ × 24″

LAUNDRY TUBS

22″ × 22″   26″ × 26″

WASHER
30″ × 28″

DRYER
30″ × 28″

TRASH COMPACTOR
20″ × 22″

DISHWASHER
24″ SQ

BROOM CLOSET
18″ × 24″

PANTRY
24″ SQ

SEWING MACHINE
22″ × 12″

WATER HEATER
24″ SQ

WASHER-DRYER COMB
36″ × 28″

IRONING BOARD
48″ × 12″

CLOTHES HAMPER
20″ × 24″

ITEM	LENGTH, INCHES (mm)	WIDTH, INCHES (mm)	HEIGHT, INCHES (mm)
COUCH	72(1829)	30(762)	30(762)
	84(2134)	30(762)	30(762)
	96(2438)	30(762)	30(762)
LOUNGE	28(711)	32(813)	29(737)
	34(864)	36(914)	37(940)
COFFEE TABLE	36(914)	20(508)	17(432)
	48(1219)	20(508)	17(432)
	54(1372)	20(508)	17(432)
DESK	50(1270)	21(533)	29(737)
	60(1524)	30(762)	29(737)
	72(1829)	36(914)	29(737)
STEREO CONSOLE	36(914)	16(406)	26(660)
	48(1219)	17(432)	26(660)
	62(1575)	17(432)	27(660)
END TABLE	22(559)	28(711)	21(533)
	26(660)	20(508)	21(533)
	28(711)	28(711)	20(508)
TV CONSOLE	38(965)	17(432)	29(737)
	40(1016)	18(457)	30(762)
	48(1219)	19(483)	30(762)
SHELF MODULES	18(457)	10(254)	60(1524)
	24(610)	10(254)	60(1524)
	36(914)	10(254)	60(1524)
	48(1219)	10(254)	60(1524)
DINING TABLE	48(1219)	30(762)	29(737)
	60(1524)	36(914)	29(737)
	72(1829)	42(1067)	28(711)
BUFFET	36(914)	16(406)	31(787)
	48(1219)	16(406)	31(787)
	52(1321)	18(457)	31(787)
DINING CHAIRS	20(508)	17(432)	36(914)
	22(559)	19(483)	29(737)
	24(610)	21(533)	31(787)

	DIAMETER, INCHES (mm)		HEIGHT, INCHES (mm)
DINING TABLE (ROUND)	36(914)		28(711)
	42(1067)		28(711)
	48(1219)		28(711)

Fig. 8-4 Furniture sizes.

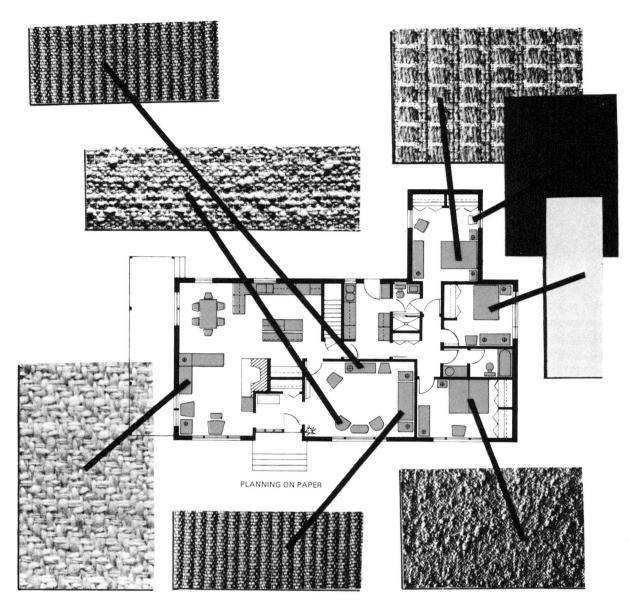

PLANNING ON PAPER

Fig. 8-5   Furniture templates on floor plan.

	LIVING ROOM, FT²/m²	DINING ROOM, FT²/m²	KITCHEN, FT²/m²	BEDROOMS, FT²/m²	BATH, FT²/m²
SMALL HOME	200/18.5	155/14.4	110/10.2	140/13.0	40/3.7
AVERAGE HOME	250/24.2	175/16.2	135/12.5	170/15.7	70/6.5
LARGE HOME	300/27.8	195/18.1	165/15.3	190/17.6	100/9.3

Fig. 8-6   Room sizes.

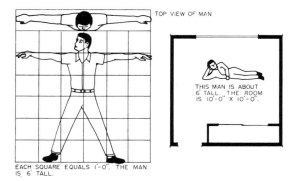

THIS MAN IS ABOUT 6' TALL. THE ROOM IS 10'-0" X 10'-0".

EACH SQUARE EQUALS 1'-0". THE MAN IS 6' TALL.

Fig. 8-7 Method of checking sizes.

If you have determined a room is too small, proceed with preparing an overlay with the additional space added. Always add space to outside walls whenever possible, because altering interior space will require adjusting other room sizes and can cause a chain reaction in moving walls. However, if for lack of space or for budgetary reasons the overall dimensions of the house must remain the same, then adding space to one room will obviously necessitate reducing the size of another. For example, to increase the size of the bedrooms in Fig. 8–8, the size of the entry space in the living area was diminished. This change not only provided more space for the bedrooms but also created more privacy for the kitchen and bath from the living area. Remember, when increasing room sizes, position walls on even modules. Also keep in mind that in removing any portion of a bearing partition (a center wall upon which ceiling joists rest) the ceiling framing must be changed or additional beam support added.

Room location changes Sometimes the general layout and relationship of rooms is appropriate for one family's needs but not for another's. Or the location of specific rooms may be ideal for one site or neighborhood but not another. Room locations are also often changed to provide new facilities as a trade-off for others; to take advantage of a view, prevailing winds, or solar orientation; or to avoid an unsightly view or noise. For example, the rooms in the plan shown in Fig. 8–9 have been relocated to allow the bedrooms to take advantage of a cool breeze, to provide the family room with an outstanding view, and to recluster the bedrooms together in the sleeping area. This change also relocates the kitchen adjacent to the family room and the dining room.

Altering room shapes Rectangular and sometimes square rooms normally function best with normal furniture or facilities. However, irregularly shaped rooms can function well if furniture is predesigned or selected for the room. Room shapes are normally changed, however, to alter a room with awkward effects or disproportioned

ratios of width to length. For example, the shape of the bedroom shown in Fig. 8–10 was altered to eliminate an offset created by the addition of a closet without balancing the offset space. In this plan, the kitchen was also moved from the front of the house and the dining room and living room locations were reversed. This move placed the kitchen adjacent to both the family room and the dining room. It also located the living room next to the foyer, which is much more desirable than entering through the gathering room. Notice also how two additional bedrooms and a bath were designed into an open attic area.

Moving doors and windows Relocating doors or windows in the design process is usually a by-product of wall changes. However, sometimes doors and windows are moved or sizes changed because of a change in the type of door or window used.

Doors Doors are primarily designed for privacy, safety, security, and climate control. For example, interior bedroom and bath doors are designed for personal privacy, while closet doors are designed to hide stored objects. Exterior doors are used primarily to secure the house, control heat loss or gain, and keep dirt and odors from penetrating the house. The front door should be so designed that it becomes an integral part of the main entrance to the house. All outside doors should offer privacy and protection from weather and intruders.

Door types. Doors are of two types—paneled or flush—and may be installed to swing, slide, or fold. Both types can have windows. Paneled doors are mainly used on traditional homes, while flush doors are best suited to modern or contemporary homes. Doors are constructed of wood, plastic, glass, or metal. The solid wood doors of the past were handsome but heavy. Today, the majority of wood doors are of hollow-core construction, which makes them lighter, less expensive, and less likely to warp.

Door styles. Swing doors are by far the most popular door used in home design today. It is

BEFORE

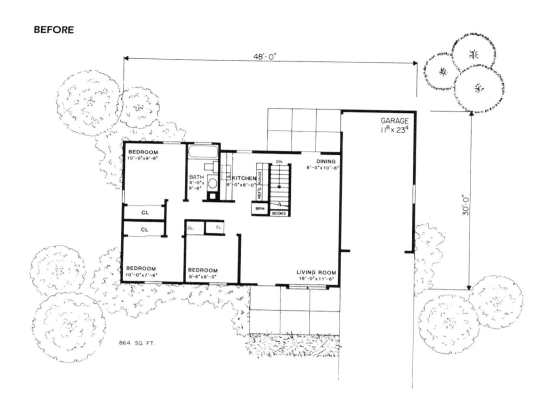

48'-0"

GARAGE
11⁸ x 23⁴

30'-0"

BEDROOM
10'-0"x9'-6"

BATH
5'-0"x
9'-6"

KITCHEN
8'-0"x8'-0"

DINING
8'-0"x10'-6"

DN.

REF'G. RANGE

BRM.

BOOKS

CL

CL

CL.

CL

BEDROOM
10'-0"x7'-6"

BEDROOM
8'-6"x8'-0"

LIVING ROOM
16'-0"x11'-6"

864 SQ. FT.

AFTER

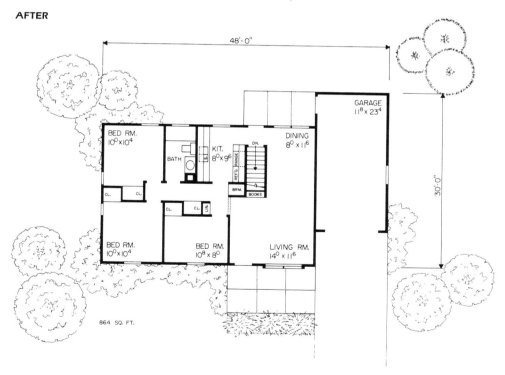

48'-0"

GARAGE
11⁸ x 23⁴

30'-0"

BED RM.
10⁰x10⁴

BATH

KIT.
8⁰x9⁶

DINING
8⁰ x 11⁶

DN.

REF'G. RANGE

BRM.

BOOKS

CL

CL

CL.

CL.

LIN.

BED RM.
10⁰x10⁴

BED RM.
10⁸ x 8⁰

LIVING RM.
14⁰ x 11⁶

864 SQ. FT.

Fig. 8-8   Increasing bedroom sizes. (Design 2163)

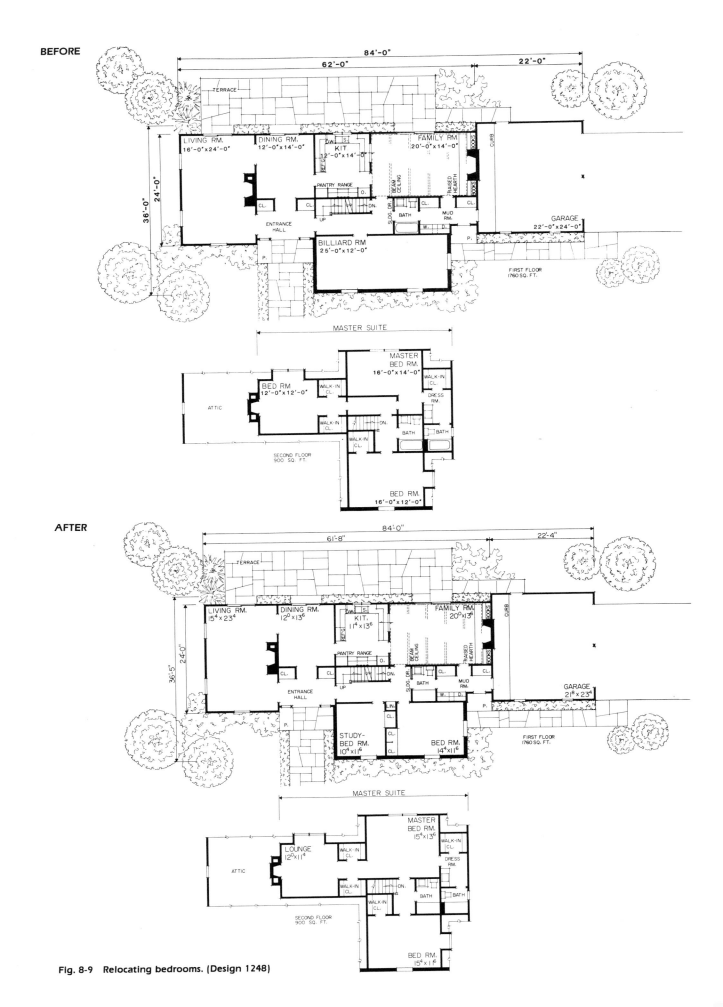

BEFORE

TERRACE

84'-0"
62'-0"
22'-0"

LIVING RM.
16'-0" x 24'-0"

DINING RM.
12'-0" x 14'-0"

KIT
12'-0" x 14'-0"

FAMILY RM.
20'-0" x 14'-0"

CURB

36'-0"
24'-0"

PANTRY RANGE

CL.

CL.

DN.
UP

BEAM CEILING

RAISED HEARTH

CL.

CL.

MUD RM.

ENTRANCE HALL

SLDG. DR.

BATH

W. D.

P.

GARAGE
22'-0" x 24'-0"

BILLIARD RM
25'-0" x 12'-0"

FIRST FLOOR
1760 SQ. FT.

MASTER SUITE

MASTER BED RM.
16'-0" x 14'-0"

WALK-IN CL.

BED RM
12'-0" x 12'-0"

WALK-IN CL.

ATTIC

WALK-IN CL.

DRESS RM.

DN.

WALK-IN CL.

BATH

BATH

SECOND FLOOR
900 SQ. FT.

BED RM.
16'-0" x 12'-0"

AFTER

TERRACE

84'-0"
61'-8"
22'-4"

LIVING RM.
15⁴ x 23⁴

DINING RM.
12⁰ x 13⁶

KIT.
11⁴ x 13⁶

FAMILY RM.
20⁰ x 13⁶

CURB

36'-5"
24'-0"

PANTRY RANGE

CL.

CL.

DN.
UP

BEAM CEILING

RAISED HEARTH

CL.

CL.

MUD RM.

ENTRANCE HALL

SLDG. DR.

BATH

W. D.

P.

GARAGE
21⁸ x 23⁴

STUDY-BED RM.
10⁴ x 11⁶

LIN CL.

CL.

BED RM.
14⁴ x 11⁶

FIRST FLOOR
1760 SQ. FT.

MASTER SUITE

MASTER BED RM.
15⁴ x 13⁶

WALK-IN CL.

LOUNGE
12⁰ x 11⁴

WALK-IN CL.

ATTIC

WALK-IN CL.

DRESS RM.

DN.

WALK-IN CL.

BATH

BATH

SECOND FLOOR
900 SQ. FT.

BED RM.
15⁴ x 11⁶

Fig. 8-9   Relocating bedrooms. (Design 1248)

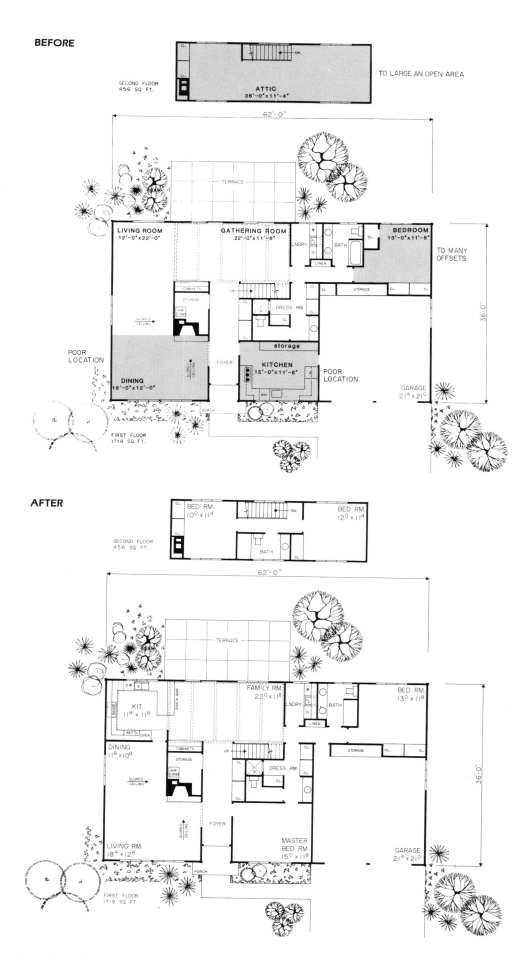

Fig. 8-10   Altering bedroom shape. (Design 2309)

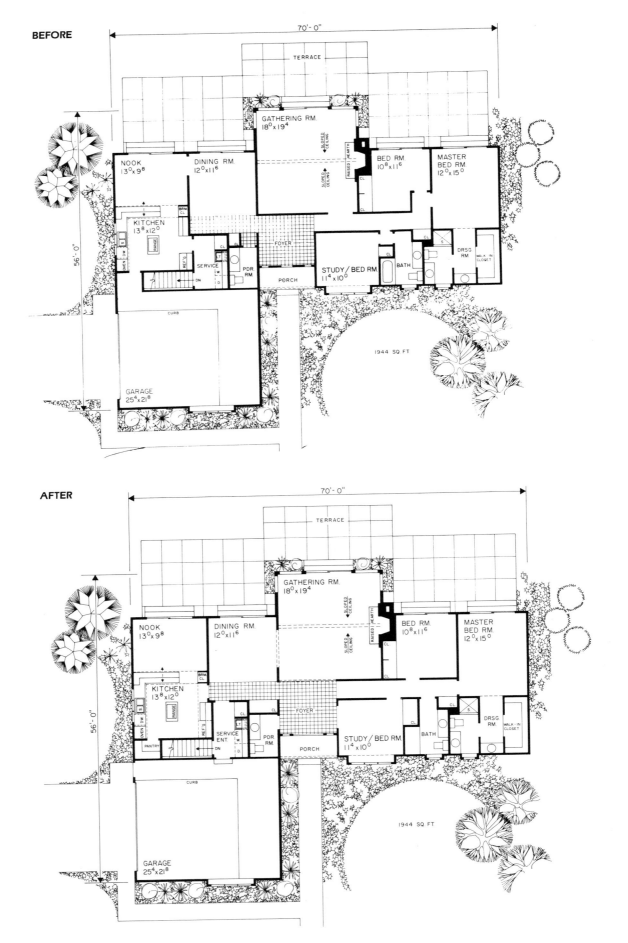

Fig. 8-11 Moving doors. (Design 2792)

hinged on one side usually opening against a wall. Swing doors also work well in pairs, but because of the additional swing space needed, their use is limited.

Sliding doors ride on an overhead track and are usually guided on bottom rails. Pocket and slide-by doors are made for places where swing space is limited or where swinging doors create a furniture placement problem. They are excellent for dining rooms, bedrooms, and closets. Solid-glass sliding doors are ideally suited as outside doors when the exit is onto a patio or balcony. If you don't need a door at all times, or if the door remains open much of the time, then consider sliding pocket doors that slide into or past a wall. But remember, no plumbing or electrical equipment can be installed in the wall pocket area.

Folding doors are hinged and may be solid or louvered in design. Folding doors can separate one room from another without using much space. They are often used to separate a kitchen from a dining room, or a living room from a dining room. They're appropriate for closets, too, because they are easy to open and close.

Accordion doors are similar to folding doors but are constructed in smaller modular widths.

Double (cafe) doors swing in both directions and are effective in providing semiprivacy without sacrificing the convenience of easy access. Their use is limited because of the need to provide swing space on both sides.

The design of the garage door greatly affects the appearance of the house, especially if the garage is front facing. Several types of garage doors are available, including the two-leaf swinging, overhead, four-leaf swinging, and sectional roll-up types.

Interior room doors range in width from 2'–6" to 3'–0". Closet doors usually range from 1'–8" to 2'–6" wide, while exterior doors are usually 2'–8" to 3'–6" wide. After you have chosen the type, style, and size door for each room, carefully select the door location on each wall to provide the best possible traffic flow and minimize interference with furniture placement. If you have prepared furniture templates for each room, place them in position and check for door swing clearance. Whenever possible place interior doors near a perpendicular wall, since furniture cannot be placed behind the swing area. Also keep in mind the swing of the door can be designed in either direction, left-hand swing or right-hand swing. The door should always open into the open area of a room, not to the wall side.

Notice the door position alterations shown in Fig. 8–11. By moving the master bedroom door nearer to the wall, an awkward portion of the hall was eliminated and more furniture placement space was created for the room. Also, note the elimination of an extra door between the study and the bath. In Fig. 8–11 the entrance from the garage directly to the kitchen was changed to access through the service (laundry or mud room) to the kitchen. The wall separating the gathering room and the foyer was removed, thus creating an effective open plan. Always question the need for a door. If it's not needed for privacy, safety, or security, do you need it?

Windows Windows are most often changed to allow more light to enter dark interior areas, to take advantage of or hide a view, to add or diminish solar gain, or to provide a source of additional ventilation. Different types of windows provide different effects and admit varying amounts of ventilation and light.

There are three basic types of windows used in home construction: sliding, swinging, and fixed. Within these types there are many varieties of design. All windows are available with wood, metal, or plastic frames. Wood frames do not transmit heat readily and as a result do not become as cold as metal frames. Metal frames, being stronger, are not as bulky as wooden frames. Plastic frames are available in a variety of colors, slide smoothly, and do not decay or absorb moisture.

Architects and designers select prebuilt window types and sizes to fit the architectural style of the home. Figure 8–12 shows examples of the most common types. The following is a more complete listing of window types with the optional treatment.

Slanting Windows. Follows the line of a slanting roof. Simplest treatment is the use of traverse draperies. Leave top uncurtained or have draperies custom-made to fit slant.

Clerestory. Shallow windows set near ceiling for indoor privacy. Sometimes placed in slope of a beamed ceiling, in which case they are often left uncurtained.

Corner Windows. Any windows that come together at a corner. Best decorating effect is to treat windows as one.

Fixed Center, Double-hung Sides. One large, fixed pane, or fixed pane with movable sections. Make sure drapes are hung so as to allow opening to admit air at side.

Large, Fixed, Hopper Bottom. Usually a group of basic window units that form a vertical *wall* of windows. Can be treated as one wide window or as individual units.

In-swinging Casement. If it is not decorated properly, curtains and draperies may tangle with the window as it is opened.

Awning Type. Has wide, horizontal sashes that

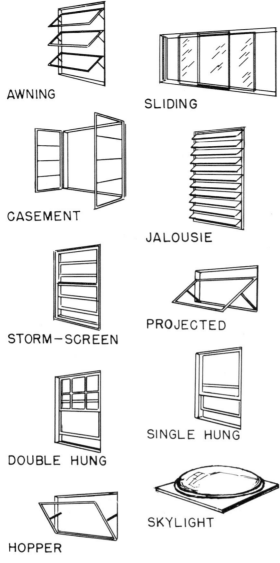

AWNING

SLIDING

CASEMENT

JALOUSIE

STORM—SCREEN

PROJECTED

DOUBLE HUNG

SINGLE HUNG

HOPPER

SKYLIGHT

Fig. 8-12 Window styles.

open outward to any angle. Unless it is awkwardly placed, it is an easy one to decorate.

Sliding Glass Doors. Often set into a wall construction, but sometimes part of a modern "glass wall." Make sure drapes draw away from opening.

Double-hung. Two sashes. Unless too high or too narrow, easy to decorate, using traverse draperies or cafe curtain treatment.

Jalousie Window. Narrow horizontal strips of glass that crank open to any desirable angle. A problem only when shape or location is unusual.

Fixed Arched Window. Any window arched at top. Easily treated with flexible aluminum rodding.

Ranch Windows. Most often a wide window, set high on the wall. Common to ranch-type and contemporary houses. Permits the placement of furniture against wall area below the window.

Bay. Three or more windows set at an angle to each other. You can use lots of imagination here to make it a room's main decorative feature.

Glass-pane Door. Often in pairs, need special decorating to look their best and to open easily. Just don't leave them bare.

Out-swinging Wood Frame. Opens outward by use of a crank, or operated by hand. Easily decorated in any of the standard ways.

Fixed Dormer Window. Usually a small window projecting from the roof in any alcovelike extension. This can use any of the usual treatments.

Bow Window (circular bay). The key to decorating this window lies in the selection of hardware. Curved rods are needed if draped.

Once the window style is selected, then the location must be carefully studied in relation to the need for light, a view, or ventilation. Windows were changed in Fig. 8–13 to provide more light in the bedroom and give access to an attractive view from the left. In this case, not only could the window be expanded but the type could be changed to sliding glass doors, thus providing the living room wall with an access to an outdoor living area patio. When considering window sizes for bedrooms, it is important to know that many building codes require a minimum area of window space in proportion to the size of the room.

Altering traffic space More than any other feature, traffic areas, particularly halls, create the greatest problem for the floor plan designer. Almost any architectural plan can work if you can live with excessive hall space. Thus, an inordinate amount of hall space in a design is one of the marks of a poor design, since hall space is not living space. Conversely, reducing hall space by providing traffic routes directly through rooms to access other rooms is also to be avoided. So, as in many areas of design, finding the right balance or compromise between these two extremes is the key to success. An excellent example of reducing excessive hall space and making a floor plan more efficient is shown in Fig. 8–14. Only two changes were required in this case to make a clumsy design effective. First, the long hall offset connecting the two front bedrooms was eliminated and replaced with access doors facing the hall. The space for these doors was taken from the bedroom closet. Second, the direct access to the bath was eliminated and converted to an access only from the master bedroom. This change not only eliminated the long hall but provided more privacy for the master bedroom bath.

Moving stair locations or changing stair types

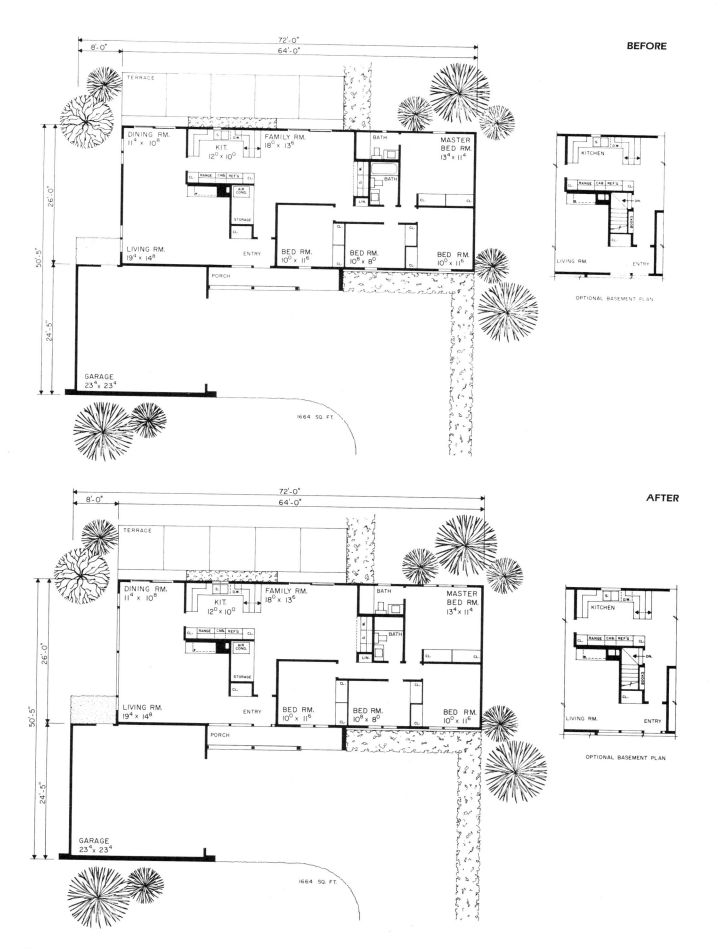

BEFORE

TERRACE

DINING RM.
11⁴ × 10⁸

KIT.
12⁰ × 10⁰

S. D.W.

FAMILY RM.
18⁰ × 13⁶

BATH

MASTER
BED RM.
13⁴ × 11⁴

CL. RANGE CAB. REF'G CL.

AIR
COND.

BATH

STORAGE

CL.

LIN.

CL. CL.

LIVING RM.
19⁴ × 14⁸

ENTRY

BED RM.
10⁰ × 11⁶

CL.

BED RM.
10⁸ × 8⁰

CL.

BED RM.
10⁰ × 11⁶

CL.

PORCH

GARAGE
23⁴ × 23⁴

1664 SQ. FT.

72'-0"
64'-0"
8'-0"
26'-0"
50'-5"
24'-5"

KITCHEN

S. D.W.

RANGE CAB. REF'G

DN.

BOOKS

CL.

LIVING RM.

ENTRY

OPTIONAL BASEMENT PLAN

AFTER

TERRACE

DINING RM.
11⁴ × 10⁸

KIT.
12⁰ × 10⁰

S. D.W.

FAMILY RM.
18⁰ × 13⁶

BATH

MASTER
BED RM.
13⁴ × 11⁴

CL. RANGE CAB. REF'G CL.

AIR
COND.

BATH

STORAGE

CL.

LIN.

CL. CL.

LIVING RM.
19⁴ × 14⁸

ENTRY

BED RM.
10⁰ × 11⁶

CL.

BED RM.
10⁸ × 8⁰

CL.

BED RM.
10⁰ × 11⁶

CL.

PORCH

GARAGE
23⁴ × 23⁴

1664 SQ. FT.

72'-0"
64'-0"
8'-0"
26'-0"
50'-5"
24'-5"

KITCHEN

S. D.W.

RANGE CAB. REF'G

DN.

BOOKS

CL.

LIVING RM.

ENTRY

OPTIONAL BASEMENT PLAN

Fig. 8-13 Changing windows. (Design 1313)

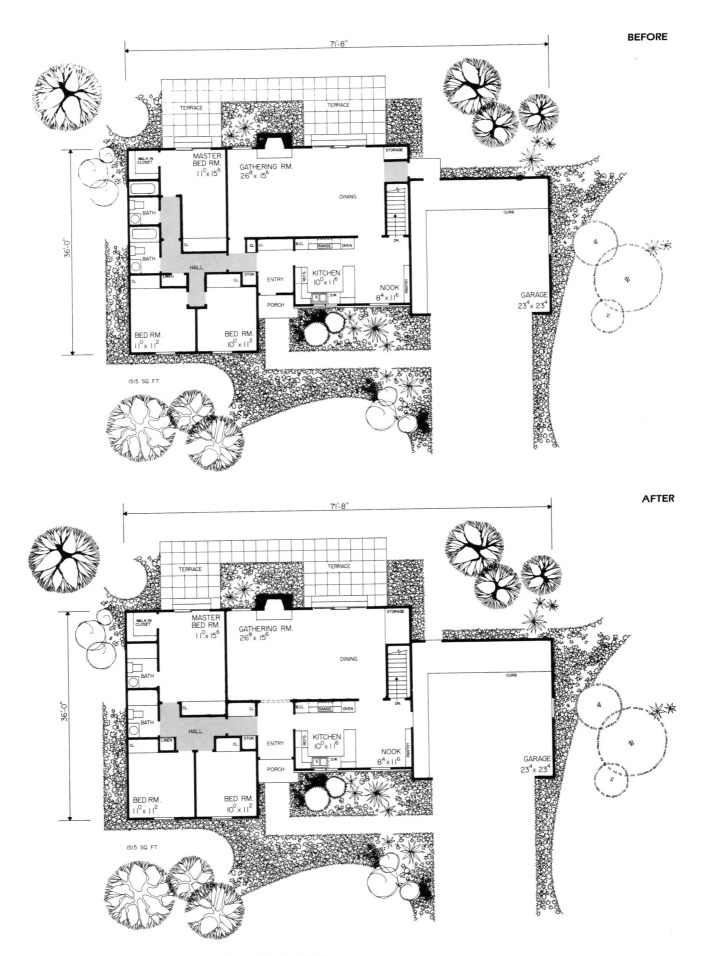

Fig. 8-14 Reducing excessive hall space. (Design 2597)

usually results from a need to condense or reapportion space. But often stairs must be moved to align with other design changes. Always remember when a stair location or type is changed on one level, all intersecting stairs at other levels must also be changed. For example, when the straight-run stairs on the first level in Fig. 8–15 were moved and changed to a U-shape type, the second-level plan also needed to be altered. In general, long straight-run stairs are more difficult to integrate into a design because of the amount of lineal space required. For this reason, choose the most critical level and establish the maximum area for stair space, then design the system to fill that space.

Expanding living space. Space can be added to an existing plan either by adding horizontal space (width or length) or by adding additional levels (height). The easiest method to expand a plan is to move a wall a specific distance outward, as shown in Fig. 8–16. In this plan an entire living area, including living room, dining room, and family room, was too small for the needs and wants established. The original space would not accommodate a grand piano in the living room or a pool table in the family room without sacrificing other needs. Thus, the solution to move the entire back wall 6 feet outward was relatively simple.

Regardless of how simple a solution may seem, be sure to look for potential secondary problems caused by each design change. For example, this change resulted in the master bedroom window partially facing the new living room wall. The solution, of course, is to either move the window further to the rear of the same wall or to move the window to one of the other two master bedroom walls. But if this is done perhaps the original furniture placement plan in relation to the door or closet may not work, and this may require an additional design adjustment. This is the type of design alteration chain reaction that can create chaos if not carefully planned. The effective designer must constantly consider the consequences of one feature over another. This is why one of the greatest skills of a designer is the ability to establish appropriate priorities for maximizing strong, significant design features and minimizing the negative aspects of compromised features. Thus, effective architectural design, especially design changes, establishes a balance between needs and the varying levels of wants without compromising the aesthetic and practical elements of the plan.

One of the most common types of design changes involves the addition of bedrooms. Families can often get by without many living area wants if necessary, but sacrificing the appropriate number of bedrooms is extremely difficult. This is why listing a specific number of bedrooms is nearly always high on the list of absolute needs. So important is the number of bedrooms in a house

that houses are classified by that statistic—a three-bedroom house, a four-bedroom house, and so forth. Adding bedrooms horizontally is usually one of the simplest design tasks if the sleeping area is clustered into a rectangular wing or end of the house. In adding the bedrooms to the house in Fig. 8–17, the designer simply extended the entire house rectangle to the left and extended the hall until the maximum length provided the necessary access to the far-left bedrooms. Then a closet was added to fill the otherwise dead space at the end of the hall, thus eliminating awkward offsets in the bedrooms. The number of bedrooms in this plan could also have been expanded by adding to the front or rear of the house. But this type of expansion would have resulted in an excessively long T-shaped hall and an L-shaped extension to the house, which is less normally desirable and more expensive than a straight-line expansion. However, sometimes an L-shaped expansion is the only alternative if only part of the plan is involved. Figure 8–18 shows an L-shaped expansion of part of the service area, which was designed to give the kitchen a desk space and expand the storage area into a home workshop.

When horizontal space is limited or budgetary reasons preclude horizontal expansion, one of the most convenient methods of expansion is to add an additional level. If the roof pitch is steep, dormer windows can be added to the roof and windows to the gable ends to convert the attic into living space. If, however, the roof pitch is low, as in Fig. 8–19, then adding a second level requires significant redesigning of the exterior in addition to the design of the second-level floor plan. In designing a second level, the key factor is the alignment of the outside walls, stairwell openings, and plumbing walls for the soil stack. At times, adjustments in the lower level design may be necessary to provide the needed space or alignments necessary on the second level. Notice how this was accomplished in Fig. 8–19. Since three bedrooms were added to the second level, the study-bedroom area on the first floor could be converted to a more expansive dressing room and bath for the master bedroom. If a second level is planned to cover the entire first floor then alignment of outside walls is simple. However, if only a partial second level is to be added, the alignment of second-level outside walls must be directly over first-level outside walls or directly over a first-floor bearing wall partition. Notice how the second-level right bath wall aligns with the first-level wall and all other walls align with outside walls.

When adding a second level to an existing plan, always integrate both vertical and horizontal building lines and match material texture and color. Also, be careful to match roof, window, and door styles with the existing design. Notice how this was done on the second-level addition shown in Fig. 8–19.

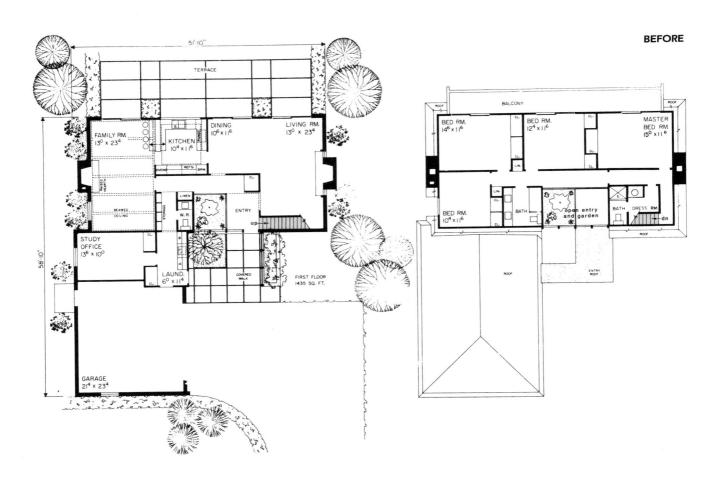

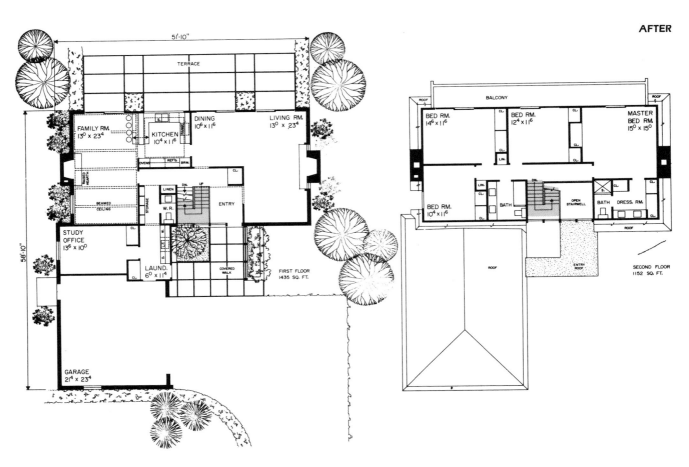

Fig. 8-15 Changing stairs. (Design 2187)

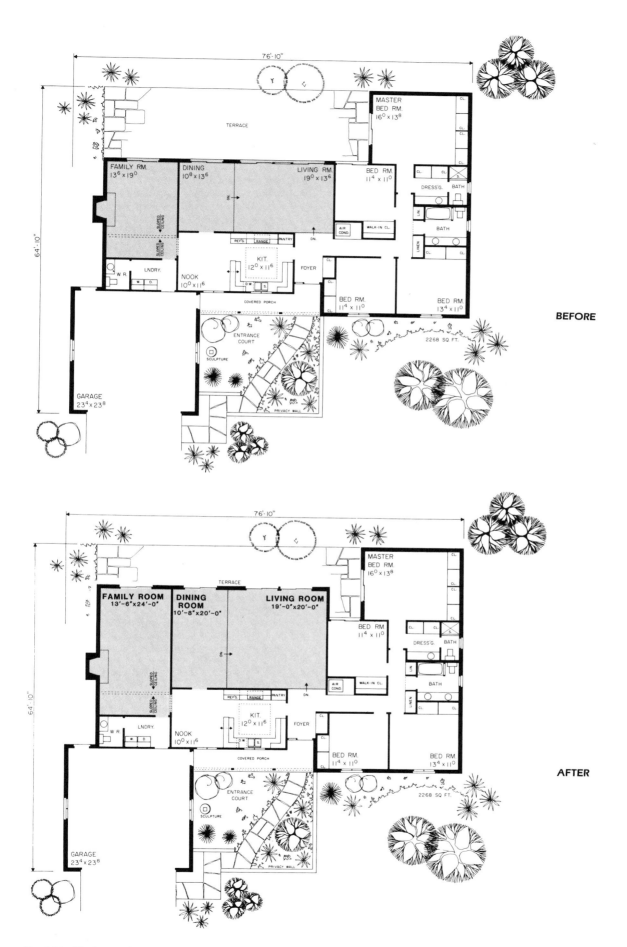

BEFORE

AFTER

Fig. 8-16 Moving walls to gain space. (Design 2329)

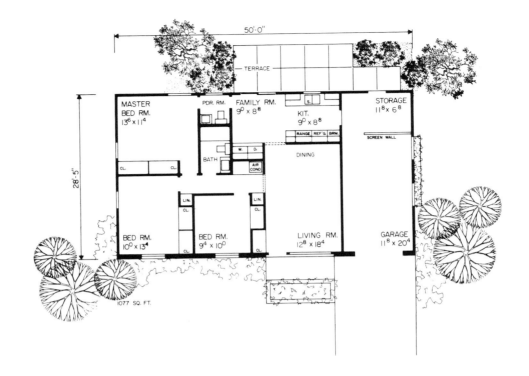

Fig. 8-17 Adding bedrooms. (Design 2159)

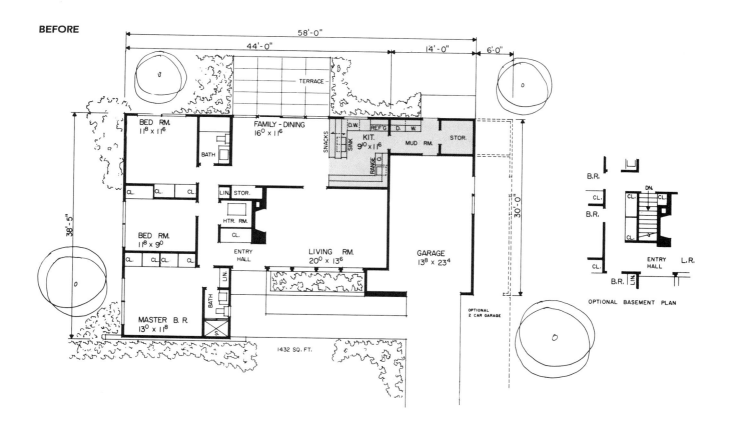

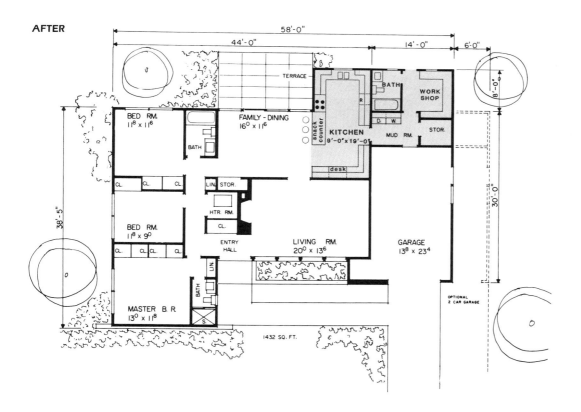

Fig. 8-18   Extending L shapes. (Design 1021)

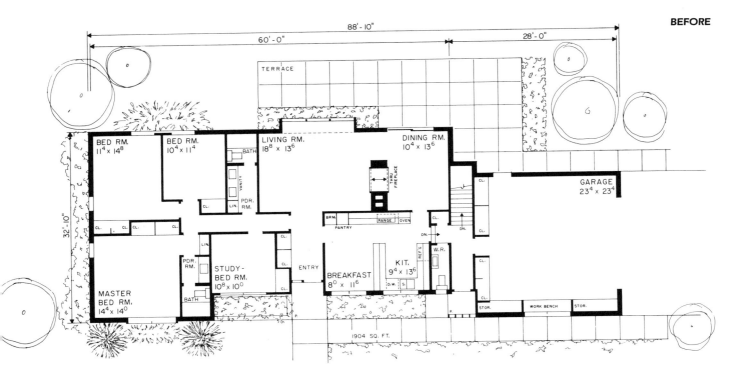

88'-10"

60'-0"   28'-0"

TERRACE

| BED RM.
11^4 x 14^8 | BED RM.
10^4 x 11^4 | BATH | LIVING RM.
18^8 x 13^6 | DINING RM.
10^4 x 13^6 |

THRU FIREPLACE

CL.

GARAGE
23^4 x 23^4

VANITY

PDR. RM.

32'-10"

CL. LIN.

CL. CL. CL.   CL.

BRM.   RANGE OVEN
PANTRY

DN.   DN.

CL.

CL.

LIN   CL.

MASTER
BED RM.
14^4 x 14^0

PDR.
RM.

STUDY-
BED RM.
10^8 x 10^0 CL.   ENTRY   BREAKFAST
8^0 x 11^6 KIT.
9^4 x 13^6 W.R.

BATH   CL.   REF'G.

D.W.   S

CL.

CL.

STOR.   WORK BENCH   STOR.

1904 SQ. FT.

BEDROOM 10'-0" x 17'-0"	BEDROOM 9'-0" x 17'-0"	
CL	BATH
	LT
	LAUN	W D
CL	LIN	DN
CL	BEDROOM 17'-0" x 11'-6"	SEWING 8'-0" x 7'-0"

Fig. 8-19 Upper level expansion. (Design 1129)

Lofts are also an additional method of adding living space to a design without adding to the total volume of the house. But the same guidelines apply to adding lofts as apply to adding second levels. Lofts supported by posts may also create a secondary problem of having no solid walls which can be used for plumbing. So baths in lofts must be kept to the rear or align with some first-level wall that can house water lines, waste lines, and soil stack.

Converting a basementless plan to a plan with either a full or partial basement requires solving the same alignment problems as does adding a second level. Space for a stairwell must be created from some existing first-level space. If a stairwell exists to the second level, then the space under the existing stairs can be used. If not, a realignment of space on the first level will be required, as shown in Fig. 8–21. Some stock plans dually design first-level plans to include an optional stairwell feature which can be implemented if a basement is anticipated and used for another purpose.

Because of limitations of time or money, it is sometimes desirable to construct a house over a long period of time. When this occurs or if construction is delayed, the house can be built in several steps. The basic part of the house can be constructed first. Then additional rooms (usually bedrooms) can be added in future years as the need develops or changes. When future expansion of the plan is anticipated, the complete floor plan should be drawn before the initial construction begins, even though the entire plan may not be complete at that time. If only part of the building is planned and built and an addition is made later, the addition will invariably look tacked on or extreme sacrifices or drastic changes will need to be made to the existing plan. This problem can be avoided by predesigning the floor plan for expansion. But regardless of whether you design an expandable plan or are only making design adjustments to a basic plan, always work in even, modular distances of 2 feet, preferably 4 feet if possible.

Solar adaptations Design revisions are also sometimes needed to make a house more passively or even actively solar efficient. The plan shown in Fig. 8–22 has been adapted to utilize passive solar features and also an active solar system. Passive features include the solarium with large glass areas to absorb solar heat. Here the sun's heat input can be controlled by summer shades and the amount of heat accepted into the main house can be controlled by sliding doors. The active features, of course, require exterior solar collectors but also require additional indoor space for storage. In this plan the solar storage facilities are housed with the remainder of the house's mechanical equipment such as furnace, air conditioning, and hot water tank. Notice how the roof line on this house has been adjusted to the proper solar angle to accommodate the solar collectors, thus integrating the active solar system into the total design of the structure without that tacked on look. Fig. 8-20 shows another application of passive solar planning.

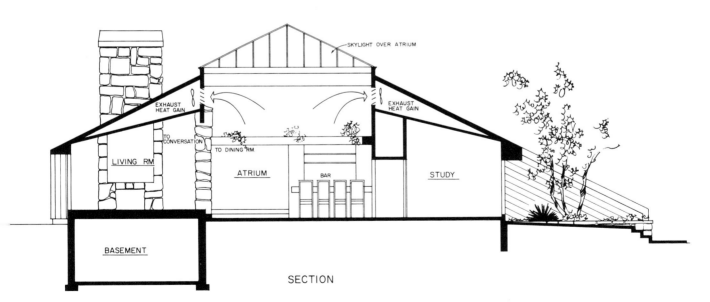

Fig. 8-20 **Passive solar design features. (Design 2832)**

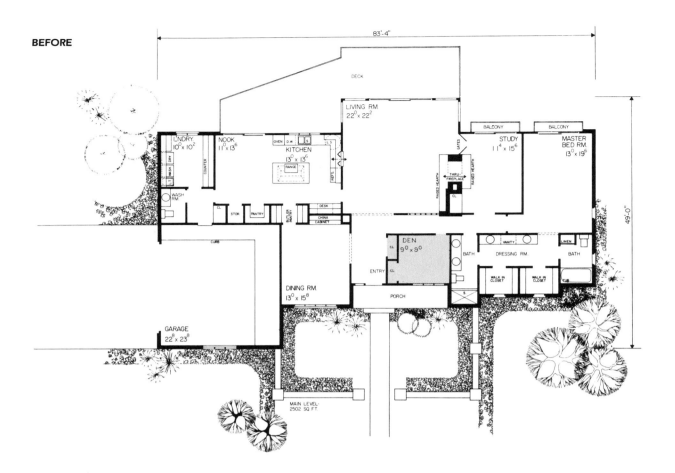

BEFORE

STREET VIEW

Fig. 8-21   Expanding basement space. (Design 2560)

AFTER

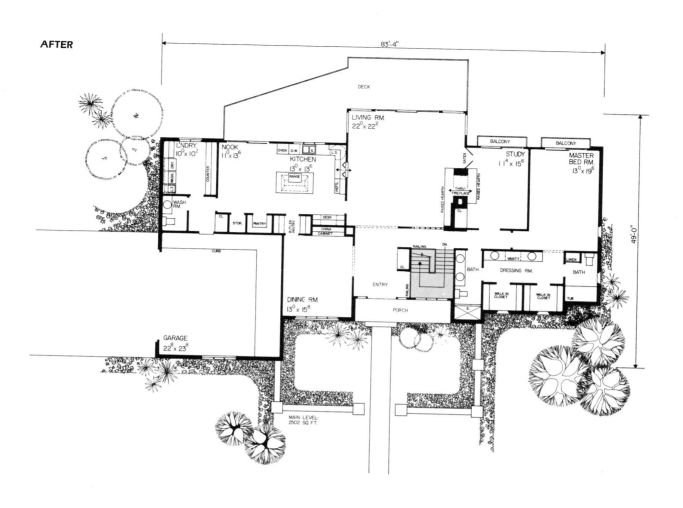

83'-4"

49'-0"

DECK

LIVING RM.
22⁰ x 22²

LNDRY.
10⁰ x 10²

NOOK
11⁰ x 13⁶

KITCHEN
13⁰ x 13⁶

OVEN D.W. S

I.L.S.

COUNTER

RANGE

REF.

WASH RM.

BALCONY

BALCONY

STUDY
11⁴ x 15⁶

MASTER
BED RM.
13⁰ x 19⁶

GATES

RAISED HEARTH

THRU-FIREPLACE

RAISED HEARTH

CL

CL

STOR.

PANTRY

BTLR PANTRY

DESK

CHINA CABINET

RAILING

DN.

CL

VANITY

LINEN

BATH

DRESSING RM.

BATH

CURB

ENTRY

STAIRS

BATH

WALK IN CLOSET

WALK IN CLOSET

TUB

DINING RM.
13⁰ x 15⁶

PORCH

GARAGE
22⁸ x 23⁸

MAIN LEVEL·
2502 SQ. FT.

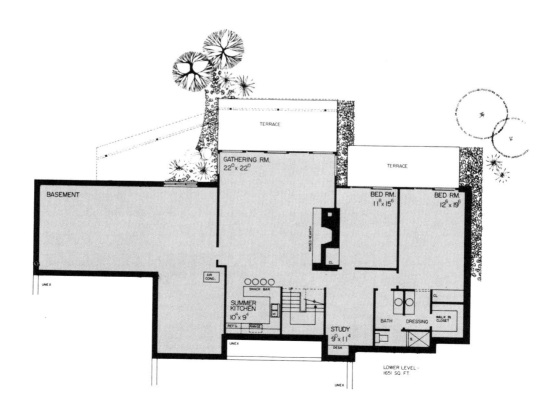

TERRACE

GATHERING RM.
22⁰ x 22⁰

TERRACE

BASEMENT

BED RM.
11⁸ x 15⁶

BED RM.
12⁶ x 19⁶

RAISED HEARTH

CL

UNEX

AIR COND.

SNACK BAR

UP

BATH

DRESSING

WALK IN CLOSET

CL

SUMMER KITCHEN
10⁴ x 9⁴

REFG. RANGE

STUDY
9⁰ x 11⁴

DESK

UNEX

UNEX

LOWER LEVEL·
1651 SQ. FT.

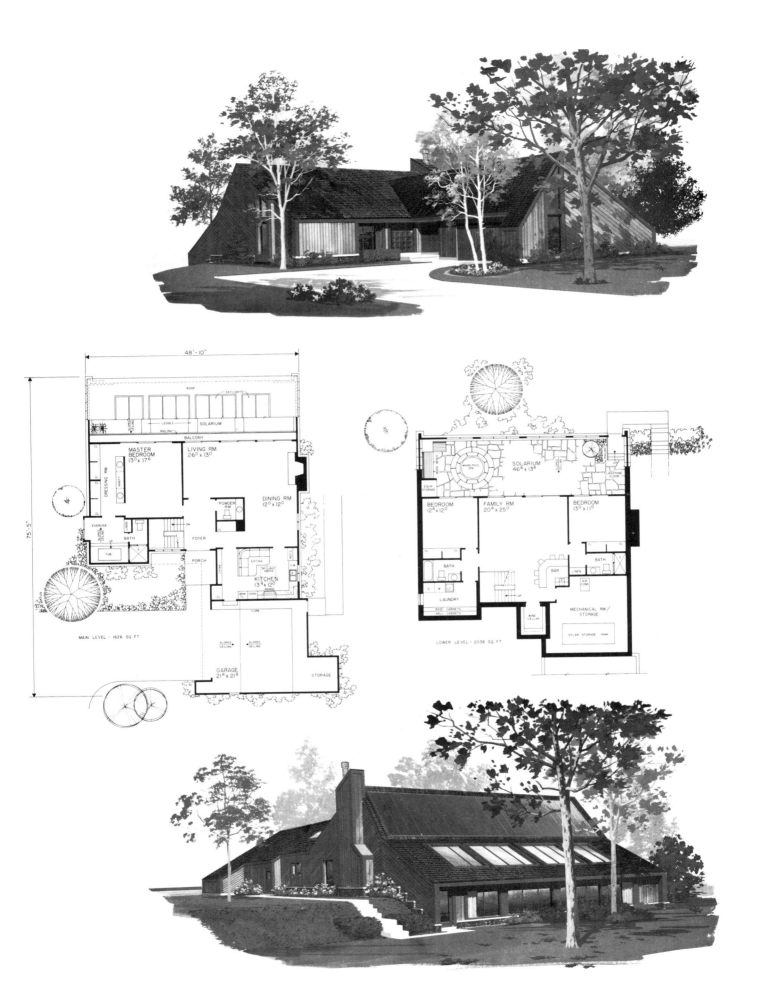

48'-10"

ROOF
SKYLIGHTS
LEDGES SOLARIUM
RAILING
BALCONY

MASTER
BEDROOM
13⁰ x 17⁶

LIVING RM.
26⁰ x 13⁰

DRESSING RM

POWDER
RM

DINING RM
12⁰ x 12⁰

EXERCISE

BATH

FOYER

TUB

PORCH

KITCHEN
13⁴ x 12⁰

EATING
SKYLIGHT
ABOVE

BRM OVEN RANGE

CURB

75'-5"

MAIN LEVEL - 1626 SQ FT

SLOPED
CEILING   SLOPED
CEILING

GARAGE
21⁸ x 21⁸

STORAGE

EQUIP
STORAGE

WHIRLPOOL
SPA

SOLARIUM
46⁶ x 13⁸

FLAGSTONE
FLOOR

BEDROOM
12⁸ x 12⁰

FAMILY RM.
20⁴ x 25⁰

BEDROOM
13⁰ x 11⁰

BATH

BAR LINEN

BATH

AIR
COND

LAUNDRY

BASE CABINETS
WALL CABINETS

WINE
CELLAR

MECHANICAL RM /
STORAGE

SOLAR STORAGE TANK

LOWER LEVEL - 2038 SQ FT

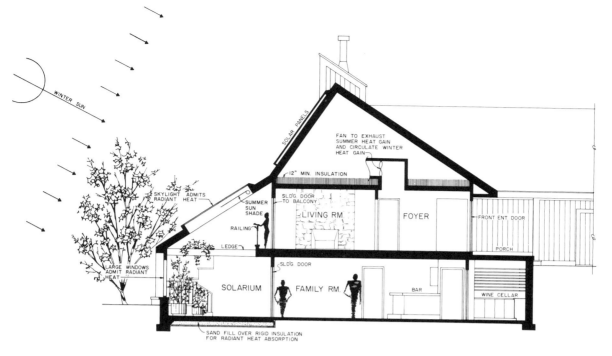

WINTER SUN

SOLAR PANELS

FAN TO EXHAUST
SUMMER HEAT GAIN
AND CIRCULATE WINTER
HEAT GAIN

12" MIN. INSULATION

SKYLIGHT ADMITS RADIANT HEAT

SLD'G. DOOR
TO BALCONY

SUMMER
SUN
SHADE

RAILING

LEDGE

LARGE WINDOWS
ADMIT RADIANT
HEAT

LIVING RM.

FOYER

FRONT ENT DOOR

PORCH

SLD'G. DOOR

SOLARIUM

FAMILY RM.

BAR

WINE CELLAR

SAND FILL OVER RIGID INSULATION
FOR RADIANT HEAT ABSORPTION

SECTION

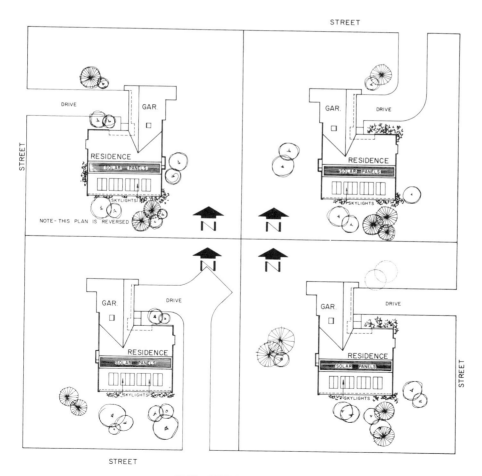

STREET

DRIVE

GAR.

RESIDENCE

SOLAR PANELS

STREET

SKYLIGHTS

NOTE- THIS PLAN IS REVERSED

N

GAR.

DRIVE

RESIDENCE

SOLAR PANELS

SKYLIGHTS

N

N

GAR.

DRIVE

RESIDENCE

SOLAR PANELS

SKYLIGHTS

STREET

GAR.

DRIVE

RESIDENCE

SOLAR PANELS

SKYLIGHTS

STREET

STREET

SITE ORIENTATION

Fig. 8-22 Passive solar design. (Design 2835)

CHAPTER 9

Adapting Elevation Styles

Elevation Design

Regardless of the efficiency and appropriateness of the floor plan in meeting individual needs and wants, if the exterior of a house does not meet the aesthetic needs of the occupant the home design will be considered a failure. Although the design of the floor plan should, and usually does, precede the design of the elevation, the complete design process requires a continual relationship between the elevation and the floor plan.

Much flexibility is possible in the design of elevations, even in those designed from the same floor plan. When the location of doors, windows, and chimneys has been established on the floor plan, the development of an attractive and functional elevation for the structure still depends on the factors of roof style, overhang, grade-line position, and the relationship of windows, doors, and chimneys to the building line. Figure 9–1 clearly shows that choosing a desirable elevation design is not an automatic process which follows the floor plan design, but a development which requires a careful blending of these elements. The designer should keep in mind that only horizontal distances (width and length) can be established on the floor plan. All vertical distances (heights), such as the position of the grade line, eave line, roof ridge line, chimney shape, and heights of windows and doors, must be designed and shown on the elevation. As these vertical heights are established, the appearance of the outside and the functioning of the heights as they

affect the internal functioning of the house must be considered.

The basic architectural style of a building is more closely identified with the design of the elevation than with any other factor. Consequently, the selection of the basic type of structure must be compatible with the architectural style of the elevation. The elevation design can be changed to create the appearance of different architectural styles, but only if the basic building type is consistent with that style. For example, Fig. 9–2 shows four distinctly different elevation styles projected from the same floor plan. Look carefully at the pictorial rendering of these houses and you will see the same detail positioning of the distinguishing features, such as garage, entry, and chimney. Although it is relatively simple to change an elevation style, total deviation from the lines created by the floor plan can produce an aesthetically unpleasant design. For example, if a floor plan is designed in a single-level rambling form, then adding second levels with dormers or two-story columns would be inappropriate. As you observe the style changes in options in this chapter you will find there are distinct limits beyond which alteration is neither aesthetically pleasing nor practical.

Form and space The total appearance of the elevation depends upon the relationship among the areas of the elevation such as surfaces, doors, windows, and chimneys. The balance of these areas, the emphasis placed on various compo-

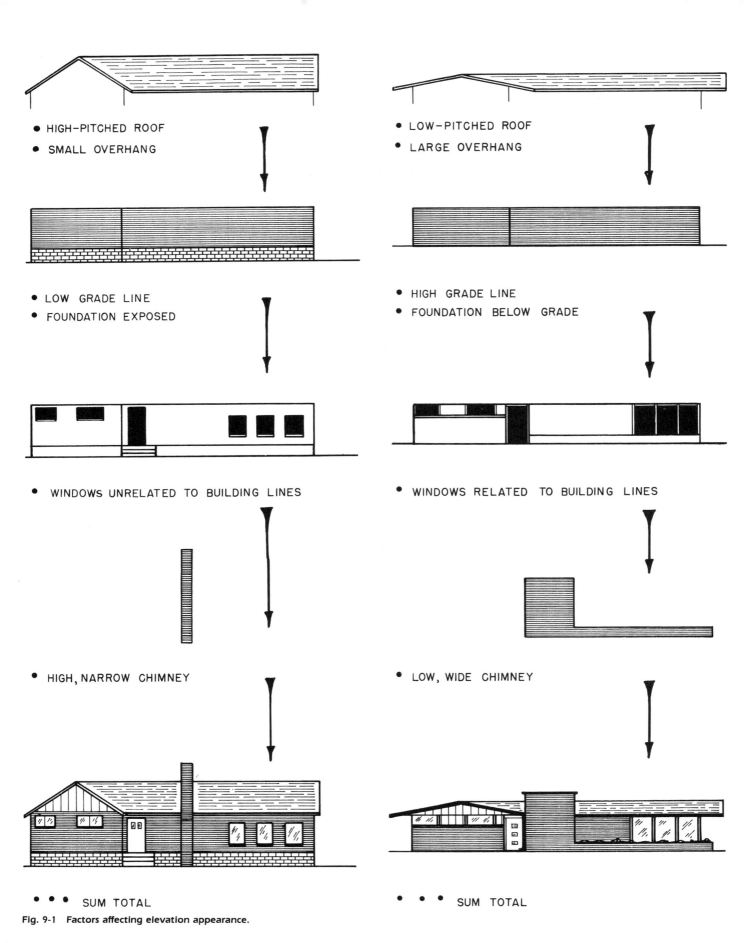

- HIGH-PITCHED ROOF
- SMALL OVERHANG

- LOW-PITCHED ROOF
- LARGE OVERHANG

- LOW GRADE LINE
- FOUNDATION EXPOSED

- HIGH GRADE LINE
- FOUNDATION BELOW GRADE

- WINDOWS UNRELATED TO BUILDING LINES

- WINDOWS RELATED TO BUILDING LINES

- HIGH, NARROW CHIMNEY

- LOW, WIDE CHIMNEY

- • • SUM TOTAL

- • • SUM TOTAL

Fig. 9-1 Factors affecting elevation appearance.

nents of the elevation, the texture, the light, the color, and the shadow patterns all affect greatly the general appearance of the elevation.

The elevation should appear as one integral and functional facade, rather than as a surface in which holes have been cut for windows and doors and to which structural components, such as chimneys, have been added without reference to the other areas of the elevation. Doors, windows, and chimney lines should constitute part of the general pattern of the elevation and should not exist in isolation.

When the vertical lines of the windows are extended to the eave line from the ground line, planter line, or some division line in the separation of materials, the vertical lines become related to the building. Horizontal lines of a window extending from one post to another, or from one vertical separation in the elevation to another, as between a post and a chimney, also help to relate the window to the major lines of the elevation. Doors can also easily be related to the major lines of the house by extending the area above the door at the ridge line, or divider, and making the side panel consistent with the door size.

Lines dominate the appearance of an elevation. The lines of an elevation are horizontal and are called the ground line, eave line, and ridge line. The lines of an elevation can help to create horizontal or vertical emphasis. If the ground line, ridge line, and eave line are accented, the emphasis will be placed on the horizontal. If the emphasis is placed on corner posts and columns, the emphasis will be vertical. In general, low buildings will usually appear longer and lower if the emphasis is placed on horizontal lines.

Lines should be consistent. The lines of an elevation should appear to flow together as one integrated line pattern. It is usually better to continue a line through an elevation for a long distance than to break the line and start it again. Rhythm can be developed by the use of lines, and lines can be repeated in various patterns. When a line is repeated, the basic consistency of the elevation is considerably strengthened.

Roof styles Nothing affects the silhouette of a house more than the roof line. The most common roofs are the gable roof, hip roof, flat roof, and shed roof. A change in the roof style of a structure greatly affects the appearance of the elevation even when all other factors remain constant.

Gable roofs are used extensively on Cape Cod and Ranch homes. The pitch (angle) of a gable roof varies from the high-pitch roofs found on the chalet-style building to the low-pitch roofs found on most ranch homes.

Hip roofs are used when roof-line protection is desired around the entire perimeter of the building. Hip-roof overhangs shade the windows of the house. For this reason hip roofs are very popular in warm climates. Hip roofs are commonly used on Regency and French Provincial homes.

Flat roofs are used to create a low silhouette on many modern homes. Since no support is achieved by the leaning together of rafters, slightly heavier rafters are needed for flat roofs. Built-up asphalt construction is often used on flat roofs. Water may be used as an insulator and solar heater on flat roofs.

Shed roofs are flat roofs that are higher at one end than at the other. They may be used effectively when two levels exist and where additional light is needed. The use of clerestory windows between two sheds provides skylight illumination. The double shed is really very advantageous on hillside, split-level structures.

Sufficient roof overhang should be provided to afford protection from the sun, rain, and snow. The length and angle of the overhang will greatly affect its appearance and its functioning in providing protection. When the pitch is low, a larger overhang is needed to provide protection. However, with a high-pitch roof the overhang may be extended and block the view from the inside. To provide protection and at the same time allow sufficient light to enter the windows, slatted overhangs may be used.

Design adjustment guidelines Except for windows and door styles selection, the appearance of an elevation can be adjusted to many different architectural styles regardless of the floor plan. For example, in Fig. 9–3 Colonial and Contemporary exteriors were created from the identical floor plan. The basic difference lies in the use of siding materials and window style. Even the roof style is relatively unaltered between the two exterior styles. However, in Fig. 9–4 primarily the roof style was changed to convert a New England Colonial to a Dutch Colonial, French Mansard, or Georgian style from the same floor plan. Siding material, trim, and details play a major role in creating the difference. The main reason these styles could be adjusted so easily is related to the nature of the basic floor plan. For example, the floor plan in Fig. 9–4 could not easily or should not even be used as a basis for a Contemporary Ranch-style adaptation. However, the floor plan shown in Fig. 9–2 could easily be converted to a Contemporary Ranch style through the conversion of window styles, courtyard and patio walls, roof, and siding materials without any change in the basic lines of the elevation.

Fig. 9-2 Different elevations from same plan. (Designs 2815, 2816, 2817, and 2814)

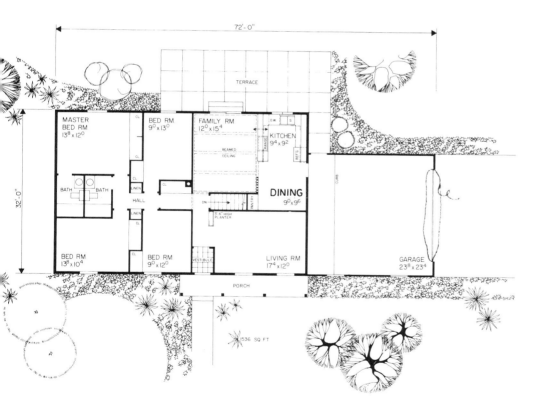

72'-0"

TERRACE

MASTER
BED RM
13⁸ x 12⁰

BED RM
9⁰ x 13⁰

FAMILY RM
12⁰ x 15⁴

KITCHEN
9⁴ x 9²

BEAMED
CEILING

RANGE

D.W.

S

REF'G

32'-0"

BATH   BATH

HALL

LINEN

CL

CL

LINEN

CL

DN

3'-6" HIGH
PLANTER

DINING
9⁰ x 9⁶

BED RM
13⁸ x 10⁴

BED RM
9⁰ x 12⁰

VESTIBULE

LIVING RM
17⁴ x 12⁰

GARAGE
23⁸ x 23⁴

CURB

PORCH

1536 SQ FT

MASTER
BED RM

BED RM
9⁰ x 12⁰

FAMILY RM

HALL

LINEN

CL

AIR
COND

STORAGE   WASH   DRY

PAN-
TRY

3'-6" HIGH
PLANTER

LINEN

CL

BED RM

CL

BED RM
9⁰ x 9⁸

VESTIBULE

LIVING RM

PORCH

OPTIONAL CRAWL SPACE FLOOR PLAN

DINING

CURB

LIVING RM

GARAGE

PORCH

OPTIONAL FRONT ENTRANCE GARAGE

Fig. 9-3   Colonial and Tudor exteriors from same floor plan. (Designs 1933 and 2190)

BED RM.
12⁰ x 11⁶

BATH

MASTER
BED RM.
15⁸ x 11⁶

ROOF

ROOF

ROOF

ROOF

CL.
CL.

DN.

CL.

CL. CL.

CL.

CL.

LIN.

BATH

BED RM.
12⁰ x 10⁴

BED RM.
11⁰ x 11⁰

CL.

ROOF

SECOND FLOOR
884 SQ. FT.

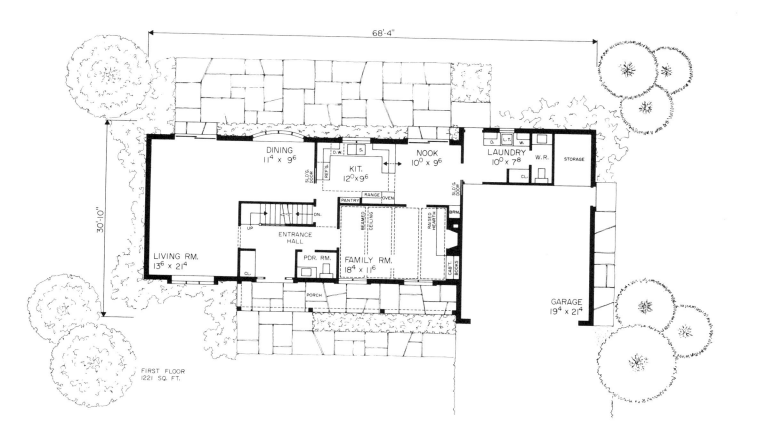

68'-4"

30'-10"

DINING
11⁴ x 9⁶

SLD'G
DOOR

REF'G.

D.W.

S.

KIT.
12⁰x9⁶

NOOK
10⁰ x 9⁶

LAUNDRY
10⁰ x 7⁸

D.

L.T.

W.

W.R.

STORAGE

CL.

PANTRY

RANGE

OVEN

SLD'G
DOOR

BRM.

UP

DN.

ENTRANCE
HALL

BEAMED
CEILING

RAISED
HEARTH

CAB'T.
BOOKS

LIVING RM.
13⁶ x 21⁴

CL.

PDR. RM.

FAMILY RM.
18⁴ x 11⁶

GARAGE
19⁴ x 21⁴

PORCH

FIRST FLOOR
1221 SQ. FT.

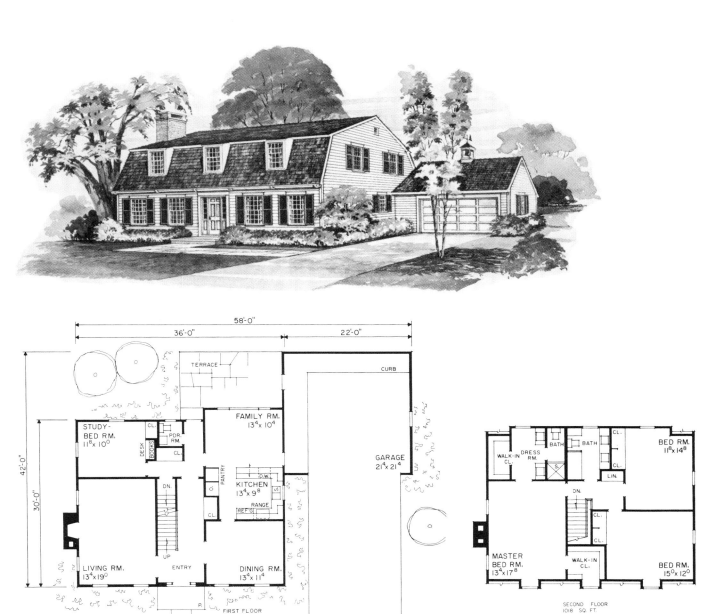

Fig. 9-4 (opposite and above) Effect of roof style change. (Designs 1834, 1831, 1833, and 1832)

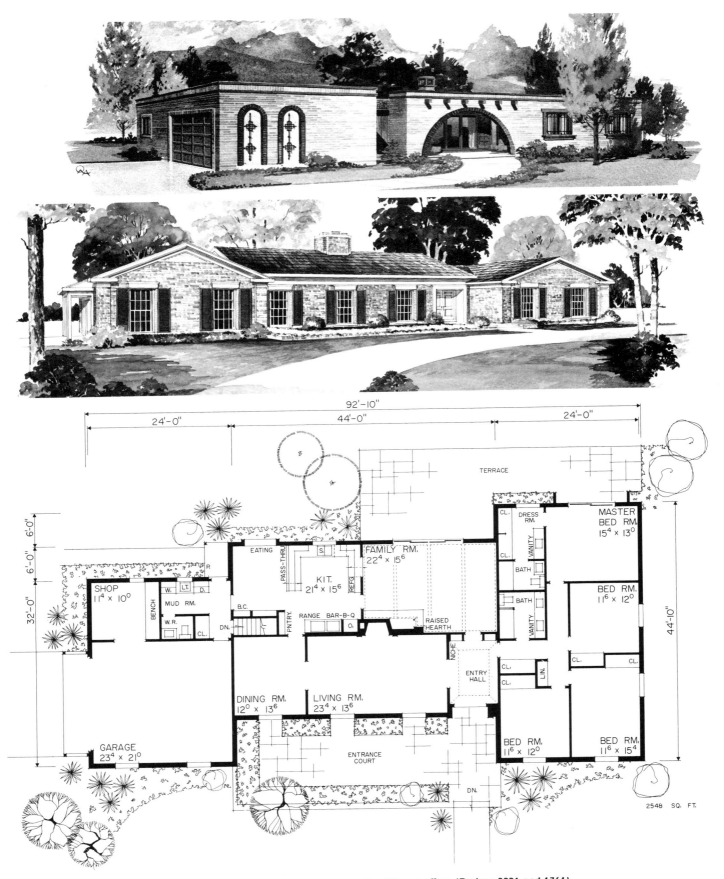

92'-10"

24'-0"   **44'-0"**   **24'-0"**

TERRACE

6'-0"
6'-0"
6'-0"
32'-0"

SHOP
11⁴ × 10⁰

BENCH
W.
LT.
D.
MUD RM.
W.R.
CL.
DN.
R
EATING
PASS-THRU
S
KIT.
21⁴ × 15⁶
REFG.
B.C.
PNTRY.
RANGE
BAR-B-Q
O.
FAMILY RM.
22⁴ × 15⁶
RAISED HEARTH

CL.
DRESS RM.
CL.
VANITY
BATH
BATH
VANITY

MASTER BED RM.
15⁴ × 13⁰

BED RM.
11⁶ × 12⁰

44'-10"

NICHE
ENTRY HALL

CL.
CL.
LIN.
CL.
CL.

DINING RM.
12⁰ × 13⁶
LIVING RM.
23⁴ × 13⁶

GARAGE
23⁴ × 21⁰

ENTRANCE COURT

DN.

BED RM.
11⁶ × 12⁰

BED RM.
11⁶ × 15⁴

2548 SQ. FT.

Fig. 9-5   **Roof and window differences create the different effect. (Designs 2231 and 1761)**

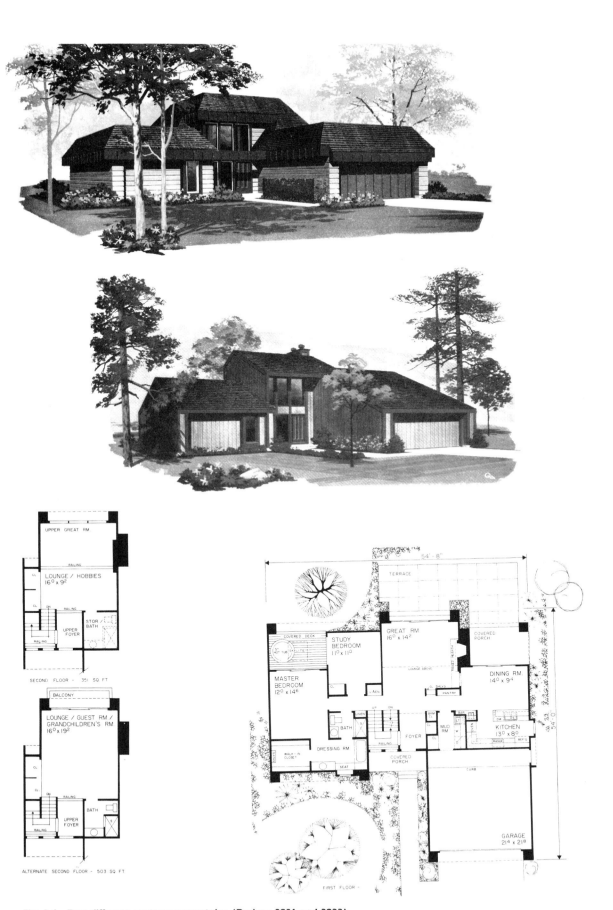

SECOND FLOOR - 351 SQ FT

UPPER GREAT RM.

LOUNGE / HOBBIES
16⁰ x 9²

STOR.
BATH

UPPER
FOYER

ALTERNATE SECOND FLOOR - 503 SQ FT

BALCONY

LOUNGE / GUEST RM /
GRANDCHILDREN'S RM
16⁰ x 19²

BATH

UPPER
FOYER

54' - 8"

TERRACE

COVERED DECK

STUDY
BEDROOM
11⁰ x 11⁰

GREAT RM
16⁰ x 14²

COVERED
PORCH

MASTER
BEDROOM
12⁰ x 14⁶

LOUNGE ABOVE

PANTRY

DINING RM.
14⁰ x 9⁴

BATH

FOYER

MUD
RM

KITCHEN
13⁰ x 8⁰

DRESSING RM

WALK-IN
CLOSET

SEAT

COVERED
PORCH

CURB

GARAGE
21⁴ x 21⁸

FIRST FLOOR -

Fig. 9-6 Two different contemporary styles. (Designs 2821 and 2822)

The elevation style difference is even more prominent and distinct in the plan shown in Fig. 9–5. In this plan the contrast between the Spanish style flat roof, sheltered entrance, and arched windows and the conventional gable roof and Colonial lighted windows makes a comparison with the same floor plan seem almost impossible. But if you look carefully at the floor plan, you will find the primary difference lies in the windows and roof lines used. Although this example is extremely distinct, most elevation options are developed within the same architectural style. For example, it is unlikely for anyone designing their own home to want to consider a wide range of elevation options. Usually one's architectural preference restricts the choice of elevations to a relatively narrow range. For example, the two options shown in Fig. 9–6 are both Contemporary in style. The basic differences lie in the execution of that style, and not in considering another style.

A Final Word on Styles

Reference plans are organized under broad architectural style categories. Normally architectural styles are based on either country of origin, historical period, or some regional or climatic requirements.

The purpose of this section is not to characterize architectural styles in any finite manner as an architectural historian might do, but to organize home plans under broad style categories to help the home planner in selecting the most appropriate plan to fit individual needs and wants and the most appealing exterior to satisfy personal preferences. The general categories used here include European, Early American, Later American, and Contemporary styles. For convenience and ease of identification these categories are further subdivided into specific style types. For example, the European styles are broken down into English and French styles and the English styles are further categorized under specific style headings such as Tudor, Elizabethan, Cotswold, or Georgian. Likewise, the Early American styles are divided into specific styles such as New England Colonial, Early American Farmhouse, Saltbox, Cape Cod, Garrison, and so forth.

Regardless of the basis for identification, there are few homes past or present which are totally pure examples of a specific architectural style. This is primarily because in the historical development of styles, architectural change was constantly evolving from one region to another, from one climate to another, and/or from one time period to another. And these changes were usually in transition simultaneously. For example, the European influence was brought to this country by many different ethnic groups and continued to change and evolve as we passed through the Colonial, Georgian-Federal, and Romantic periods into the Contemporary period. And though

dates are applied to these periods (Colonial 1600 to 1700; Georgian 1700 to 1775; Federal 1775 to 1800; and Romantic 1820 to 1860), there was considerable overlap in these periods and in the architectural styles developed and used during those times. To further amplify this point, remember that when the English landed at Plymouth in 1620 they brought with them much of their architectural heritage, which out of necessity was adapted to meet the needs, materials, skills, and tools available in the new world. Later, the Dutch, French, and Spanish emulated or adapted some of these architectural styles in the houses they built in this country. These styles existed in different yet overlapping parts of the country from 1600 through 1800, when many other European architectural styles including Italian and Greek, were introduced. Consequently, it is also difficult to precisely purify or identify any specific architectural style with a country of origin or time period. Nevertheless, there are common and dominant characteristic features which do help us communicate architectural style preferences. And those general features are the ones that have been used in this book to categorize the house plans.

European styles Since most of the early settlers of this country emigrated from England and France, the European styles that dominated early American residential architecture naturally include those from England and France. English styles include Old English (Cotswold), Tudor, Elizabethan, and Georgian. English styles included in this chapter can be distinguished from each other by some very different specific features. However, there are also many common features to these styles. For example, English styles all have relatively high-pitch roofs, massive chimneys, light leaded windows, and masonry siding. But the Cotswold is a small cottage, the Elizabethan is distinguished by its half-timber construction, the Tudor by its multiple gables, and the Georgian by its classic box form.

English styles can range from the very simple, as in the Cotswold, to the very lavish, as in the Elizabethan. The Cotswold is derived from two words, Cots ("cottage") and Wald ("wood"), meaning cottage in the woods. In contrast, the English Tudor, Elizabethan, and Georgian styles are extremely formal, austere, and commanding. The Tudor, developed during the reign of the House of Tudor, with extremely imposing fortress silloutte and heavy masonry, became popular in this country in the late 1880s. The Elizabethan, with its half-timber overhanging second story, is only slightly less formal.

But of all the English styles brought to this country, the Georgian style, developed during the reign of four King Georges, became the most copied by the beginning of the 1700s. Houses based on this style were later adapted and evolved into the Williamsburg and Southern Colonial styles. In fact, the most famous house in the United States, the White House, is of Georgian origin.

Late Georgian (1776 to 1840) is often referred to as Early Federal and was the predominant style in this country after 1790. This overlapping of styles and periods reinforces the statements made earlier concerning the relatively impure nature of residential architecture at any specific time and place in history.

Since the French styles were brought to this country much later than the English styles, from 1700 to 1800, their impact on Colonial residential architecture was far less pronounced. However some French styles—the Regency, Mansard, Provincial, and Château—were accepted and used in many areas. The Regency style actually found its way to this country through England during the early 1800s. The Provincial style was first popularized during the reign of Louis XIV, by the wealthy French who wanted to emulate royalty. The French Château is a less formal adaptation of the Provincial, while the Mansard was developed during the reign of Napoleon III in the mid 1800s. Developed by François Mansard, its distinguishing characteristic, the Mansard roof, is enjoying a current revival and is indeed being adapted in many contemporary homes.

European architectural styles normally refer to northern European styles while southern European styles are usually classified under the Mediterranean heading.

Early American styles   The label "Early American styles" is somewhat of a misnomer since all styles that found their way to America during our early development can also be labeled "Early American." There is probably as much or more overlapping of characteristics among Early American styles than in the European styles, since all of these styles have a northern European base. Early American styles covered in this book include the New England Colonial, Early American Farmhouse, Saltbox, Cape Cod, Garrison, Dutch Colonial, Southern Colonial, and French Colonial. The New England Colonial, Early American Farmhouse, Saltbox, Cape Cod, Garrison, and Dutch Colonial share many common features. Primarily the roof styles and size set these styles apart. Likewise the Southern Colonial and French Colonial are very similar except for porch and trim treatments. As you look at examples of these styles note the similarities and differences.

Later American styles   After the Colonial period, architectural styles either evolved from existing styles or climatic needs, or were copied from southern European styles as part of the Classical Revival movement. Styles that developed during this period include the Federal, Victorian, Classical Revival, Gothic Revival; several Spanish Western styles include the Western Ranch, Western Adobe, Monterey, and Spanish Mediterranean. The Federal style evolved from much of the Georgian influence combined with the Greek and Roman Classical influences. During this period, the Victorian style, which came from Italy through England, became extremely popular. Its ornate decoration, like the Gothic Revival style, provided an outlet for new construction power technology. But it was often overdone, resulting in ornate edifices on a grand scale. And from it all evolved the epitome of nonstyles—the Traditional. Traditional styling implies the use of all traditional values and characteristics in one design. When done with taste and attention to the basic elements and principles of design, the result can be effective. But without careful aesthetic balance and control the results can be offensive.

Although the Classical architecture of Italy and Greece had a significant influence on Classical Revival during this period, another southern European country, Spain, also had a profound influence on regional architecture during this period. Partially from Spanish influence and partially from climatic factors, the Western Ranch, Western Adobe, Monterey, and Spanish Mediterranean styles evolved in the West and Southwest. Warm climate and open spaces naturally led to the use of large horizontal spaces for Ranch-style homes and the availability of clay roof styles. But the more formal Monterey and Spanish Mediterranean styles grew out of Spanish architectural preference. In fact, the Monterey was the direct result of a New England businessperson building what was thought to be a New England Colonial using classic Spanish styling. Thus, a new style was inadvertently created from several existing styles. And so the evolution in residential architecture continues.

Contemporary styles   Styles of today are based on, and often dominated by, the materials and technology of today. Consequently, Contemporary homes tend to accent large, open areas with less structural restriction. Lines become simpler, bolder, and are less cluttered. Proponents of the Contemporary style remind us that any deviation from any pure historical style always includes some compromise with architectural style authenticity. For example, Colonial homes were designed and built with small window lites (panes) because large-dimension glass could not be manufactured in those times. Today, glass size is not a design restriction; however, to design a truly pure Colonial house, the designer must use small window lites. To many designers this is a waste of a technological advancement. So the designer must decide how much liberty should be taken in the cause of architectural authenticity and how many modern features can or should be incorporated into the design.

The architectural styles presented in this book are a product of those compromises. Some plans are relatively pure, others combine many style-family features, and some carefully incorporate Contemporary materials into the design. But within the broad architectural style categories, the principles and elements of design are consistent.

As you work with any existing plan to better adjust it to your wants and needs, avoid combining general categories such as European, Colonial, or Contemporary, into one house design. However you can, with aesthetic care, combine the features of different specific styles within one family into a single plan. For example, since there was considerable overlap in the use of different Colonial styles during the 1600s and 1700s—such as Cape Cod, Garrison, and New England Colonial —the combining of the features or characteristics of these styles is not generally objectionable in the creation of a comprehensive Early American design. A plan combining these different features will not be truly Cape Cod or Garrison, but will be truly a general Early American design.

Thus the designer's aesthetic licence normally extends to the broad, general architectural style categories but not beyond. For a more complete catalog of residential styles contact: Home Planners, Inc., Dept. MH, 23761 Research Drive, Farmington Hills, Michigan 48024.

Index